Quick SCRIPTURE REFERENCE for Counseling Men

KEITH R. MILLER

BakerBooks
a division of Baker Publishing Group
Grand Rapids, Michigan

Published by Baker Books
a division of Baker Publishing Group
P.O. Box 6287, Grand Rapids, MI 49516-6287
www.bakerbooks.com

Printed in the United States of America

Library of Congress Cataloging-in-Publication Data
Miller, Keith R.
    Quick scripture reference for counseling men / Keith R. Miller.
        pages cm
    ISBN 978-0-8010-1588-5 (pbk.)
    1. Men—Pastoral counseling of. 2. Church work with men.
3. Christian men—Religious life. I. Title.
BV4440.M55 2014
259.0811—dc23   2014018900

14   15   16   17   18   19   20   7   6   5   4   3   2   1

To my wife, Pat.
There's no one in the world I'd rather
spend time with than you!

To all those who love the Word of God.

Our relationship to the Scriptures must be a
lifelong quest to:

> Know what you believe
> Know why you believe it
> Know where to find it
> Choose to obey it
> Share it with others

> "The grass withers, the flower fades
> but the word of our God
> will stand forever."

Isaiah 40:8 ESV

Subject Guide

Acknowledgments

First of all, thanks to my wife, Pat, who had the vision in the beginning for *Quick Scripture Reference for Counseling Women*.

Pat and I both teach at Calvary Bible College in Kansas City. Thanks also to faculty, staff, and students of CBC who contributed ideas for topics, practical steps, and resources. Thanks to proofreaders Bill Gorman, our son-in-law, and Dr. Jim Clark, our college president. Thanks to librarian Eidene Anderson, who worked tirelessly to locate quality books to include in the resources sections for all three books in this series.

Thanks to Chad Allen and Mary Wenger of Baker Publishing for their confidence and assistance.

Introduction

The Purpose of This Book

This book is grounded on the sufficiency of the Word of God for faith and practice, for living the life that God desires, and for direction and counseling. It is written for men who are going through challenging times, as well as for those who desire to help others who struggle.

Context and Principles

I have made every effort to be true to biblical context. For those texts for which the context does not totally fit, I believe the principles (timeless, universal truths) do apply to the topic at hand. Many of the Old Testament passages refer, in context, to Israel. Yet the principles reflecting God's care for his people and interest in their welfare can clearly be seen.

My use of passages from the Mosaic Law reflects my conviction that the traditional moral, civil, and ceremonial distinctions for that code are correct. God's moral law, as summarized in the Ten Commandments, is applicable for all people, for all time. Though the civil and ceremonial laws are not our rule of life in this age of grace, they do reflect the mind of God on issues of right and wrong. Thus principles are drawn from them for the topics.

What to Look For

- The Gospel is the first topic in this book. It is necessary that we be prepared to lead individuals into a personal relationship with Jesus Christ as Savior and into a committed relationship with him as Lord of their lives.

- The "see also" heading at the beginning of each topic points to related helpful topics.

- Many of the chapters begin with a paragraph of introduction that defines key words and concepts, setting the stage for what follows in the body of statements and supporting Scripture.

- The "Biblical Narratives" are guides into the lives of people in Scripture who experienced situations and events similar to the issues in that particular topic.

- The "Practical Steps" are homework action ideas or growth steps. Use them as a starting point to stimulate your own creativity for additional steps.

- The "Resources" section is a guide to books and booklets helpful for further research and understanding.

- Because of length limitations, many verses are not printed, with biblical references listed for further study and application. *It is imperative to look up these verses for additional help with the topics.*

Who Might Benefit

- First and foremost this book is designed to assist counselors, pastors, and anyone who desires to help men in the struggles and issues of life.

- Pastors could use this book with their church boards to encourage individual growth, studying different topics as a part of regular board meetings.

- Men who desire to live their lives under the authority and blessing of God's Word can use this book for personal study and application of the various topics.

- This book can be used as a devotional. While the book is designed to help those who are struggling, it could also be a tool used each day for a man's time alone with the Lord. Taking two days for reading and study of each topic would provide over six months of meaningful involvement in Scripture.
- Teachers could use the various topics to present to Sunday school classes. Similar topics could be grouped together to cover a thirteen-week quarter.

The Gospel

A counselor's first task is to determine if an individual has a personal relationship with God through Christ. When a person has trusted Jesus Christ and him alone for salvation, Scripture will be effective in the person's life.

Steps in Guiding an Individual to Christ

1. **Each person is separated from God because of sin.**

   Romans 3:23 For all have sinned and fall short of the glory of God. (NKJV)
   Isaiah 53:6; 64:6; Romans 3:10

2. **Sin must be punished—separation from God, hell.**

   Romans 6:23 For the wages of sin is death, but the gift of God is eternal life in Christ Jesus our Lord. (NKJV)

3. **There is nothing a person can do to gain status with God or to earn their salvation. We cannot earn forgiveness.**

   Ephesians 2:8–9 For by grace you have been saved through faith. And this is not your own doing; it is the gift of God, not a result of works, so that no one may boast. (ESV)
   Titus 3:5

4. **God's love in sending Jesus is the answer.**

   John 3:16 For God so loved the world that He gave His only begotten Son, that whoever believes in Him should not perish but have everlasting life. (NKJV)
   Romans 5:8; 10:9

5. Each person must repent of their sin and personally believe (i.e., trust) in Jesus Christ as Savior.

   John 3:36 Whoever believes in the Son has eternal life, but whoever rejects the Son will not see life, for God's wrath remains on him. (NIV)
   Luke 15:7–10; John 1:12

6. Salvation is then assured—not a "maybe" or "hope so"—it is God's gift.

   John 5:24 Truly, truly, I say to you, whoever hears my word and believes him who sent me has eternal life. He does not come into judgment, but has passed from death to life. (ESV)
   1 John 5:13

Biblical Narratives

- Nicodemus, John 3
- Serpent in the wilderness, Numbers 21:4–9 with John 3:14
- Woman at the well, John 4
- The Ethiopian, Acts 8:26–40
- Cornelius, Acts 10
- Philippian jailor, Acts 16:16–40

Practical Steps

- For the best model or illustration of what the gospel looks like, do a comparison study of the serpent in the wilderness, Numbers 21:4–9, with John 3:14.
- Study carefully the Gospel of John. Note the multiple times "believe" is used.
- Question to ask: "If you were to die soon, why would you expect God to allow you to join him in heaven?"

Resources

- *What's So Amazing About Grace?* Philip Yancey. Zondervan.
- *A Gospel Primer for Christians*. Milton Vincent. Focus.
- *Assurance* (booklet). Susan Heck. Focus.
- *The Reason for God*. Timothy Keller. Dutton.

Abortion

See also Decision Making, Fear, Hope, Selfishness

Abortion is often seen as primarily a woman's issue. Yet any man who is the father of a child still in the womb is very much responsible for the welfare of that baby. Men must be vitally involved. Scripture is clear about this issue of life from conception and that an abortion is never the will of God.

The Need to Choose Life

1. **Birth is not the beginning of life; it is the arrival. The baby in the womb is a living human being from conception.**

    Psalm 139:13–15 For you formed my inward parts; you knitted me together in my mother's womb. I praise you, for I am fearfully and wonderfully made. Wonderful are your works; my soul knows it very well. My frame was not hidden from you, when I was being made in secret, intricately woven in the depths of the earth. (ESV)

2. **God is actively and personally involved in the life of every unborn person, including plans for each day of his or her life.**

    Psalm 139:16 Your eyes saw my unformed substance; in your book were written, every one of them, the days that were formed for me, when as yet there was none of them. (ESV)
    Genesis 25:21–23

3. **The prophets comprehended that God knew them as persons before they were born.**

    Jeremiah 1:5 I knew you before I formed you in your mother's womb. Before you were born I set you apart and appointed you as my prophet to the nations. (NLT)

Isaiah 49:1 Listen to me, you islands; hear this, you distant nations: before I was born the LORD called me; from my mother's womb he has spoken my name. (NIV)

4. **Elizabeth's unborn baby was aware of Jesus, Mary's unborn baby. Through a unique situation (the God-man in the womb), evidence is provided for personhood in the womb.**

Luke 1:44 As soon as the sound of your greeting reached my ears, the baby in my womb leaped for joy. (NIV) (See verses 39–44.)

5. **Following what we want, rather than what God wants, is sin and leads to heartache and trouble.**

Psalm 19:13 Keep your servant from deliberate sins! Don't let them control me. Then I will be free of guilt and innocent of great sin. (NLT)

Proverbs 14:12 There is a way that seems right to a man, but its end is the way to death. (ESV)

Proverbs 16:2

6. **Our actions are not hidden from God.**

2 Chronicles 16:9 The LORD keeps close watch over the whole world, to give strength to those whose hearts are loyal to him. (GNT)

Hebrews 4:13 Nothing in all creation is hidden from God's sight. Everything is uncovered and laid bare before the eyes of him to whom we must give account. (NIV)

Psalm 139:9–12

7. **Children are a gift from God, no matter the circumstances of their conception.**

Psalm 127:3–4 Behold, children are a gift of the LORD, the fruit of the womb is a reward. Like arrows in the hand of a warrior, so are the children of one's youth. (NASB)

8. Our bodies, our very lives, belong not to us but to God.

> **1 Corinthians 6:19–20** Don't you realize that your body is the temple of the Holy Spirit, who lives in you and was given to you by God? You do not belong to yourself, for God bought you with a high price. So you must honor God with your body. (NLT)
> **Romans 12:1–2; 2 Corinthians 6:16**

9. Choose life! Escaping from a pregnancy and its consequences is selfishness and sin. Choosing God's way might be difficult but is a decision that leads to life and peace.

> **Romans 8:5–6** Those who live according to the flesh have their minds set on what the flesh desires; but those who live in accordance with the Spirit have their minds set on what the Spirit desires. The mind governed by the flesh is death, but the mind governed by the Spirit is life and peace. (NIV)
> **Joshua 1:9; 24:14–15; Philippians 1:9–10**

Biblical Narratives

- Mary and Elizabeth, joys of motherhood, Luke 1:26–45
- Job, fashioned by God, Job 10:8–12
- Those needing rescue from death, Proverbs 24:11–12
- Harm to a mother and baby, Exodus 21:22–23. The death of a mother and baby are seen as of equal standing

Practical Steps

- You must understand the baby's development. Ask that an ultrasound be done.
- Memorize Psalm 139:16. Write it on a card and review often.
- Memorize Isaiah 43:1–2. Concentrate on "I will be with you."

Resources

Pro-life Answers to Pro-choice Arguments. Randy Alcorn. Multnomah.

If an Abortion Has Occurred

See also Confession, Forgiveness from God, Grief, Past Memories

1. When God's forgiveness is requested, it is given freely.

> **Psalm 32:5** I acknowledged my sin to You, and my iniquity I
> have not hidden. I said, "I will confess my transgressions to the
> LORD," and You forgave the iniquity of my sin. (NKJV)

2. God can take our broken spirits and produce joy.

> **Psalm 51:12, 14** Restore to me the joy of Your salvation, and
> uphold me by Your generous Spirit. . . . Deliver me from the guilt
> of bloodshed, O God, the God of my salvation, and my tongue
> shall sing aloud of Your righteousness. (NKJV)

3. God offers restoration and freedom.

> **Psalm 40:1–3** I waited patiently for the LORD; he turned to me
> and heard my cry. He lifted me out of the slimy pit, out of the
> mud and mire; he set my feet on a rock and gave me a firm place
> to stand. He put a new song in my mouth, a hymn of praise to
> our God. (NIV)
>
> **John 8:32, 36** Then you will know the truth, and the truth
> will set you free. . . . So if the Son sets you free, you will be free
> indeed. (NIV)

4. God understands the Israelites weeping for children they would
   never see again. He understands our grief over the loss of a baby.

> **Jeremiah 31:15** Thus says the LORD: a voice was heard in
> Ramah, lamentation and bitter weeping, Rachel weeping for
> her children, refusing to be comforted for her children, because
> they are no more. (NKJV)

5. As the Israelites in captivity were not to dwell on past mistakes, we also should not dwell on the past once it is forgiven.

> Isaiah 43:18–19 Forget the former things; do not dwell on the past. See, I am doing a new thing! Now it springs up; do you not perceive it? I am making a way in the desert and streams in the wasteland. (NIV)
> Micah 7:18–19

6. God is our source of relief and comfort when we grieve.

> Psalm 18:1–2, 6 How I love you, LORD! You are my defender. The LORD is my protector; he is my strong fortress. My God is my protection, and with him I am safe. He protects me like a shield; he defends me and keeps me safe. . . . In my trouble I called to the LORD; I called to my God for help. In his temple he heard my voice; he listened to my cry for help. (GNT)
> Isaiah 25:8 The Sovereign LORD will destroy death forever! He will wipe away the tears from everyone's eyes and take away the disgrace his people have suffered throughout the world. The LORD himself has spoken. (GNT)

Practical Steps

- Study carefully the topics Forgiveness from God and Grief in this book.

Resources

- *When the Pain Won't Go Away: Dealing with the Effects of Abortion* (booklet). RBC Ministries.
- *Healing after Abortion* (booklet). David Powlison. New Growth.
- *Hope Again.* Charles Swindoll. Thomas Nelson.

Abuse

See also Anger, Bitterness, Forgiveness from God, Forgiving Others, Grief, Past Memories, Repentance

It is always wrong to abuse anyone in any way—verbally, physically, emotionally, sexually, politically, or economically! If you have suffered abuse, God has great provision for recovery and healing.

For Those Who Are Tempted to Abuse or Have Abused Others

1. **Afflicting or oppressing the helpless is forbidden. God hears their cry.**

   Exodus 22:21–23 You shall not wrong a stranger or oppress him, for you were strangers in the land of Egypt. You shall not afflict any widow or orphan. If you afflict him at all, and if he does cry out to Me, I will surely hear his cry. (NASB)

   Isaiah 3:14–15 "It is you who have devoured the vineyard; the plunder of the poor is in your houses. What do you mean by crushing My people and grinding the face of the poor?" declares the Lord GOD of hosts. (NASB)

   Psalm 40:14; Proverbs 30:14; Amos 5:11–13; Micah 2:1–2, 9

2. **Abusive words cause great pain.**

   James 3:8–9 No one can tame the tongue. It is restless and evil, full of deadly poison. Sometimes it praises our Lord and Father, and sometimes it curses those who have been made in the image of God. (NLT)

   Proverbs 12:18 Some people make cutting remarks, but the words of the wise bring healing. (NLT)

   Proverbs 15:4

3. Those who abuse can expect God's judgment.

Psalm 10:12–14 Arise, O LORD; O God, lift up Your hand. Do not forget the afflicted. Why has the wicked spurned God? He has said to himself, "You will not require it." You have seen it, for You have beheld mischief and vexation to take it into Your hand. The unfortunate commits himself to You; You have been the helper of the orphan. (NASB)

Matthew 18:5–6 And whoever receives one such child in My name receives Me; but whoever causes one of these little ones who believe in Me to stumble, it would be better for him to have a heavy millstone hung around his neck, and to be drowned in the depth of the sea. (NASB)

Psalm 9:12; 37:17; Isaiah 10:1–3

4. What to do: repent, confess, and make it right. Get help.

1 John 1:8–9 If we say that we have no sin, we are deceiving ourselves and the truth is not in us. If we confess our sins, He is faithful and righteous to forgive us our sins and to cleanse us from all unrighteousness. (NASB)

Isaiah 1:16–17

For Those Who Have Been Abused

1. We must not allow past events to control the present. When there is nothing we can do to correct the past, we must entrust it to God's care.

Isaiah 43:18–19 Do not cling to events of the past or dwell on what happened long ago. Watch for the new thing I am going to do. It is happening already—you can see it now! I will make a road through the wilderness and give you streams of water there. (GNT)

Matthew 10:26; Philippians 3:13

2. Revenge is not an acceptable option. We must leave the matter to God.

Romans 12:17, 19 Repay no one evil for evil, but give thought to do what is honorable in the sight of all. . . . Beloved, never avenge yourselves, but leave it to the wrath of God, for it is written, "Vengeance is mine, I will repay, says the Lord." (ESV)
Proverbs 20:22; 24:29; 1 Thessalonians 5:15

3. Genuine forgiveness of an abuser is difficult but necessary. Holding on to anger or bitterness only hurts oneself.

Colossians 3:13–14 Bear with each other and forgive one another if any of you has a grievance against someone. Forgive as the Lord forgave you. And over all these virtues put on love, which binds them all together in perfect unity. (NIV)
Ephesians 4:31–32; Hebrews 12:14–15

4. To move beyond past abuse, we must refocus our thinking on all that God has done for us, his gracious provision.

Psalm 63:6–8 On my bed I remember you; I think of you through the watches of the night. Because you are my help, I sing in the shadow of your wings. I cling to you; your right hand upholds me. (NIV)
Philippians 4:8 And now, dear brothers and sisters, one final thing. Fix your thoughts on what is true, and honorable, and right, and pure, and lovely, and admirable. Think about things that are excellent and worthy of praise. (NLT)
Psalm 143:5–8

Biblical Narratives

- Hagar suffered at the hand of Sarah, Genesis 16
- Joseph, Genesis 37
- Job, the suffering of the abused, Job 24
- David, abused by Saul, 1 Samuel 18–26
- Tamar, abused by Amnon, 2 Samuel 13:1–25
- Description of abuse, Psalm 10:7–11

Practical Steps

- Immerse yourself in Scripture, especially the Psalms of refuge and comfort—34; 37; 46; 63; 64; 91; 121; 145.
- Write out your story and share it with a trusted close friend or counselor.
- As you are able to move past the hurt and disgust, be open to helping others who have had similar experiences.
- If you are abusing others in any way, repent and confess this evil, seek immediate counsel, become accountable to others who can help.

Resources

- *Abused: Finding Hope in Christ* (booklet). John Henerson. P & R.
- *Abused: How You Can Find God's Help*. Richard and Lois Klempel. Fairway.
- *Recovering from Abuse* (booklet). David Powlison. CCEF.
- *Rid of My Disgrace: Hope and Healing for Victims of Sexual Abuse*. Justin and Lindsey Holcomb. Crossway.

Adultery

See also Confession, Forgiveness from God, Forgiving Others, Integrity, Marriage, Pornography, Sexual Purity, Temptation

Adultery is any sexual involvement with someone other than your wife or (if you are single) who is the wife of someone else. It includes thoughts, touching, or intercourse.

Adultery Is Sin

1. **Adultery is a sin against God. He forbids it; it is against his law. Absolutely, case closed.**

   Exodus 20:14 You shall not commit adultery. (NKJV)

   Genesis 39:9 There is no one greater in this house than I, and he has withheld nothing from me except you, because you are his wife. How then could I do this great evil and sin against God? (NASB)

   Proverbs 5:20; Romans 13:9–10

2. **It is sin to desire or take what belongs to another—another man's wife.**

   Exodus 20:15, 17 You shall not steal. . . . you shall not covet your neighbor's wife. (ESV)

   1 Thessalonians 4:6–7 Never harm or cheat a Christian brother in this matter by violating his wife, for the Lord avenges all such sins, as we have solemnly warned you before. God has called us to live holy lives, not impure lives. (NLT)

   Jeremiah 5:7–8

3. Lustful thinking—imagining what it would be like to be with someone else—is mental and emotional adultery—sin. Like Job, men need commitment to "bouncing their eyes" away from the object of lust.

> **Job 31:1** I made a covenant with my eyes not to look with lust at a young woman. (NLT)
>
> **Matthew 5:28** But I say to you that everyone who looks at a woman with lustful intent has already committed adultery with her in his heart. (ESV)

4. An individual has no right to separate what God has placed together.

> **Mark 10:8–9** And the two shall become one flesh. So they are no longer two but one flesh. What therefore God has joined together, let not man separate. (ESV)

Consequences of Adultery

1. Adultery, like all sin, separates us from God. Only Jesus Christ offers us freedom.

> 1 Corinthians 6:9–13

2. Adultery leads to destruction.

> **Proverbs 6:27–29, 32** Can you carry fire against your chest without burning your clothes? Can you walk on hot coals without burning your feet? It is just as dangerous to sleep with another man's wife. Whoever does it will suffer. . . . But a man who commits adultery doesn't have any sense. He is just destroying himself. (GNT)
>
> Proverbs 5:20–23

Steps for Preventing Adultery

1. Realize its source. Adultery happens when a person's heart is not focused on Christ.

> **Matthew 15:19** For out of the heart come evil thoughts, murders, adulteries, fornications, thefts, false witness, slanders. (NASB)
>
> 2 Corinthians 5:17; Hebrews 12:1–2

2. **Adultery is prevented by changing our thinking and accepting it as the sin it is.**

   Romans 8:5–6 Those who are dominated by the sinful nature think about sinful things, but those who are controlled by the Holy Spirit think about things that please the Spirit. So letting your sinful nature control your mind leads to death. But letting the Spirit control your mind leads to life and peace. (NLT)
   Romans 12:1–2

3. **With God's help, temptation can be resisted.**

   1 Corinthians 10:13–14 No temptation has overtaken you but such as is common to man; and God is faithful, who will not allow you to be tempted beyond what you are able, but with the temptation will provide the way of escape also, so that you will be able to endure it. Therefore, my beloved, flee from idolatry [includes other sins]. (NASB)

4. **We must renew our commitment to honor our vows.**

   Hebrews 13:4 Marriage is to be honored by all, and husbands and wives must be faithful to each other. God will judge those who are immoral and those who commit adultery. (GNT)
   Malachi 2:13–16

5. **Exercising wisdom and self-control is essential.**

   1 Thessalonians 4:3–4 It is God's will that you should be sanctified: that you should avoid sexual immorality; that each of you should learn to control your own body in a way that is holy and honorable. (NIV)
   Proverbs 2:16 Wisdom will save you also from the adulterous woman, from the wayward woman with her seductive words. (NIV)

6. **A healthy sexual relationship within marriage is helpful.**

   1 Corinthians 7:2–3 But because there is so much sexual immorality, each man should have his own wife, and each woman should have her own husband. The husband should fulfill his wife's sexual needs, and the wife should fulfill her husband's needs. (NLT)

If Adultery Has Occurred

1. If a man falls into the sin of adultery, he must confess, repent, and seek God's forgiveness and restoration with his wife.

   1 John 1:9 If we confess our sins, He is faithful and just to forgive us our sins and to cleanse us from all unrighteousness. (NKJV)

   Psalm 32:1, 5 Blessed is the one whose transgression is forgiven, whose sin is covered. . . . I acknowledged my sin to you, and I did not cover my iniquity; I said, "I will confess my transgressions to the LORD," and you forgave the iniquity of my sin. (ESV)

2. If your wife has failed in this area and responds with confession and repentance, forgiveness and restoration are now your responsibility.

   Colossians 3:12–13 Put on then, as God's chosen ones, holy and beloved, compassionate hearts, kindness, humility, meekness, and patience, bearing with one another and, if one has a complaint against another, forgiving each other; as the Lord has forgiven you, so you also must forgive. (ESV)

   Hosea 3:1 The LORD said to me, "Go again and show your love for a woman who is committing adultery with a lover. You must love her just as I still love the people of Israel, even though they turn to other gods and like to take offerings of raisins to idols." (GNT)

   Ephesians 4:32

Biblical Narratives

- David, 2 Samuel 11:2–5 with Psalm 51
- Wayward Israelites, 1 Corinthians 10:6–8, 11; Exodus 32:1–10
- Joseph, resisting temptation, Genesis 39

- Two unnamed women, Luke 7:37–47; John 8:1–11
- Warnings against adultery, Proverbs 5; 6:20–35; 7

Practical Steps

- Take pictures of your wife and children to work with you. Place them strategically around your office to let other women know you are unavailable. Take them on business trips as well, to look at and show others.
- When tempting thoughts come, pray quickly for help. Pray, "Lord, please remove that thought from me," or "Lord, through your Spirit, I reject that thought."
- If adultery has happened, consider the possibility of how you might have contributed to the infidelity (your own or your wife's). Create a plan and take radical steps to prevent it from happening again—Matthew 5:29–30. (A metaphorical, not literal, statement from Jesus.)
- Seek restoration. Distance yourself from past relationships. Date your wife. Write letters to her. Seek accountability.

Resources

- *After Adultery* (booklet). Robert Jones. New Growth.
- *Help! My Spouse Committed Adultery* (booklet). Winston Smith. CCEF.
- "Maintaining Moral Purity" in *The Measure of a Man*. Gene Getz. Regal.
- "You Shall Not Commit Adultery" in *Pathway to Freedom: How God's Laws Guide Our Lives*. Alistair Begg. Moody.
- "Sexual Temptations and Lust" in *Character Counts*. Rod Handley. Cross Training.

Aging/Retirement

See also Contentment, Purpose for Living, Trust, Widower

In our youth-oriented society, aging is seen by many as something to avoid at all costs. The Bible addresses the inevitability of aging and provides positive encouragement. What about the "American dream" of retirement? What should be the Christian's response? Is it a biblical concept at all?

1. **Aging, along with the brevity of life, can be frustrating.**

   Job 14:1–2, 5 How frail is humanity! How short is life, how full of trouble! We blossom like a flower and then wither. Like a passing shadow, we quickly disappear. . . . You have decided the length of our lives. You know how many months we will live, and we are not given a minute longer. (NLT)

   James 4:14 Yet you do not know what tomorrow will bring. What is your life? For you are a mist that appears for a little time and then vanishes. (ESV)

   Psalm 39:5–6; 90:3–12

2. **The fact that the stages of life move by so quickly is a reminder to make the best of the years we are allowed, glorifying God each day.**

   Psalm 115:1 Not to us, O LORD, not to us, but to your name give glory, for the sake of your steadfast love and your faithfulness! (ESV)

   2 Corinthians 5:9 More than anything else, however, we want to please him, whether in our home here or there. (GNT)

   Psalm 34:12–15; 72:19; 79:9; 1 Corinthians 10:31

3. That God allows us to live to an advanced age is something for which we should be thankful.

Proverbs 16:31 Gray hair is a crown of splendor; it is attained in the way of righteousness. (NIV)
Psalm 118:24; Proverbs 20:29

4. God understands every stage of life and is worthy of our trust.

Psalm 31:14–15 But I trust in you, O LORD; I say, "You are my God. My times are in your hand." (ESV)
Psalm 34:8–9; 91:11–12

5. God provides for every season of life.

Isaiah 46:4 Even to your old age and gray hairs I am he, I am he who will sustain you. I have made you and I will carry you; I will sustain you and I will rescue you. (NIV)
Isaiah 35:3–4 Strengthen the weak hands, and make firm the feeble knees. Say to those who have an anxious heart, "Be strong; fear not! Behold, your God will come with vengeance, with the recompense of God. He will come and save you." (ESV)
Psalm 71:9; Isaiah 40:29–31; 58:11

6. Our senior years should be a productive time. If retirement means slowing down and not working as much to make money, that is acceptable, but we should always be serving Christ and others all of our days.

Psalm 71:18 So even to old age and gray hairs, O God, do not forsake me, until I proclaim your might to another generation, your power to all those to come. (ESV)
Psalm 92:12–14 But the godly will flourish like palm trees and grow strong like the cedars of Lebanon. For they are transplanted to the LORD's own house. They flourish in the courts of our God. Even in old age they will still produce fruit; they will remain vital and green. (NLT)
Job 12:12; Galatians 6:9; 1 Corinthians 15:58; 2 Thessalonians 3:13

Biblical Narratives

- Job, blessed in his latter days, Job 42:12–17
- Abraham and Sarah, used of God in their old age, Genesis 17:1–18:15
- Jacob, at the end of his life, Genesis 48–49
- Caleb, who refused to retire, Joshua 14:1–15
- Paul's testimony, 2 Timothy 4:6–8

Practical Steps

- Be active with frequent physical exercise. This is essential for mental and emotional health.
- Seek wise advice for financial planning and big decisions.
- Minister to others at nursing homes or as a hospital volunteer. Reach out through calls and letters. Invest in the lives of others. See 2 Timothy 2:2.
- Keep your mind active and sharp through word and number games.
- Make a time line of important life events, thanking God for his care.
- Write Isaiah 46:4 on a three-by-five-inch card. Post it or carry it. Review often.

Resources

- *The Art of Aging*. Howard Eyrich. Focus.
- *The Joys of Successful Aging*. George Sweeting. Moody.
- *Lost in the Middle: Midlife and the Grace of God*. Paul Tripp. Shepherd.
- "Retirement" and "Aging" in *The Strength of a Man: 50 Devotionals to Help Men Find Their Strength in God*. David Roper. Discovery House.

Anger/Rage

See also Bitterness, Confession, Forgiving Others, Selfishness, Thought Life

Anger is a strong emotional reaction brought about by an offense against us. Rage suggests violent emotion and loss of self-control. Both anger and rage can be expressed in thoughts, words, or actions.

Becoming Angry

Righteous or indignant anger is appropriate, according to Scripture, when sin is being committed.

1. **God expresses righteous anger against sin.**

   Numbers 32:13 And the LORD's anger was kindled against Israel, and he made them wander in the wilderness forty years, until all the generation that had done evil in the sight of the LORD was gone. (ESV)
   Exodus 32:10; Numbers 11:1; Deuteronomy 9:8; Jeremiah 6:11

2. **Jesus also expressed righteous anger.**

   Mark 3:5 He looked around at them angrily and was deeply saddened by their hard hearts. (NLT)
   Mark 11:15; Matthew 21:12–13 (in the temple)

3. **The believer can also express righteous anger. There are times when we need to be angry about sin.**

   Ephesians 4:26 Be angry, and yet do not sin; do not let the sun go down on your anger. (NASB)

Unrighteous Anger

Unrighteous or sinful anger is when we choose to become angry because of being personally affronted in some way.

1. **Anger is included in a list of troubling sins.**

   Galatians 5:19–21 What human nature does is quite plain. It shows itself in immoral, filthy, and indecent actions; in worship of idols and witchcraft. People become enemies and they fight; they become jealous, angry, and ambitious . . . get drunk, have orgies, and do other things like these. I warn you now as I have before: those who do these things will not possess the Kingdom of God. (GNT)
   Proverbs 29:22

2. **Anger is loss of self-control and must be dealt with immediately.**

   Proverbs 29:11 A fool always loses his temper, but a wise man holds it back. (NASB)
   Ephesians 4:31 Let all bitterness and wrath and anger and clamor and slander be put away from you, along with all malice. (ESV)
   Psalm 37:8; Colossians 3:8

3. **To avoid anger, men need to listen more, talk less, slow down, and not react poorly.**

   James 1:19–20 Remember this, my dear brothers! Everyone must be quick to listen, but slow to speak and slow to become angry. Man's anger does not achieve God's righteous purpose. (GNT)
   Proverbs 14:17 People with a hot temper do foolish things; wiser people remain calm. (GNT)
   Proverbs 20:3; Ecclesiastes 7:9

4. Married men, and those with children, must be doubly cautious to rid themselves of anger. Inappropriate or poorly expressed anger is a major factor in family problems.

Ephesians 5:25, 28–29 Husbands, love your wives, just as Christ loved the church and gave himself up for her. . . . In this same way, husbands ought to love their wives as their own bodies. He who loves his wife loves himself. After all, no one ever hated their own body, but they feed and care for their body, just as Christ does the church. (NIV)

Ephesians 6:4 Fathers, do not exasperate your children. (NIV)

Colossians 3:19–21

Responding to Anger

1. Practicing a gentle and kind response and avoiding irritation will greatly reduce episodes of anger.

Proverbs 15:1 A gentle answer turns away wrath, but a harsh word stirs up anger. (NASB)

Proverbs 15:18 A hot-tempered man stirs up strife, but he who is slow to anger quiets contention. (ESV)

Proverbs 20:22; 25:15; Romans 12:19

2. If anger is experienced, the issue should be resolved that day between those involved. At the very least, a specific plan must be made for a resolution in the near future.

Ephesians 4:26–27 And "don't sin by letting anger control you." Don't let the sun go down while you are still angry, for anger gives a foothold to the devil. (NLT)

Psalm 4:4

3. Respond with patience—the opposite of anger. Patience is a slow, reasoned, and understanding response to a situation.

Proverbs 15:18 A hot-tempered person stirs up conflict, but the one who is patient calms a quarrel. (NIV)

Proverbs 14:29; 16:32; 19:11

4. People who have a tendency toward anger are not the best choices for close friends or marriage partners.

> **Proverbs 22:24–25** Make no friendship with a man given to anger, nor go with a wrathful man, lest you learn his ways and entangle yourself in a snare. (ESV)
> **Proverbs 21:19** Better to dwell in the wilderness, than with a contentious and angry woman. (NKJV)
> **Psalm 119:63; Proverbs 19:9; 25:24**

Biblical Narratives

- Cain and Abel, Genesis 4:1–15
- Gideon responds gently to accusations, Judges 8:1–3; see Proverbs 15:1
- Nabal's rage, 1 Samuel 25:9–17
- Asa's sinful anger, 2 Chronicles 16:10
- Jonah, angry with God, Jonah 4

Practical Steps

- If you are a "road rage" person, you must correct this unbiblical and dangerous behavior immediately. Think carefully though this and other similar situations that push you toward anger. Seek mature, godly men and biblical solutions to help you.
- Do not attempt to reason with someone when they are angry; wait until you both can communicate with reason.
- Every time you confess your anger to God (and others you have affected), redirect your energy toward a solution to the problem. Center on Scripture.
- Write James 1:19–20 on a card. Memorize the passage and keep it close at hand.

Resources

- "Anger—Burning Fuse of Hostility" in *Three Steps Forward, Two Steps Back*. Charles Swindoll. Thomas Nelson.
- *Basics for Angry Believers*. Jim Berg. BJU.
- *Living with an Angry Spouse* (booklet). Ed Welch. New Growth.
- *Overcoming Emotions That Destroy: Practical Help for Those Angry Feelings That Ruin Relationships*. Chip Ingram. Baker.
- "Sinful Anger" in *Feelings and Faith: Cultivating Godly Emotions in the Christian Life*. Brian Borgman. Crossway.
- *Anger and Stress Management God's Way*. Wayne Mack. Calvary Press.

Anxiety/Worry

See also Depression, Failure, Fear, Thought Life, Trust

Anxiety in Scripture is expressed with a number of different Hebrew and Greek words, most of which have to do with negative thinking. Anxious thinking is beyond the normal reasoning process. Descriptions for it include dread, apprehension, hesitation, agitation, uneasiness, loss of control, doubt, a "gnawing away," or worry.

1. **Anxiety results in heaviness of heart and provides no relief to the situation.**

   Proverbs 12:25 Anxiety in a man's heart weighs him down, but a good word makes him glad. (ESV)

   Job 6:2–3 If my misery could be weighed and my troubles be put on the scales, they would outweigh all the sands of the sea. (NLT)

2. **We must live by faith and not by sight. Anxiety pulls us down when we focus on what** *might be* **rather than what** *is*.

   Psalm 73:2–3 But I had nearly lost confidence; my faith was almost gone because I was jealous of the proud when I saw that things go well for the wicked. (GNT)

   Psalm 142:4–5 When I look beside me, I see that there is no one to help me, no one to protect me. No one cares for me. LORD, I cry to you for help; you, LORD, are my protector. (GNT)

   Job 23:8–10; Philippians 4:8; 2 Timothy 1:7

3. Giving the problem back to God, asking for his help, is the proper response to anxiety.

   1 Peter 5:7 Give all your worries and cares to God, for he cares about you. (NLT)
   Philippians 4:6 Don't worry about anything; instead, pray about everything. Tell God what you need, and thank him for all he has done. (NLT)
   Isaiah 41:10–13

4. Anxiety is linked to envy and jealousy.

   Proverbs 24:19–20 Fret not yourself because of evildoers, and be not envious of the wicked, for the evil man has no future; the lamp of the wicked will be put out. (ESV)
   Psalm 37:1–9

5. God's sufficient resources are more than enough for our every concern.

   2 Corinthians 12:9 But he said to me, "My grace is sufficient for you, for my power is made perfect in weakness." Therefore I will boast all the more gladly of my weaknesses, so that the power of Christ may rest upon me. (ESV)
   Ephesians 1:3; Philippians 4:13–19; Romans 8:32

6. Trusting God's sovereignty replaces anxiety with peace. He has our best interests at heart.

   Isaiah 26:3–4 You keep him in perfect peace whose mind is stayed on you, because he trusts in you. Trust in the LORD forever, for the LORD GOD is an everlasting rock. (ESV)
   Psalm 139:16; Isaiah 45:5–7

7. Knowing that God has plans all laid out for us removes anxiety about the future.

   Jeremiah 29:11–13 For I know the plans I have for you, declares the LORD, plans for welfare and not for evil, to give you a future and a hope. Then you will call upon me and come and pray to me, and I will hear you. You will seek me and find me, when you seek me with all your heart. (ESV)

Matthew 6:33–34 But seek first the kingdom of God and his righteousness, and all these things will be added to you. Therefore do not be anxious about tomorrow, for tomorrow will be anxious for itself. Sufficient for the day is its own trouble. (ESV)

John 14:1–3; James 4:15

8. **God can use any situation for good, even those that trouble us.**

Romans 8:28 And we know that for those who love God all things work together for good, for those who are called according to his purpose. (ESV)

Biblical Narratives

- Hannah, anxious because she was childless, 1 Samuel 1
- Jeremiah, concerned about committing to God's plan to purchase property, Jeremiah 32:24–27
- David, realizing he must focus on God and not his enemies, Psalm 13

Practical Steps

- Memorize Isaiah 41:10.
- Read chapter 22 in *The Knowledge of the Holy* by A. W. Tozer.
- Listen to Christian music that speaks of God's provision, strength, and guidance.
- Keep a prayer list and write down when God answers. Review God's answers when your faith is weak.
- Physical exercise is a must at least three times a week for thirty minutes. It makes a huge difference in mental attitude.

Resources

- *Anxiety: Anatomy and Cure* (booklet). Robert Kellerman. P & R.
- *Anxious for Nothing.* John MacArthur. Victor.
- *Anger, Anxiety,* and Fear (booklet). Stuart Scott. Focus.
- "Fear, Anxiety, and Worry" in *Feelings and Faith: Cultivating Godly Emotions in the Christian Life.* Brian Borgman. Crossway.
- *God's Attributes: Rest for Life's Struggles* (booklet). Brad Hambrick. P & R.
- *Running Scared: Fear, Worry, and the God of Rest.* Ed Welch. New Growth.

Attitude/Mind

See also Forgiving Others, Priorities, Purpose for Living, Selfishness, Thought Life

Having a godly, positive attitude will make all the difference in enjoying happiness, success, and contentment in life. "Words can never adequately convey the incredible impact of our attitude toward life. The longer I live the more convinced I become that life is 10 percent what happens to us and 90 percent how we respond to it. . . . When my attitude is right, there's no barrier too high, no valley too deep, no dream too extreme, no challenge too great for me" (Charles Swindoll, *Strengthening Your Grip*).

1. **Loving and serving God must have first priority in our thinking.**

   Deuteronomy 10:12–13 Now, people of Israel, listen to what the LORD your God demands of you: Worship the LORD and do all that he commands. Love him, serve him with all your heart, and obey all his laws. I am giving them to you today for your benefit. (GNT)
   Joshua 23:11; 24:14–15; Matthew 22:37

2. **We must maintain an eternal perspective in our thinking.**

   Colossians 3:2 Set your minds on things that are above, not on things that are on earth. (ESV)
   2 Corinthians 4:18 We look not to the things that are seen but to the things that are unseen. For the things that are seen are transient, but the things that are unseen are eternal. (ESV)
   Matthew 16:23–25; Romans 14:7–8

3. **Our minds must be focused on spiritual things—what God desires for us.**

   Romans 8:5 Those who live according to the flesh have their minds set on what the flesh desires; but those who live in accordance with the Spirit have their minds set on what the Spirit desires. (NIV)

4. **We must have transformed, renewed minds and must not think as unbelievers think.**

   Romans 12:2 Do not be conformed to this world, but be transformed by the renewal of your mind, that by testing you may discern what is the will of God, what is good and acceptable and perfect. (ESV)
   Ephesians 4:17–24

5. **We must think sacrificially, placing others ahead of ourselves.**

   John 15:13 Greater love has no one than this, that someone lays down his life for his friends. (ESV)
   Ephesians 4:2; Philippians 2:3–7

6. **A humble attitude is pleasing to God. Sinful pride he clearly hates.**

   Proverbs 8:13 The fear of the LORD is hatred of evil. Pride and arrogance and the way of evil and perverted speech I hate. (ESV)
   Romans 12:3 For by the grace given to me I say to everyone among you not to think of himself more highly than he ought to think, but to think with sober judgment, each according to the measure of faith that God has assigned. (ESV)
   Proverbs 11:2; 16:18; 18:12; Romans 12:16

7. **When others have wronged us, an attitude of forgiveness is commanded. Bitterness must be put away.**

   Ephesians 4:30–32 And do not grieve the Holy Spirit of God, by whom you were sealed for the day of redemption. Let all bitterness and wrath and anger and clamor and slander be put away from you, along with all malice. Be kind to one another, tenderhearted, forgiving one another, as God in Christ forgave you. (ESV)

Romans 12:17–21

Biblical Narratives

- Cain, his bad attitude, Genesis 4:5–7
- Joseph, his good attitude toward his brothers, Genesis 50:15–21
- Jesus, sacrificial thinking, Philippians 2:5–8
- Paul, his attitude of contentment, Philippians 4:10–13

Practical Steps

- Complete a biblical word study of the many uses of the words *mind*, *thinking*, and *thoughts* to better understand God's thoughts on our thoughts.
- Ask this question often: what difference will this make in eternity? Keep perspective when you are frustrated over little things.
- Study Romans 12:2. Make a list of areas that need to change and how you plan to bring about that change. Remember, behavior changes when the mind changes.

Resources

- *The Christian Mind: How Should a Christian Think?* (an older classic). Harry Blamires. Servant.
- "Discipline of Mind" in *Disciplines of a Godly Man*. Kent Hughes. Crossway.
- *Lord, Change My Attitude*. James MacDonald. Moody.
- *You Can Change: God's Transforming Power for Our Sinful Behavior and Negative Emotions*. Tim Chester. Crossway.

Authority/Rebellion

See also Complaining, Integrity, Work Ethic

1. **God is the ultimate authority for every person. He requires obedience.**

> **Job 42:2** I know that you can do all things, and that no purpose of yours can be thwarted. (ESV)
>
> **Isaiah 43:13** From eternity to eternity I am God. No one can snatch anyone out of my hand. No one can undo what I have done. (NLT)
>
> **Jeremiah 7:23** But this command I gave them: "Obey my voice, and I will be your God, and you shall be my people. And walk in all the way that I command you, that it may be well with you." (ESV)
>
> **Psalm 119:59–60; Proverbs 16:9; Ecclesiastes 12:13–14**

2. **Church leaders are to be respected and obeyed as long as they are true to God's Word.**

> **Hebrews 13:17** Obey your leaders and submit to them, for they are keeping watch over your souls, as those who will have to give an account. Let them do this with joy and not with groaning, for that would be of no advantage to you. (ESV)
>
> **1 Thessalonians 5:12–13**

3. **God has established governmental authorities for our good.**

> **Romans 13:1, 5** Everyone must submit to governing authorities. For all authority comes from God, and those in positions of authority have been placed there by God. . . . So you must submit to them, not only to avoid punishment, but also to keep a clear conscience. (NLT)
>
> **1 Peter 2:13–15**

4. Civil disobedience is acceptable when authorities try to restrict the spread of the gospel.

> Acts 4:19–20 But Peter and John answered them, "Whether it is right in the sight of God to listen to you rather than to God, you must judge, for we cannot but speak of what we have seen and heard." (ESV)
> Acts 5:27–29

5. Respectful obedience is due your employer. If you are the employer justice and fairness are due to employees. (For application in today's culture, substitute "workers" for "slaves" and "employers" for "masters.")

> Colossians 3:22–24 Slaves, obey your earthly masters in everything; and do it, not only when their eye is on you and to curry their favor, but with sincerity of heart and reverence for the Lord. Whatever you do, work at it with all your heart, as working for the Lord, not for human masters, since you know that you will receive an inheritance from the Lord as a reward. It is the Lord Christ you are serving. (NIV)
> Colossians 4:1 Masters, provide your slaves with what is right and fair, because you know that you also have a Master in heaven. (NIV)
> Ephesians 6:5–9; Titus 2:9–10; 1 Timothy 6:1–2; 1 Peter 2:18–19

6. While adults are no longer under parental authority, parents must be given honor and respect.

> Exodus 20:12 Honor your father and your mother, that your days may be long in the land that the LORD your God is giving you. (ESV)
> Proverbs 23:22 Listen to your father, who gave you life, and don't despise your mother when she is old. (NLT)

7. Rebellious attitudes and actions are sinful and will bring God's discipline.

Isaiah 1:19–20 If you are willing and obedient, you shall eat the good of the land; but if you refuse and rebel, you shall be eaten by the sword; for the mouth of the LORD has spoken. (ESV)
1 Samuel 15:22–23; Isaiah 63:10; 65:2

8. Submissive obedience to God's authority brings blessing. God has our best interests at heart.

Deuteronomy 8:1, 6 Every commandment which I command you today you must be careful to observe, that you may live and multiply, and go in and possess the land of which the LORD swore to your fathers. . . . Therefore you shall keep the commandments of the LORD your God, to walk in His ways and to fear Him. (NKJV)
John 15:10–11 If you keep My commandments, you will abide in My love, just as I have kept My Father's commandments and abide in His love. These things I have spoken to you, that My joy may remain in you, and that your joy may be full. (NKJV)
Deuteronomy 10:20–21

Biblical Narratives

- Tower of Babel, mankind doing its own thing, Genesis 11
- Esau, Genesis 28:6–9
- Sons of Eli, rebellious, out of control, 1 Samuel 2:22–25
- Saul, partially obedient, 1 Samuel 15
- Prodigal, rebelled but returned, Luke 15:11–32
- Jesus, all authority comes from God, John 19:11

Practical Steps

- Complete a biblical word study on *rebellion* and *obedience*. Ask God to make his view of authority your view.

- Avoid watching movies or TV where fathers and husbands are mocked, portrayed as ignorant, weak, or poor leaders. This is especially important for your family viewing times.

- Study this question: why does God give us rules and standards to live by? Make a list of what happens when people obey God, and what happens when we get outside of God's boundaries.

Resources

- *Authority Issues: When It's Hard Being Told What to Do.* Robert Smith. New Growth.

- "Replace a Rebellious Attitude . . . with an Attitude of Submission" in *Lord, Change My Attitude.* James MacDonald. Moody.

Birth Control

See also Decision Making, Fathering, Marriage

Husbands should not expect their wives to be solely responsible for birth control and need to be actively involved in decisions that are made. We are to be good stewards of our fertility. Scripture does not speak specifically to this issue; however, these principles apply.

1. Children are God's gift and blessing.

Psalm 127:3–5 Behold, children are a heritage from the LORD, the fruit of the womb a reward. Like arrows in the hand of a warrior are the children of one's youth. Blessed is the man who fills his quiver with them! He shall not be put to shame when he speaks with his enemies in the gate. (ESV)

Proverbs 17:6 Children's children are a crown to the aged, and parents are the pride of their children. (NIV)

Genesis 1:27–28; Psalm 128:3–4; Matthew 18:5

2. Decisions need to be made prayerfully, seeking God's wisdom for guidance.

James 1:5 If any of you lacks wisdom, you should ask God, who gives generously to all without finding fault, and it will be given to you. (NIV)

Ephesians 5:15–17 Look carefully then how you walk, not as unwise but as wise, making the best use of the time, because the days are evil. Therefore do not be foolish, but understand what the will of the Lord is. (ESV)

Proverbs 2:6–7; 3:5–6; James 3:17

3. God is sovereign; he will do what he wants to do, birth control or no birth control.

> Job 42:2 I know that you can do all things, and that no purpose of yours can be thwarted. (ESV)
>
> Isaiah 14:27 For the LORD of hosts has planned, and who can frustrate it? And as for His stretched-out hand, who can turn it back? (NASB)
>
> Isaiah 43:13; Jeremiah 32:17, 27; Ephesians 1:11

4. Any birth control method that destroys the newly conceived embryo is wrong and unacceptable. That embryo is a real person from the instant of conception as God forms it in the womb.

> Psalm 139:13–14 For you formed my inward parts; you knitted me together in my mother's womb. I praise you, for I am fearfully and wonderfully made. (ESV) (See also verses 15–16.)
>
> Isaiah 44:24 Thus says the LORD, your Redeemer, who formed you from the womb: "I am the LORD, who made all things, who alone stretched out the heavens, who spread out the earth by myself." (ESV)

Practical Steps

- You and your wife need to discuss openly and pray about birth control decisions. Evaluate your reasons for using birth control.

- If possible, see a Christian medical expert (pro-life) for answers to questions.

- Research types of birth control. Look for conception-blocking (prevents conception) methods. Stay away from implantation-blocking methods (the baby is alive but cannot grow if it is not implanted).

- If pregnancy does occur while you and your wife are using birth control, take joy in God's sovereignty.

Resources

- "Demonstrating Wisdom" in *The Measure of a Man*. Gene Getz. Regal.
- *Does the Birth Control Pill Cause Abortions?* Randy Alcorn. EPM.
- *God's Will: Finding Guidance for Everyday Decisions*. J. I. Packer. Baker.
- "In Times of Confusion" in *Finding God When You Need Him the Most*. Chip Ingram. Baker.
- "Sex and Birth Control" in *Ethics for a Brave New World*. 2nd ed. John and Paul Feinberg. Crossway.

Bitterness

See also Anger, Disappointment, Failure, Forgiving Others, Grief, Jealousy, Thought Life

Bitterness is deep and painful resentment that festers and does not go away; it includes an unwillingness to forgive. Envy can be a factor. Bitterness can be against others who have wronged or mistreated us. It could be against God because of bad things that have happened in our lives. If not removed, it becomes an emotional cancer that eats body and soul.

1. **Bitterness is unacceptable to God and must be replaced with kindness, compassion, and forgiveness.**

   Hebrews 12:14–15 Pursue peace with all men, and the sanctification without which no one will see the Lord. See to it that no one comes short of the grace of God; that no root of bitterness springing up causes trouble, and by it many be defiled. (NASB)

   James 3:14 But if in your heart you are jealous, bitter, and selfish, don't sin against the truth by boasting of your wisdom. (GNT)

   Ephesians 4:31–32

2. **Jesus provides the great example.**

   1 Peter 2:21–23 For to this you were called, because Christ also suffered for us, leaving us an example, that you should follow His steps: "Who committed no sin, nor was deceit found in His mouth"; who, when He was reviled, did not revile in return; when He suffered, He did not threaten, but committed Himself to Him who judges righteously. (NKJV)

3. Although we don't always understand God's plan, we must trust his sovereignty and will. Job is a great example.

Job 1:20–22 Then Job arose, tore his robe, and shaved his head; and he fell to the ground and worshiped. And he said: "Naked I came from my mother's womb, and naked shall I return there. The LORD gave, and the LORD has taken away; blessed be the name of the LORD." In all this Job did not sin nor charge God with wrong. (NKJV)
Job 2:10; Isaiah 55:8–9; Romans 8:28

4. Bitterness is a characteristic of the unsaved and is an unacceptable emotion for a believer.

James 3:10–11 Words of thanksgiving and cursing pour out from the same mouth. My friends, this should not happen! No spring of water pours out sweet water and bitter water from the same opening. (GNT)
Acts 8:23; Romans 3:9–18

5. In his time, God will judge the unrighteous and unrepentant.

Psalm 37:1–2 Don't be worried on account of the wicked; don't be jealous of those who do wrong. They will soon disappear like grass that dries up; they will die like plants that wither. (GNT)
Romans 12:17–19 Repay no one evil for evil, but give thought to do what is honorable in the sight of all. If possible, so far as it depends on you, live peaceably with all. Beloved, never avenge yourselves, but leave it to the wrath of God, for it is written, "Vengeance is mine, I will repay, says the Lord." (ESV)

6. If our own failure to resist temptation is the cause of our bitterness, we must gain assurance that God's restoration comes with his forgiveness.

Psalm 51:10–12 Create in me a clean heart, O God, and renew a right spirit within me. Cast me not away from your presence, and take not your Holy Spirit from me. Restore to me the joy of your salvation, and uphold me with a willing spirit. (ESV)
Psalm 42:5; 85:4–7; Micah 7:18–19

7. Each believer has his own areas of bitterness to work on.

Proverbs 14:10 Each heart knows its own bitterness, and no one else can fully share its joy. (NLT)

Biblical Narratives

- Job, lack of bitterness, Job 1:21–22; 2:10
- Naomi, bitter over her losses, Ruth 1:20
- Esau with Jacob, Genesis 32–33
- David's trust in the Lord, Psalm 37

Practical Steps

- Write about your area of bitterness. Talk to God about the injustice you feel. Write steps to move toward forgiveness and freedom.
- Read the topic Forgiving Others in this book. Make a list of those you need to forgive.
- Study Matthew 18:15–20. What steps do you need to take to move toward reconciliation?
- Pray for God to soften your heart so you are willing to give up bitterness. Commit to pray for those who have hurt you.

Resources

- *Freedom from Resentment* (booklet). Robert Jones. New Growth.
- *Bitterness* (booklet). Lou Priolo. P & R.
- *Overcoming Emotions That Destroy*. Chip Ingram. Baker.
- *When Disappointment Deceives*. Jeff Olson. RBC Ministries.
- *When You've Been Wronged: Moving from Bitterness to Forgiveness*. Erwin Lutzer. Moody.

Boundaries/Limits

See also **Abuse, Authority, Forgiveness from God, Peer Pressure**

In today's world, a rebellious, push the limits, "nobody tells me what to do" attitude is seen as a positive masculine image. Not being satisfied with the status quo can be a good thing, but we need to make sure that our "outside the box" thinking is not disobedience to God. There is also the danger of pushing ourselves on others or not allowing them to establish their own boundaries.

1. **God establishes boundaries for our good, for our happiness, health, and holiness. He desires to protect us and provide for us.**

   Deuteronomy 32:46–47 He [Moses] said, "Be sure to obey all these commands that I have given you today. Repeat them to your children, so that they may faithfully obey all of God's teachings. These teachings are not empty words; they are your very life. Obey them and you will live long in that land across the Jordan that you are about to occupy." (GNT)

   Jeremiah 6:16 Thus says the LORD: "Stand by the roads, and look, and ask for the ancient paths, where the good way is; and walk in it, and find rest for your souls. But they said, 'We will not walk in it.'" (ESV)

   Joshua 1:8; Psalm 74:12–17

2. **Satan's primary, number one attack has always been to question God's Word and his authority to establish boundaries. "Did God really say that?"**

   Genesis 3:1 Now the serpent was more crafty than any other beast of the field that the LORD God had made. He said to the

53

woman, "Did God actually say, 'You shall not eat of any tree in the garden'?" (ESV) (See verses 2–4.)

3. **Refusing to obey God's boundaries—sin—always has negative consequences.**

Romans 5:12 Therefore, just as sin came into the world through one man, and death through sin, and so death spread to all men because all sinned. (ESV)

Judges 2:12 And they abandoned the LORD, the God of their fathers, who had brought them out of the land of Egypt. They went after other gods, from among the gods of the peoples who were around them, and bowed down to them. And they provoked the LORD to anger. (ESV) (See verses 10–15.)

Genesis 3:16–17; Hosea 8:5–8; Romans 1:18–32

4. **The world's secular culture is in rebellion against God's boundaries and worships the gods of personal freedom.**

Psalm 2:1–3 Why do the nations rage and the peoples plot in vain? The kings of the earth set themselves, and the rulers take counsel together, against the LORD and against his Anointed, saying, "Let us burst their bonds apart and cast away their cords from us." (ESV)

Jeremiah 2:12–13 Be appalled, O heavens, at this; be shocked, be utterly desolate, declares the LORD, for my people have committed two evils: they have forsaken me, the fountain of living waters, and hewed out cisterns for themselves, broken cisterns that can hold no water. (ESV)

Judges 17:6

5. **True freedom is in Christ. He redeemed us out of slavery to sin. We now are free to serve him. We must have this attitude: I do what I do because Christ gave himself for me and now I want to please him, always with an awareness of God's expectations, standards, and commands for me.**

Galatians 5:1, 13 Freedom is what we have—Christ has set us free! Stand, then, as free people, and do not allow yourselves to become slaves again. . . . As for you, my friends, you were called to be free. But do not let this freedom become an excuse for letting your physical desires control you. Instead, let love make you serve one another. (GNT)

Galatians 2:19–20 I have been put to death with Christ on his cross, so that it is no longer I who live, but it is Christ who lives in me. This life that I live now, I live by faith in the Son of God, who loved me and gave his life for me. (GNT)

Romans 12:1–2; 1 John 4:19

6. A blessed, happy life comes as we establish godly, biblical boundaries, delighting in the Word of God

Psalm 1:1–3 Blessed is the man who walks not in the counsel of the wicked, nor stands in the way of sinners, nor sits in the seat of scoffers; but his delight is in the law of the LORD, and on his law he meditates day and night. He is like a tree planted by streams of water that yields its fruit in its season, and its leaf does not wither. In all that he does, he prospers. (ESV)

Exodus 23:2

7. Boundaries that must be established (selected).

Thinking—**Philippians 4:8**
Purity—**Matthew 5:27–30; 1 Thessalonians 4:3; 1 Corinthians 7:1–4**
Use of the tongue—**James 3**
Partnerships only in Christ—**2 Corinthians 6:14**
Honoring our parents—**Ephesians 6:1–3**
Telling the truth; no lying—**Ephesians 4:25**
Not involved in the works of darkness—**Ephesians 5:11–12**

In our busy lives, with so much pressure to perform, we must be careful to establish biblical priorities and not follow those others impose on us. Though living sacrificially is good, allowing others to take advantage of us is unacceptable. Balance is needed. We need not permit everyone into our lives, nor is there a need to keep everyone out.

Biblical Narratives

- Adam and Eve, eating the fruit in the garden, Genesis 1–3
- Laban, taking advantage of Jacob, Genesis 29–31
- Israel, at the mountain of God, Exodus 19
- Intermarriage with non-Israelites, Deuteronomy 7:3; Judges 3:6
- Israel crosses God's boundaries, 2 Kings 17:7–18
- Partnerships (including marriage) with non-Christians, 2 Corinthians 6:14
- Ministry roles, 1 Timothy 2:11–14; 3:2

Practical Steps

- Are you in violation of any scriptural boundaries? Take a fresh look at your life, asking God to empower you for making the necessary course corrections.
- Set a boundary to "go primitive" (no use of electronics of any kind) after 9:00 p.m. (or earlier).
- Are you allowing others to take advantage of you or pressure you into activities in which you would rather not be involved? Evaluate each activity and learn to say no with finality.
- Are others asking you to set boundaries in your relationships in their presence? If so, make a list of how you can honor godly boundaries with them.

Resources

- "Boundaries in Relationships" in *Journal of Biblical Counseling*. Spring 2004. Ed Welch.
- *Disciplines of a Godly Man*. Kent Hughes. Crossway.
- *The Measure of a Man*. Gene Getz. Regal.
- *Pathway to Freedom: How God's Laws Guide Our Lives*. Alistair Begg. Moody.
- *When People Are Big and God Is Small: Overcoming Peer Pressure, Co-Dependency, and Fear of Man*. Ed Welch. CCEF.

Burnout/Rest

See also Boundaries, Priorities, Sleep Struggles, Time Management, Trust

Burnout is the overwhelming sense that life and work or ministry have become too much to bear, and life has lost its joy. A much repeated saying is, "I'd rather burn out than rust out," to which one could reply, "Are those the only two options?"

1. **A burned-out Timothy needs a fresh rekindling of God's grace in his life.**

   2 Timothy 1:3–7 I thank God whom I serve, as did my ancestors, with a clear conscience, as I remember you constantly in my prayers night and day. As I remember your tears, I long to see you, that I may be filled with joy. I am reminded of your sincere faith, a faith that dwelt first in your grandmother Lois and your mother Eunice and now, I am sure, dwells in you as well. For this reason I remind you to fan into flame the gift of God, which is in you through the laying on of my hands, for God gave us a spirit not of fear but of power and love and self-control. (ESV)

2. **Having received devastating news, Habakkuk needs to get away alone for thinking, praying, listening, and waiting on God. Waiting on God is a familiar theme in Scripture.**

   Habakkuk 2:1 I will take my stand at my watchpost and station myself on the tower, and look out to see what he will say to me, and what I will answer concerning my complaint. (ESV)
   Habakkuk 2:20 But the LORD is in his holy temple; let all the earth keep silence before him. (ESV)
   Psalm 27:14 Wait for the LORD; be strong, and let your heart take courage; wait for the LORD! (ESV)
   Psalm 37:7–9; 40:1–3

3. **Jesus often sought solitude to pray and rest, and he encouraged his disciples to do the same.**

> **Mark 1:35** And rising very early in the morning, while it was still dark, he departed and went out to a desolate place, and there he prayed. (ESV)
>
> **Mark 6:30–32** The apostles returned to Jesus and told him all that they had done and taught. And he said to them, "Come away by yourselves to a desolate place and rest a while." For many were coming and going, and they had no leisure even to eat. And they went away in the boat to a desolate place by themselves. (ESV)
>
> **Matthew 11:28–30; Mark 6:45–47; Luke 4:42**

Practical Steps

- A health checkup is advisable (blood work for vitamin D and B-12, thyroid, testosterone). Exercise daily.

- Evaluate all you are doing—you are probably overly involved in far too many projects or responsibilities and need major cutting back. Work on delegating to others.

- Make one day a week, preferably Sunday, a true day of rest.

- Learn how to say no and mean it. Don't let others pressure you with their priorities.

- Use the commentary *The Minor Prophets*, vol. 2, by James Boice, pages 83–89, for a discussion on Habakkuk's need to get some time alone.

- Take some needed time off, vacation time alone or with your wife to get recharged for life's challenges.

- One of the spiritual disciplines is solitude. As Jesus took time away to restore, how can you? Make a list of the possibilities of daily and larger increments of time dedicated to restoration. Vacation!

Resources

- *Balancing Life's Demands: Biblical Priorities for a Busy Life*. DVD series. Chip Ingram. Living on the Edge Ministries.
- *Basics for Pressured Believers*. Jim Berg. BJU.
- *Burned Out: Trusting God with Your To Do List* (booklet). Winston Smith. New Growth.
- *Burnout: Resting in God's Fairness*. Brad Hambrick. P & R.
- *Margin—the Overload Syndrome: Learning to Live within Your Limits*. Richard A. Swenson. NavPress.
- *The Rest of God: Restoring Your Soul by Restoring Sabbath*. Mark Buchanan. Thomas Nelson.

Career/Employment

See also Burnout, Character, Decision Making, Priorities, Purpose for Living, Work Ethic

Our career path is the choice we make of what we do with our lives vocationally, earning money to live, caring for our family, making a contribution to society, all the while bringing honor to the Lord.

1. **God's plan for work was established with Adam and Eve in the garden for their benefit and for ours.**

   Genesis 2:15 The LORD God took the man and put him in the garden of Eden to work it and keep it. (ESV)

   2 Thessalonians 3:10–12 While we were with you, we used to tell you, "Whoever refuses to work is not allowed to eat." We say this because we hear that there are some people among you who live lazy lives and who do nothing except meddle in other people's business. In the name of the Lord Jesus Christ we command these people and warn them to lead orderly lives and work to earn their own living. (GNT)

   1 Thessalonians 4:11–12

2. **Seeking God's wisdom in our career/employment choices is vital.**

   James 1:5 But if any of you lack wisdom, you should pray to God, who will give it to you; because God gives generously and graciously to all. (GNT)

   Psalm 111:10 The way to become wise is to honor the LORD; he gives sound judgment to all who obey his commands. (GNT)

   Proverbs 4:5; 14:33; James 3:17

3. As we place total trust in God, allowing him to give us direction for the pathways of our lives, we can be certain that he will lead us.

Psalm 20:4–5 May He grant you according to your heart's desire, and fulfill all your purpose. We will rejoice in your salvation, and in the name of our God we will set up our banners! May the LORD fulfill all your petitions. (NKJV)

Jeremiah 6:16 This is what the LORD says: "Stand at the crossroads and look; ask for the ancient paths, ask where the good way is, and walk in it, and you will find rest for your souls." (NIV)

Proverbs 3:5–6

4. Sometimes God chooses people to serve him in a special way. Could you be one of these?

Genesis 12:1–2 Now the LORD had said to Abram: "Get out of your country, from your family and from your father's house, to a land that I will show you. I will make you a great nation; I will bless you and make your name great; and you shall be a blessing." (NKJV)

John 1:6–7 There was a man sent from God, whose name was John. This man came for a witness, to bear witness of the Light, that all through him might believe. (NKJV)

Acts 9:15–16 But the Lord said to him, "Go, for he [Paul] is a chosen vessel of Mine to bear My name before Gentiles, kings, and the children of Israel. For I will show him how many things he must suffer for My name's sake." (NKJV)

Exodus 3:10 (Moses); Judges 6:14 (Gideon); Jeremiah 1:5 (Jeremiah)

5. The big picture for every believer is our calling to a life of serving Jesus. Therefore, whatever our career calling, a Christian vocation or in the secular realm, it is of great value to God.

Ephesians 1:4 Even before he made the world, God loved us and chose us in Christ to be holy and without fault in his eyes. (NLT)

Colossians 3:17 Whatever you do in word or deed, do all in the name of the Lord Jesus, giving thanks through Him to God the Father. (NASB)

John 15:16; Ephesians 2:10; 2 Timothy 1:9; 2 Peter 1:10

6. Whatever career choice is made, all work must be done ultimately for God's glory.

Psalm 115:1 Not to us, O LORD, not to us, but to your name give glory, for the sake of your steadfast love and your faithfulness! (ESV)

Colossians 3:23 Whatever you do, do your work heartily, as for the Lord rather than for men. (NASB)

1 Corinthians 10:31; 1 Peter 4:11

7. A man who chooses to be a husband and father must make that calling his first and foremost career responsibility. Family before work.

Ephesians 5:25, 28–29 Husbands, love your wives, as Christ loved the church and gave himself up for her. . . . In the same way husbands should love their wives as their own bodies. He who loves his wife loves himself. For no one ever hated his own flesh, but nourishes and cherishes it, just as Christ does the church. (ESV)

Deuteronomy 6:6–7 And these words that I command you today shall be on your heart. You shall teach them diligently to your children, and shall talk of them when you sit in your house, and when you walk by the way, and when you lie down, and when you rise. (ESV)

Psalm 128:1–4; Matthew 7:9–11

Biblical Narratives

- Other men and women chosen for special service: Deborah, Judges 4; Amos, Amos 7:14–15; Isaiah, Isaiah 6; Anna, Luke 2:37–38; Barnabas, Acts 13:2; Philip's daughters, Acts 21:9; Priscilla and Aquila, Acts 18.

- Jacob worked hard for his father-in-law, Laban, Genesis 29–30
- Paul did double duty as a tent maker, Acts 18:3; 1 Corinthians 4:12

Practical Steps

- If you are still deciding about your career, explore many avenues and opportunities to determine likes and dislikes. Go to job fairs. Ask others about your gifts and talents. Interview successful, experienced men in your church about their work paths and decisions.
- Use employment inventories to scale your talents and interests.
- If you are one who moves quickly from job to job, ask others who have longevity in their fields how they are able to stay so long. Move toward responsibility, discipline, and patience in your workplace.
- Ask God to direct you and show you his vocational calling for you.

Resources

- *Choosing Your Career: The Christian's Decision Manual*. Martin Clark. P & R.
- *Every Good Endeavor: Connecting Your Work to God's Work*. Timothy Keller. Dutton.
- *Kingdom Calling: Vocational Stewardship for the Common Good*. Amy Sherman. IVP.
- *The Call: Finding and Fulfilling the Central Purpose of Your Life*. Os Guinness. Thomas Nelson.
- *Work Matters*. Tom Nelson. Crossway.

Church Involvement

See also **Leadership, Priorities, Spiritual Gifts, Time Management**

God's plan is that Christians be involved in a local body of believers. This not only honors God but enables us to learn and grow, while supporting and ministering to others.

1. **Believers need each other for the body of Christ to function as God planned.**

   Romans 12:4–6 For as in one body we have many members, and the members do not all have the same function, so we, though many, are one body in Christ, and individually members one of another. Having gifts that differ according to the grace given to us, let us use them. (ESV)
   1 Corinthians 12:12–26

2. **Serving others in the body of Christ, relating to one another in sacrificial ways, is commanded.**

   Galatians 5:13 Use your freedom to serve one another in love. (NLT)
   Philippians 2:2–4 Then make me truly happy by agreeing wholeheartedly with each other, loving one another, and working together with one mind and purpose. Don't be selfish; don't try to impress others. Be humble, thinking of others as better than yourselves. Don't look out only for your own interests, but take an interest in others, too. (NLT)
   1 Thessalonians 5:11 Therefore encourage one another and build one another up, just as you are doing. (ESV)
   Romans 12:10; 15:7; Galatians 6:2; Ephesians 4:2, 32; 1 Thessalonians 5:15; Hebrews 3:13; James 5:16

3. The church requires spiritually strong, qualified men to serve as its primary leaders. Perhaps you would be one of these.

Ephesians 4:11–12 And He gave some as apostles, and some as prophets, and some as evangelists, and some as pastors and teachers, for the equipping of the saints for the work of service, to the building up of the body of Christ. (NASB)

1 Timothy 3:1–2 This is a faithful saying: If a man desires the position of a bishop, he desires a good work. A bishop then must be blameless, the husband of one wife, temperate, sober-minded, of good behavior, hospitable, able to teach. (NKJV) ("Bishop" is equivalent to "overseer"; see also verses 3–7.)

4. Believers are not to neglect their meeting together.

Hebrews 10:24–25 And let us consider how to stir up one another to love and good works, not neglecting to meet together, as is the habit of some, but encouraging one another, and all the more as you see the Day drawing near. (ESV)

Psalm 122:1

5. Submission to the leadership of church authorities is God's will, as long as they are submissive to God's Word. They are to be honored and respected.

Hebrews 13:17 Obey your leaders and submit to them, for they are keeping watch over your souls, as those who will have to give an account. Let them do this with joy and not with groaning, for that would be of no advantage to you. (ESV)

1 Thessalonians 5:12–13

6. Understand that not everyone who is a member or attendee of a church is a true believer. Some have not yet come to faith and are still searching for the truth.

Matthew 13:36–40 When Jesus had left the crowd and gone indoors, his disciples came to him and said, "Tell us what the parable about the weeds in the field means." Jesus answered, "The man who sowed the good seed is the Son of Man; the field is the world; the good seed is the people who belong to the Kingdom; the weeds are the people who belong to the Evil One; and the enemy who sowed the weeds is the Devil. The harvest is the end of the age, and the harvest workers are angels. Just as the weeds are gathered up and burned in the fire, so the same thing will happen at the end of the age. (GNT)

Matthew 15:8–9; 2 Peter 2:1

Biblical Narratives

- Parables of Jesus, describing the church he will build, Matthew 13
- The beginning and expansion of the early church, the entire book of Acts

Practical Steps

- Make the Lord's Day a day of activity for the Lord. Without becoming legalistic, keep it a special day, different from the routine activities of the other six days.
- Make a complete study of the many "one another" passages in the New Testament.
- Always attend church together as a complete family. Be involved; accept service opportunities.
- Be involved during the preaching time. Use your Bible and take notes on the message. Write down application points for your life.

Resources

- *Why Church Matters*. Joshua Harris. Multnomah.
- "Do I Need to Be a Part of the Church to Follow Jesus?" in *The Post-Church Christian: Dealing with the Generational Baggage of Our Faith*. J. Paul Nyquist. Moody.
- "Holy Day or Holiday" in *Pathway to Freedom*. Alistair Begg. Moody.
- *The Rest of God: Restoring Your Soul by Restoring Sabbath*. Mark Buchanan. Thomas Nelson.
- *Why We Love the Church*. Kevin DeYoung. Moody.

Communication/Speech

See also **Lying, Profanity, Words That Hurt**

Communication involves both what we say (content) and how we say it (tone, inflection, body language). God has given us enormous capability in this area, and we must make sure we are pleasing him with our words.

1. **Positive traits to develop in speech.**

BUILDING UP

Ephesians 4:29 Let no corrupting talk come out of your mouths, but only such as is good for building up, as fits the occasion, that it may give grace to those who hear. (ESV)

Colossians 4:6 Let your conversation be always full of grace, seasoned with salt, so that you may know how to answer everyone. (NIV)

GENTLENESS

Proverbs 15:1 A gentle answer turns away wrath, but a harsh word stirs up anger. (NASB)

Galatians 6:1

KINDNESS

Proverbs 16:24 Kind words are like honey—sweet to the soul and healthy for the body. (NLT)

Ephesians 4:32 Be kind and compassionate to one another, forgiving each other, just as in Christ God forgave you. (NIV)

Proverbs 12:25

PATIENCE

Proverbs 25:15 With patience a ruler may be persuaded, and a soft tongue will break a bone. (ESV)

SPEAKING TRUTH

Ephesians 4:25 Therefore, having put away falsehood, let each one of you speak the truth with his neighbor, for we are members one of another. (ESV)

SPEAKING AFTER LISTENING

James 1:19–20 Know this, my beloved brothers: let every person be quick to hear, slow to speak, slow to anger; for the anger of man does not produce the righteousness of God. (ESV)

Proverbs 18:13 If one gives an answer before he hears, it is his folly and shame. (ESV)

Proverbs 15:28

COMMUNICATING KNOWLEDGE

Proverbs 20:15 There is gold, and an abundance of jewels; but the lips of knowledge are a more precious thing. (NASB)

APPROPRIATE WORDS

Psalm 37:30 The mouth of the righteous utters wisdom, and his tongue speaks justice. (ESV)

Proverbs 10:19; 15:23; 25:11; 1 Timothy 4:12

2. **Negative traits to avoid in speech.**

MISUSING GOD'S NAME (IN VAIN OR WITH CONTEMPT)

Exodus 20:7 You shall not misuse the name of the LORD your God, for the LORD will not hold anyone guiltless who misuses his name. (NIV)

OBSCENE, FOOLISH, RAW HUMOR

Ephesians 4:29 Do not let any unwholesome talk come out of your mouths, but only what is helpful for building others up according to their needs, that it may benefit those who listen. (NIV)

Ephesians 5:4

FALSEHOOD, LYING

Colossians 3:9–10 Do not lie to one another, seeing that you have put off the old self with its practices and have put on the new self, which is being renewed in knowledge after the image of its creator. (ESV)

Ephesians 4:25, Zechariah 8:16

ANSWERING BEFORE LISTENING

Proverbs 18:13 If one gives an answer before he hears, it is his folly and shame. (ESV)

Proverbs 18:17

FOOLISH, IGNORANT ARGUMENTS

2 Timothy 2:23–24 But keep away from foolish and ignorant arguments; you know that they end up in quarrels. As the Lord's servant, you must not quarrel. You must be kind toward all, a good and patient teacher. (GNT)

SLANDER, GOSSIP

Proverbs 20:19 He who goes about as a slanderer reveals secrets, therefore do not associate with a gossip. (NASB)

Ephesians 4:31 Let all bitterness and wrath and anger and clamor and slander be put away from you, along with all malice. (ESV)

1 Timothy 5:13–14; Titus 3:1–2

LACK OF CONTROL

James 1:26 If you claim to be religious but don't control your tongue, you are fooling yourself, and your religion is worthless. (NLT)

COMPLAINING

Philippians 2:14 Do everything without grumbling or arguing. (NIV)

1 Corinthians 10:6–10; James 5:9

SUMMARY OF THE TONGUE'S NEGATIVE POTENTIAL

James 3:8 But no one has ever been able to tame the tongue. It is evil and uncontrollable, full of deadly poison. (GNT) (See verses 5–12.)

3. Speech can both grieve and please the Holy Spirit.

Ephesians 4:29–30 Do not use harmful words, but only helpful words, the kind that build up and provide what is needed, so that what you say will do good to those who hear you. And do not make God's Holy Spirit sad; for the Spirit is God's mark of ownership on you, a guarantee that the Day will come when God will set you free. (GNT)

4. As creation gives glory to God, so should our speech.

Psalm 19:1–4 The heavens declare the glory of God; and the firmament shows His handiwork. Day unto day utters speech, and night unto night reveals knowledge. There is no speech nor language where their voice is not heard. Their line has gone out through all the earth, and their words to the end of the world. (NKJV)

5. Additional contrasts from Proverbs.

Proverbs 12:18 Some people make cutting remarks, but the words of the wise bring healing. (NLT)

Proverbs 10:20–21 The tongue of the righteous is choice silver, but the heart of the wicked is of little value. The lips of the righteous nourish many, but fools die for lack of sense. (NIV)

Proverbs 15:4

Biblical Narratives

- Israelites, grumbling, Numbers 16:41; 17:5–10
- Abigail, calming David down, 1 Samuel 25
- Ananias and Sapphira, lying, Acts 5:1–11

Practical Steps

- As you drive home from work, commit to speaking with your family positively and without complaining.
- Be aware of your body language or nonverbal communication habits. Ask others to evaluate. Work on corrections where needed.
- Pray before you go into social situations, before calling or writing someone, or before posting on a social media site.
- Practice not responding to or laughing at rude or cruel speech or off-color humor.
- Openly communicate when you need to take a stand against sin or wrong. Your silence communicates agreement.

Resources

- *Communication and Conflict Resolution* (booklet). Stuart Scott. Focus.
- "Discipline of Tongue" in *Disciplines of a Godly Man*. Kent Hughes. Crossway.
- *War of Words*. Paul Tripp. P & R.
- *The Weight of Your Words*. Joseph Stowell. Moody.
- *Your Family God's Way*. Wayne Mack. P & R.

Compassion/Kindness

See also **Attitude, Selfishness**

Compassion is sensing the distress of others, empathizing with them, and reaching out to them in specific ways to assist in alleviating their need. A godly, Christ-centered man must include compassion as a quality of his busy, success-oriented lifestyle. If you are married, strive to have compassion for your wife and children.

1. Our model for compassion is God himself.

> **Psalm 72:12–13** For he will deliver the needy when he cries for help, the afflicted also, and him who has no helper. He will have compassion on the poor and needy, and the lives of the needy he will save. (NASB)
>
> **Lamentations 3:21–23** This I recall to my mind, therefore I have hope. The LORD's lovingkindnesses indeed never cease, for His compassions never fail. They are new every morning; great is Your faithfulness. (NASB)
>
> **Matthew 14:14** When He went ashore, He saw a large crowd, and felt compassion for them and healed their sick. (NASB)
>
> **Deuteronomy 30:3; Psalm 25:6; 51:1; Isaiah 49:10; 54:10; Micah 7:18–19; Matthew 15:32; 20:34; Luke 7:13; 10:33**

2. Compassion for others is required.

> **Zechariah 7:9** This is what the LORD Almighty said: "Administer true justice; show mercy and compassion to one another." (NIV)
>
> **Colossians 3:12–14** Therefore, as God's chosen people, holy and dearly loved, clothe yourselves with compassion, kindness, humility, gentleness and patience. Bear with each other and

forgive one another if any of you has a grievance against someone. Forgive as the Lord forgave you. And over all these virtues
put on love, which binds them all together in perfect unity. (NIV)
Proverbs 29:7; Philippians 2:1–3

3. **Compassion must be expressed in tangible ways, not just talk
   or good intentions. Those who are able should share materially
   with others.**

   Proverbs 19:17 If you help the poor, you are lending to the
   LORD—and he will repay you! (NLT)

   Psalm 41:1 Blessed is the one who considers the poor! In the
   day of trouble the LORD delivers him. (ESV)

   1 John 3:17 If we are rich and see others in need, yet close
   our hearts against them, how can we claim that we love God?
   (GNT)

   Proverbs 11:25; Matthew 25:35–36; Luke 3:11; James 2:15–16

Biblical Narratives

- David to Saul, 1 Samuel 23:21
- David to Mephibosheth, 2 Samuel 9
- Jonah's need, Jonah 4
- Nehemiah to Jerusalem, Nehemiah 1
- Jesus, Matthew 14:14; 15:32; 20:34; Mark 1:40–42
- Good Samaritan, Luke 10:25–37

Practical Steps

- Get your family involved in volunteer work for needy people. Make
  a list of those you know who are hurting; do something tangible
  to help.
- Study the parable of the Good Samaritan (Luke 10:25–37), and
  write out ten specific applications reflecting present-day needs
  around you.

- List the number of times in the Gospels something is mentioned or modeled about compassion.

- Get involved in the lives of needy people through ministries such as Christmas shoe boxes or Angel Tree. Consider sponsoring a child through organizations such as Compassion International or Samaritan's Purse.

- In showing compassion to your children, remember their age and the need to see things from their point of view. How can you show compassion in language they will understand?

- Make a list of coming events in your child's life when you will need extra compassion (start of school, new baby coming, fear of illness, losing a game in sports, etc.).

Resources

- "Determine to Love" in *Broken-Down House*. Paul Tripp. Shepherd.
- *Ministries of Mercy: The Call of the Jericho Road*. Timothy Keller. P & R.
- "The Gift That Lives On" in *The Quest for Character*. Charles Swindoll. Multnomah.

Confession/Repentance

See also Forgiveness from God, Guilt

Sin is not a popular concept. It is one of those words the secularists in our society despise. As the prophet of old reminds us, we are those "who call evil good, and good evil; who substitute darkness for light and light for darkness. . . !" (Isa. 5:20 NASB). There is nothing more needed today than a renewed passion for seeing sin exactly as it is, a total affront to our God.

1. **Hiding our sins from God is not a possibility. He knows exactly what we have done!**

    Numbers 32:23 Be sure your sin will find you out. (ESV)

    Psalm 139:7–12 Where could I go to escape from you? Where could I get away from your presence? If I went up to heaven, you would be there; if I lay down in the world of the dead, you would be there. If I flew away beyond the east or lived in the farthest place in the west, you would be there to lead me, you would be there to help me. I could ask the darkness to hide me or the light around me to turn into night, but even darkness is not dark for you, and the night is as bright as the day. Darkness and light are the same to you. (GNT)

    Isaiah 59:12–13

2. **The only path to forgiveness and freedom from guilt is repentance and confession.**

    Psalm 32:3–5 When I did not confess my sins, I was worn out from crying all day long. Day and night you punished me, LORD; my strength was completely drained, as moisture is dried up by the summer heat. Then I confessed my sins to you; I did not conceal my wrongdoings. I decided to confess them to you, and you forgave all my sins. (GNT)

Hosea 14:1–2 Return to the LORD your God, people of Israel. Your sin has made you stumble and fall. Return to the LORD, and let this prayer be your offering to him: "Forgive all our sins and accept our prayer, and we will praise you as we have promised." (GNT)

Psalm 41:4; Joel 2:12–13

3. **Confession of sin involves a commitment to stop that sin and be done with it.**

Proverbs 28:13 Whoever conceals his transgressions will not prosper, but he who confesses and forsakes them will obtain mercy. (ESV)

Ezekiel 18:30–31 Therefore I will judge you, O house of Israel, every one according to his ways, declares the Lord GOD. Repent and turn from all your transgressions, lest iniquity be your ruin. Cast away from you all the transgressions that you have committed, and make yourselves a new heart and a new spirit! Why will you die, O house of Israel? (ESV)

Isaiah 1:16

4. **Restoration and healing are available.**

1 John 1:9 If we confess our sins, he is faithful and just to forgive us our sins and to cleanse us from all unrighteousness. (ESV)

Jeremiah 24:7 I will give them a heart to know Me, for I am the LORD; and they will be My people, and I will be their God, for they will return to Me with their whole heart. (NASB)

Psalm 51; 66:18; Malachi 3:7

5. **Confession of sin may require restitution or making things right with people we have wronged.**

Proverbs 14:9 Fools mock at making amends for sin, but goodwill is found among the upright. (NIV)

Luke 19:8 But Zacchaeus stood up and said to the Lord, "Look, Lord! Here and now I give half of my possessions to the poor,

and if I have cheated anybody out of anything, I will pay back four times the amount." (NIV)
Leviticus 6:1–5; Numbers 5:6–7

6. **If we have sinned against another person, confession to them is necessary.**

Matthew 5:23–24 So if you are about to offer your gift to God at the altar and there you remember that your brother has something against you, leave your gift there in front of the altar, go at once and make peace with your brother, and then come back and offer your gift to God. (GNT)
James 5:16–17

Biblical Narratives

- Israelites under Law, restitution required, Leviticus 6:1–5; Numbers 5:6–7
- David, repenting and confessing after his sin with Bathsheba, Psalm 32; 51
- Christians at Ephesus, ridding themselves of sinful objects, Acts 19:18–19

Practical Steps

- Ask God to reveal to you specific sins. Sometimes we become so used to our sin, we no longer see it as such.
- Make a list of what God does with confessed sin—See Psalm 103:12; Isaiah 1:18; 38:17; 44:22; Hebrews 8:12; Micah 7:18–20.
- When we confess sin, what is God's response to us from the following passages—Psalm 32:1; 51:12; 103:10, 13; Isaiah 55:7; Romans 8:1–2; 2 Corinthians 5:17.
- If other people are involved, seek forgiveness by confessing to them also.

Resources

- *Not the Way It's Supposed to Be*. Cornelius Plantinga. Eerdmans.
- "The Remedy for Sin" in *Respectable Sins: Confronting the Sins We Tolerate*. Jerry Bridges. NavPress.
- "Putting Your Past Behind You" in *Winning the Inner War*. Erwin Lutzer. Cook.
- "When You've Blown It Big Time" in *Finding God When You Need Him the Most*. Chip Ingram. Baker.

Conflict

See also Anger, Attitude, Bitterness, Forgiving Others, Friendship, Jealousy, Pride, Self-Control, Speech, Wisdom

1. **Work to be at peace with others, showing forbearance as needed. Forgiving others is required.**

   Romans 12:18 If possible, so far as it depends on you, live peaceably with all. (ESV)

   Colossians 3:12–14 Put on then, as God's chosen ones, holy and beloved, compassionate hearts, kindness, humility, meekness, and patience, bearing with one another and, if one has a complaint against another, forgiving each other; as the Lord has forgiven you, so you also must forgive. And above all these put on love, which binds everything together in perfect harmony. (ESV)

   Romans 14:12–13; Ephesians 4:1–3, 30–32

2. **Don't seek your own way. Jesus is the great example.**

   Philippians 2:3–6 Don't do anything from selfish ambition or from a cheap desire to boast, but be humble toward one another, always considering others better than yourselves. And look out for one another's interests, not just for your own. The attitude you should have is the one that Christ Jesus had: He always had the nature of God, but he did not think that by force he should try to remain equal with God. (GNT)

3. **The words we speak and the way in which they are spoken have much to do with maintaining peace.**

   Proverbs 12:18 The words of the reckless pierce like swords, but the tongue of the wise brings healing. (NIV)

Proverbs 15:1 A gentle answer turns away wrath, but a harsh word stirs up anger. (NIV)
Proverbs 18:13; 25:11; Ephesians 4:29

4. If you have been hurt or have hurt someone else, go to that person for reconciliation.

Matthew 18:15 If your brother sins against you, go and tell him his fault, between you and him alone. If he listens to you, you have gained your brother. (ESV)

Matthew 5:23–24 So if you are offering your gift at the altar and there remember that your brother has something against you, leave your gift there before the altar and go. First be reconciled to your brother, and then come and offer your gift. (ESV)

5. Paying back someone who has hurt you is wrong. If someone has truly sinned against you, trust God to take care of it.

Romans 12:19–21 Beloved, do not avenge yourselves, but rather give place to wrath; for it is written, "Vengeance is Mine, I will repay," says the Lord. Therefore "if your enemy is hungry, feed him; if he is thirsty, give him a drink; for in so doing you will heap coals of fire on his head." Do not be overcome by evil, but overcome evil with good. (NKJV)
Romans 13:3–4

6. Violence is not acceptable; it is not pleasing to God.

Psalm 11:5 The LORD examines both the righteous and the wicked. He hates those who love violence. (NLT)

Proverbs 16:29 A man of violence entices his neighbor and leads him in a way that is not good. (ESV)
Psalm 7:15–16; Proverbs 24:1–2

7. Remember that God is the ultimate defender.

Psalm 37:7–9 Rest in the LORD, and wait patiently for Him; do not fret because of him who prospers in his way, because of the man who brings wicked schemes to pass. Cease from anger, and forsake wrath; do not fret—it only causes harm. For evildoers shall be cut off; but those who wait on the LORD, they shall inherit the earth. (NKJV)

Isaiah 25:4 For You have been a strength to the poor, a strength to the needy in his distress, a refuge from the storm, a shade from the heat; for the blast of the terrible ones is as a storm against the wall. (NKJV)

Psalm 59:16

Biblical Narratives

- Paul and Barnabas in disagreement, Acts 15:36–40 (The solution for them was each going his own way.)
- Euodia and Syntyche, needing to live in harmony, Philippians 4:2–3

Practical Steps

- Asking whether this will really matter in eternity is always good advice. Be willing to stand down when the conflict is over something really not all that important.

- Ask, "Am I convinced that I am right in this situation?" Be willing to take advice; ask others for their thoughts. Be willing to consider other viewpoints.

- Evaluate: Do you seem to always be involved in some conflict? Perhaps you are the problem. Do you always need to be right? Is involvement in conflict a way to make you feel powerful? Commit to corrections in this area.

- Work on saying what you say with kindness and a nonelevated emotional tone. It's not just what we say, but how we say it.

- "Breathe grace!" is a well-known biblical counseling phrase. Our mindset must always be reaching out to others with understanding and God's love.

Resources

- *Communication and Conflict Resolution* (booklet). Stuart Scott. Focus.
- *Conflict: A Redemptive Opportunity*. Timothy Land. CCEF.
- *The Peacemaker: A Biblical Guide for Resolving Personal Conflict*. Ken Sande. Baker.
- *Pursuing Peace: A Christian Guide to Handling Our Conflicts*. Robert Jones. Crossway.
- *War of Words*. Paul Tripp. P & R.
- *The Weight of Your Words*. Joseph Stowell. Moody.

Contentment

See also Jealousy, Materialism, Purpose for Living, Self-Worth

Contentment is being satisfied with one's possessions, status, and circumstances. The Old Testament concept ("blessed") includes happiness, thankfulness, rest, and relaxation of spirit. Contentment in the New Testament is "having enough or a sufficient supply."

1. **Having an abundance of possessions is no guarantee of contentment.**

   Proverbs 15:16 Better is a little with the fear of the LORD than great treasure and trouble with it. (ESV)

   Haggai 1:5–6 Now therefore, thus says the LORD of hosts: "Consider your ways! You have sown much, and bring in little; you eat, but do not have enough; you drink, but you are not filled with drink; you clothe yourselves, but no one is warm; and he who earns wages, earns wages to put into a bag with holes." (NKJV)

   Proverbs 16:8; 17:1

2. **Contentment is possible, even when others seem to be prosperous and have much.**

   Psalm 73:2–3, 16–17, 25–26 But I had nearly lost confidence; my faith was almost gone because I was jealous of the proud when I saw that things go well for the wicked. . . . I tried to think this problem through, but it was too difficult for me until I went into your Temple. Then I understood what will happen to the wicked. . . . What else do I have in heaven but you? Since I have you, what else could I want on earth? My mind and my body may grow weak, but God is my strength; he is all I ever need. (GNT)

   Psalm 37:7, 16; Proverbs 30:7–8

83

3. We can rest with confidence in our heavenly Father's provision. This trust removes the agitation of discontent.

Ecclesiastes 2:24–25 A person can do nothing better than to eat and drink and find satisfaction in their own toil. This too, I see, is from the hand of God, for without him, who can eat or find enjoyment? (NIV)

1 Timothy 6:6–8 Yet true godliness with contentment is itself great wealth. After all, we brought nothing with us when we came into the world, and we can't take anything with us when we leave it. So if we have enough food and clothing, let us be content. (NLT)

Isaiah 26:3–4; Philippians 4:19; Hebrews 13:5

4. Contentment produces thanksgiving for what God has supplied.

Psalm 107:8–9 Oh, that men would give thanks to the LORD for His goodness, and for His wonderful works to the children of men! For He satisfies the longing soul, and fills the hungry soul with goodness. (NKJV)

Psalm 100:4–5 Enter into His gates with thanksgiving, and into His courts with praise. Be thankful to Him, and bless His name. For the LORD is good; His mercy is everlasting, and His truth endures to all generations. (NKJV)

Psalm 95:1–7; 106:1–2

5. Contentment is trusting God no matter the circumstances.

Psalm 84:10–12 For a day in Your courts is better than a thousand. I would rather be a doorkeeper in the house of my God than dwell in the tents of wickedness. For the LORD God is a sun and shield; the LORD will give grace and glory; no good thing will He withhold from those who walk uprightly. O LORD of hosts, blessed is the man who trusts in You! (NKJV)

Philippians 4:11–13 And I am not saying this because I feel neglected, for I have learned to be satisfied with what I have. I know what it is to be in need and what it is to have more than enough. I have learned this secret, so that anywhere, at any time, I am content, whether I am full or hungry, whether I have too

much or too little. I have the strength to face all conditions by the power that Christ gives me. (GNT)
Psalm 118:24; 2 Corinthians 12:9–10

6. **Being content with who we are in Christ will help us be content with our present life status.**

   Jeremiah 9:23–24 Thus says the LORD: "Let not the wise man glory in his wisdom, let not the mighty man glory in his might, nor let the rich man glory in his riches; but let him who glories glory in this, that he understands and knows Me, that I am the LORD, exercising lovingkindness, judgment, and righteousness in the earth. For in these I delight," says the LORD. (NKJV)
   Ephesians 1:3–4; 2:4–7

7. **For contentment with the way God made you, for the person you are, see the topic Self-Worth.**

Biblical Narratives

- Lot's choices, leading to great tragedy, Genesis 13, 18–19
- Paul, who practiced contentment, Philippians 4:11–13
- Timothy needed warning about "love of money," 1 Timothy 6:6–19

Practical Steps

- Avoid window shopping, just walking through a mall, or looking at the new cars when having your car worked on. Why tempt yourself?
- Clean out your attic, garage, and closets of items you no longer use—give to some charitable cause. This would help you realize that life doesn't consist of "stuff."
- Study the word *blessing* in the Psalms. The meaning of the word essentially equals "contentment." Look for the phrase "Blessed is the one who . . ." Study and discover!

- Keep a "thankful list"—write down the big and small blessings. Keep this in your Bible, and when discontentment settles in, review your list.

- Before you buy something, ask, Will this really be beneficial to my family? Do we really need this? Avoid the urge for the newer, bigger, and better. Update only when the item wears out.

Resources

- "Your Struggle with Contentment" in *The 10 Greatest Struggles of Your Life*. Colin S. Smith. Moody.
- *The Secret of Contentment*. William J. Barclay. P & R.
- *Discontentment: Why Am I So Unhappy?* Lou Priolo. P & R.
- "Discontentment" in *Respectable Sins*. Jerry Bridges. NavPress.
- *Living the Cross Centered Life*. C. J. Mahaney. Multnomah.
- *Neither Poverty nor Riches*. Craig Blomberg. IVP.

Critical Spirit/Complaining

See also Attitude, Bitterness, Contentment, Forgiving Others, Selfishness

1. **A complaining and critical spirit during the wilderness wanderings got the Israelites into a lot of trouble.**

   Numbers 21:4–6 On the way the people lost their patience and spoke against God and Moses. They complained, "Why did you bring us out of Egypt to die in this desert, where there is no food or water? We can't stand any more of this miserable food!" Then the LORD sent poisonous snakes among the people, and many Israelites were bitten and died. (GNT)

   1 Corinthians 10:9–11 We must not put the Lord to the test, as some of them did—and they were killed by snakes. We must not complain, as some of them did—and they were destroyed by the Angel of Death. All these things happened to them as examples for others, and they were written down as a warning for us. (GNT)

   Exodus 15:24; 16:2; Numbers 11:1; 14:2; 16:11

2. **A complaining spirit must be replaced with kindness and forbearance.**

   Colossians 3:12–14 Since God chose you to be the holy people he loves, you must clothe yourselves with tenderhearted mercy, kindness, humility, gentleness, and patience. Make allowance for each other's faults, and forgive anyone who offends you. Remember, the Lord forgave you, so you must forgive others. Above all, clothe yourselves with love, which binds us all together in perfect harmony. (NLT)

   Philippians 2:14–15; James 5:9

3. Patient acceptance of others—a loving outlook and manner—is the path we must choose.

> Ecclesiastes 7:8–9 The end of something is better than its beginning. Patience is better than pride. Keep your temper under control; it is foolish to harbor a grudge. (GNT)
>
> Romans 15:7 Accept one another, then, for the glory of God, as Christ has accepted you. (GNT)
>
> Psalm 40:1; 1 Corinthians 13:4–5; 2 Corinthians 6:6; Galatians 5:22; Ephesians 4:2

4. The peace and contentment offered by Jesus are necessary components for a positive spirit.

> John 14:27 Peace I leave with you; my peace I give you. I do not give to you as the world gives. Do not let your hearts be troubled and do not be afraid. (NIV)
>
> Colossians 3:14–15 Beyond all these things put on love, which is the perfect bond of unity. Let the peace of Christ rule in your hearts, to which indeed you were called in one body; and be thankful. (NASB)
>
> Philippians 4:11–13

Biblical Narratives

- Israelites grumbling (see number 1 above)
- Pharisees and scribes grumbling against Jesus, Luke 15:2; 19:7; John 6:41–43
- Corinthians grumbling against Paul, 2 Corinthians 10:1–18

Practical Steps

- At the end of each day, think back to conversations that you had. Were you positive or negative about others? Work on appropriate changes.
- Ask God each day to help you make positive contributions to others around you.

- Be open to those close to you. Ask close friends or associates to help you monitor your attitude. Ask them to help you evaluate struggles in this area.

- Work together with your wife and children to give your home a positive atmosphere. Consciously commend them and each other for the affirmative statements made in conversations.

Resources

- "Replacing a Complaining Attitude with a Thankful Attitude" in *Lord, Change My Attitude*. James MacDonald. Moody.

- *Strengthening Your Grip: How to Live Confidently in an Aimless World*. Charles Swindoll. Thomas Nelson.

Death

See also Anxiety, Compassion, Fear, The Gospel, Grief, Hope, Suffering, Trust

Paul refers to death as the "last enemy to be destroyed" (1 Corinthians 15:26 ESV). From a purely human standpoint, death is that great equalizer from which no human is exempt. But through Christ, redemption, resurrection, and eternity with God are guaranteed.

Fact of Death

1. **Death is inevitable for all.**

   Genesis 3:19 In the sweat of your face you shall eat bread till you return to the ground, for out of it you were taken; for dust you are, and to dust you shall return. (NKJV)

   Psalm 90:10 The days of our lives are seventy years; and if by reason of strength they are eighty years, yet their boast is only labor and sorrow; for it is soon cut off, and we fly away. (NKJV)

   Hebrews 9:27

2. **God is sovereign over death; the timing is as he planned.**

   Psalm 39:4–5 LORD, make me to know my end, and what is the measure of my days, that I may know how frail I am. Indeed, You have made my days as handbreadths, and my age is as nothing before You; certainly every man at his best state is but vapor. (NKJV)

   Psalm 90:5–6 Yet you sweep people away in the sleep of death— they are like the new grass of the morning: in the morning it springs up new, but by evening it is dry and withered. (NIV)

   Matthew 10:29–31

Facing Death

1. Not even death can separate us from God and his love.

Psalm 23:4 Even though I walk through the valley of the shadow of death, I will fear no evil, for you are with me; your rod and your staff, they comfort me. (ESV)

Romans 8:38–39 For I am sure that neither death nor life, nor angels nor rulers, nor things present nor things to come, nor powers, nor height nor depth, nor anything else in all creation, will be able to separate us from the love of God in Christ Jesus our Lord. (ESV)

Joshua 1:9; Psalm 73:26; 116:15

2. Death for the believer means being in the presence of Christ.

Philippians 1:21–23 For to me to live is Christ, and to die is gain. If I am to live in the flesh, that means fruitful labor for me. Yet which I shall choose I cannot tell. I am hard pressed between the two. My desire is to depart and be with Christ, for that is far better. (ESV)

Psalm 49:15; Isaiah 57:1–2; John 14:1–3; 2 Corinthians 5:6–8

3. Death for the believer means receiving a changed and glorified body.

Philippians 3:21 He will take our weak mortal bodies and change them into glorious bodies like his own, using the same power with which he will bring everything under his control. (NLT)

1 Corinthians 15:51–52 But let me reveal to you a wonderful secret. We will not all die, but we will all be transformed! It will happen in a moment, in the blink of an eye, when the last trumpet is blown. For when the trumpet sounds, those who have died will be raised to live forever. And we who are living will also be transformed. (NLT)

John 6:40; 11:25–26; 1 John 3:2

4. Jesus's death and resurrection provide ultimate freedom from fear of death.

1 Peter 1:3–5 Blessed be the God and Father of our Lord Jesus Christ! According to his great mercy, he has caused us to be born again to a living hope through the resurrection of Jesus Christ from the dead, to an inheritance that is imperishable, undefiled, and unfading, kept in heaven for you, who by God's power are being guarded through faith for a salvation ready to be revealed in the last time. (ESV)
1 Corinthians 15:20–26; Hebrews 2:9–15

5. Death for the unbeliever results in the separation, darkness, and pain of hell. See the topic The Gospel.

Matthew 22:13; 2 Thessalonians 1:7–9; Revelation 20:11–15

Loss by Death

1. David expressed his grief to God.

Psalm 31:9–10 Be gracious to me, O LORD, for I am in distress; my eye is wasted from grief; my soul and my body also. For my life is spent with sorrow, and my years with sighing; my strength fails because of my iniquity, and my bones waste away. (ESV)
Psalm 56:8 You have kept count of my tossings; put my tears in your bottle. Are they not in your book? (ESV)

2. God can restore joy.

Isaiah 51:11 And the ransomed of the LORD shall return and come to Zion with singing; everlasting joy shall be upon their heads; they shall obtain gladness and joy, and sorrow and sighing shall flee away. (ESV)

3. The knowledge of God's presence gives us strength.

Psalm 46:1–3, 7 God is our shelter and strength, always ready to help in times of trouble. So we will not be afraid, even if the earth is shaken and mountains fall into the ocean depths; even if the seas roar and rage, and the hills are shaken by the violence. . . .

The Lord Almighty is with us; the God of Jacob is our refuge. (GNT)

Lamentations 3:21–23 This I call to mind and therefore I have hope: Because of the Lord's great love we are not consumed, for his compassions never fail. They are new every morning; great is your faithfulness. (NIV)

Deuteronomy 31:6; Psalm 73:26; Isaiah 26:3; 41:10

4. **We must bring comfort to those who mourn the loss of someone close.**

Romans 12:15 Rejoice with those who rejoice, weep with those who weep. (ESV)

John 11:33–36 When Jesus saw her weeping, and the Jews who had come with her also weeping, he was deeply moved in his spirit and greatly troubled. And he said, "Where have you laid him?" They said to him, "Lord, come and see." Jesus wept. So the Jews said, "See how he loved him!" (ESV)

Matthew 5:4

5. **Death will be conquered in the end.**

1 Corinthians 15:26 The last enemy to be destroyed is death. (ESV)

Isaiah 25:8; Revelation 21:4

Biblical Narratives

- Hezekiah, depressed at prospect of death, Isaiah 38:9–13
- Mary and Martha, in the loss of their brother, John 11
- Mary, at her son's death, John 19:26–27

Practical Steps

- Psalms to read when you feel fear of death: 23; 31; 34; 46; 91. Write out specific verses on cards from these Psalms and keep close at hand.

- Memorize Revelation 21:3–4.
- Make sure your time alone with God is consistent every day.
- Research and study the stages of grief.

Resources

- "After the Funeral" in *The Hand of God: Finding His Care in All Circumstances*. Alistair Begg. Moody.
- *Facing Death with Hope* (booklet). David Powlison. New Growth.
- *Heaven* (study guide available). Randy Alcorn. Tyndale.
- *The Last Enemy*. Michael Wittmer. Discovery House.
- *One Minute after You Die*. Erwin Lutzer. Moody.
- *Questions Children and Adults Ask about Death* (booklet). Wally Stephenson. RBP.
- *Surprised by Hope*. Tom Wright. Harper Collins.

Decision Making/Will of God

See also Anxiety, Career, Peer Pressure, Purpose for Living, Trust

Every man has an inner longing to be successful—in marriage, family, ministry, career—but so much depends on the choices we make each day. Followers of Jesus have a special advantage—knowing a God who loves them and has revealed himself and his pathways in his Word, giving us direction for the choices.

1. **Our sovereign God is trustworthy and has a plan in which we can have complete confidence.**

    Isaiah 25:1 O LORD, You are my God; I will exalt You, I will give thanks to Your name; for You have worked wonders, plans formed long ago, with perfect faithfulness. (NASB)
    Psalm 40:5 Many, LORD my God, are the wonders you have done, the things you planned for us. None can compare with you; were I to speak and tell of your deeds, they would be too many to declare. (NIV)
    Psalm 138:8; Isaiah 26:4; Psalm 37:23

2. **God's plans will be fulfilled; he will carry them through. We must trust him for it.**

    Job 42:2 I know that you can do all things; no purpose of yours can be thwarted. (NIV)
    Isaiah 14:24, 27 The LORD of Heaven's Armies has sworn this oath: "It will all happen as I have planned. It will be as I have decided. . . . The LORD of Heaven's Armies has spoken—who can change his plans? When his hand is raised, who can stop him?" (NLT)
    Psalm 37:3–5; Proverbs 16:9; Isaiah 43:13

3. To know the will of God, we must determine to know and obey his Word, never making a decision contrary to that Word.

Joshua 1:8 This Book of the Law shall not depart from your mouth, but you shall meditate on it day and night, so that you may be careful to do according to all that is written in it. For then you will make your way prosperous, and then you will have good success. (ESV)

Deuteronomy 32:46–47 He said to them, "Take to heart all the words by which I am warning you today, that you may command them to your children, that they may be careful to do all the words of this law. For it is no empty word for you, but your very life, and by this word you shall live long in the land that you are going over the Jordan to possess." (ESV)

Deuteronomy 5:29; 2 Timothy 3:16–17

4. Note Paul's prayer for believers to experience knowledge of God and live productive lives.

Colossians 1:9–10 And so, from the day we heard, we have not ceased to pray for you, asking that you may be filled with the knowledge of his will in all spiritual wisdom and understanding, so as to walk in a manner worthy of the Lord, fully pleasing to him, bearing fruit in every good work and increasing in the knowledge of God. (ESV)

5. For God to bless us in our decision making, a submissive heart is required.

Psalm 40:8 I desire to do your will, my God; your law is within my heart. (NIV)

Jeremiah 6:16 This is what the LORD says: "Stop at the crossroads and look around. Ask for the old, godly way, and walk in it. Travel its path, and you will find rest for your souls." (NLT)

Psalm 37:4–5; Proverbs 3:5–6; Romans 12:1–2; James 4:13–15

6. When we proceed with a submissive heart, God will provide direction, even when we must choose between equally good options.

Psalm 48:14 For this God is our God forever and ever; he will be our guide even to the end. (NIV)

Proverbs 4:11–13 I instruct you in the way of wisdom and lead you along straight paths. When you walk, your steps will not be hampered; when you run, you will not stumble. Hold on to instruction, do not let it go; guard it well, for it is your life. (NIV)
Psalm 25:12–14

7. **Prayer for wisdom in every decision is crucial.**

James 1:5 But if any of you lack wisdom, you should pray to God, who will give it to you; because God gives generously and graciously to all. (GNT)

Psalm 25:4–5 Teach me your ways, O LORD; make them known to me. Teach me to live according to your truth, for you are my God, who saves me. I always trust in you. (GNT)
James 3:17

8. **Determining God's will involves seeking the counsel of wise, mature believers.**

Proverbs 11:14 Where there is no guidance, a people falls, but in an abundance of counselors there is safety. (ESV)
Proverbs 15:22

9. **We must choose to serve God rather than the idols of this world.**

Joshua 24:15 But if serving the LORD seems undesirable to you, then choose for yourselves this day whom you will serve, whether the gods your ancestors served beyond the Euphrates, or the gods of the Amorites, in whose land you are living. But as for me and my household, we will serve the LORD. (NIV)

1 Kings 18:21 Elijah went before the people and said, "How long will you waver between two opinions? If the LORD is God, follow him; but if Baal is God, follow him." (NIV)
Psalm 40:4

Biblical Narratives

- Joshua's challenge, Joshua 24
- Lot, who made poor choices, Genesis 13–14; 18–19

- Abraham's servant, who sought God's will, Genesis 24:12–15
- How early church leaders were chosen, Acts 6:1–6

Practical Steps

- Commit to obedience to God no matter where it may lead. Make a list of areas where you need to change.
- Write out pros and cons for decisions you must make. Study Scripture to know God's thinking on the issues.
- Spend time in fasting, prayer, and meditation. Ask for wisdom and discernment.
- Involve godly, mature men who will counsel and pray with you about your decision.
- Consider the many "wait on God" teachings of Scripture. Commit to taking enough time for making a wise decision.

Resources

- "Demonstrating Wisdom" in *The Measure of a Man*. Gene Getz. Regal.
- *Finding God When You Need Him the Most*. Chip Ingram. Baker.
- *Found: God's Will*. John MacArthur. Cook.
- *God's Will: Guidance for Everyday Decisions*. J. I. Packer. Baker.

Depression

See also Anxiety, Confession, Grief, Hope, Past Memories, Self-Worth, Trust

Depression can be one of the most painful and overwhelming struggles we face. Yet Jesus taught, "You will know the truth, and the truth will make you free" (John 8:32 NASB). Christ's truth extends throughout Scripture beyond eternal life into every need of our lives.

1. **Biblical writers experienced the weight and overwhelming feelings of depression.**

    1 Kings 19:4 He himself [Elijah] went a day's journey into the wilderness and came and sat down under a broom tree. And he asked that he might die, saying, "It is enough; now, O LORD, take away my life, for I am no better than my fathers." (ESV)

    Proverbs 18:14 The spirit of a man can endure his sickness, but as for a broken spirit who can bear it? (NASB)

    Psalm 69:1–3 Save me, O God, for the waters have threatened my life. I have sunk in deep mire, and there is no foothold; I have come into deep waters, and a flood overflows me. I am weary with my crying; my throat is parched; my eyes fail while I wait for my God. (NASB)

    Psalm 5:1–3; 6:6–7

2. **God understands the feelings of despair.**

    Psalm 38:9 O Lord, all my longing is before you; my sighing is not hidden from you. (ESV)

    Psalm 9:12 God remembers those who suffer; he does not forget their cry. (GNT)

    Job 23:8–10; Matthew 26:38

3. **God has not forgotten us; hope in him is the answer for our despair.**

> **Psalm 34:5–8** The oppressed look to him and are glad; they will never be disappointed. The helpless call to him, and he answers; he saves them from all their troubles. His angel guards those who honor the LORD and rescues them from danger. Find out for yourself how good the LORD is. Happy are those who find safety with him. (GNT)

> **John 16:33** These things I have spoken to you, so that in Me you may have peace. In the world you have tribulation, but take courage; I have overcome the world. (NASB)

> **Psalm 9:18; 43:5; Isaiah 44:21**

4. **He has the power to keep us from sinking further into depression.**

> **Psalm 42:11** Why are you cast down, O my soul, and why are you in turmoil within me? Hope in God; for I shall again praise him, my salvation and my God. (ESV)

> **Isaiah 43:1–3** Israel, the LORD who created you says, "Do not be afraid—I will save you. I have called you by name—you are mine. When you pass through deep waters, I will be with you; your troubles will not overwhelm you. When you pass through fire, you will not be burned; the hard trials that come will not hurt you. For I am the LORD your God, the holy God of Israel, who saves you." (GNT)

> **Psalm 16:8; 32:5–8; 69:13–15**

5. **God will help us move toward hope. He is our refuge, our rock, our strength.**

> **Psalm 9:9** The LORD is a refuge for the oppressed, a place of safety in times of trouble. (GNT)

> **Psalm 18:2–6** The LORD is my protector; he is my strong fortress. My God is my protection, and with him I am safe. He protects me like a shield; he defends me and keeps me safe. I call to the LORD, and he saves me from my enemies. Praise the LORD! The danger of death was all around me; the waves of destruction rolled over me. The danger of death was around me, and the grave set its trap for me. In my trouble I called to the LORD;

I called to my God for help. In his temple he heard my voice; he listened to my cry for help. (GNT) (See also verses 28–29.)

Nahum 1:7 The LORD is good, a stronghold in the day of trouble; he knows those who take refuge in him. (ESV)

Psalm 37:23–24; 46:1; 55:22; Jeremiah 29:11–12; 2 Corinthians 4:16–18; Hebrews 12:2

6. A major aspect for healing is prayer and the monitoring of our thinking. Sound doctrine leads to correct thinking.

Philippians 4:6–8 Don't worry about anything; instead, pray about everything. Tell God what you need, and thank him for all he has done. Then you will experience God's peace, which exceeds anything we can understand. His peace will guard your hearts and minds as you live in Christ Jesus. And now, dear brothers and sisters, one final thing. Fix your thoughts on what is true, and honorable, and right, and pure, and lovely, and admirable. Think about things that are excellent and worthy of praise. (NLT)

7. If sin is the cause of depression, confession must take place for the healing process to begin.

Psalm 32:3–5 When I did not confess my sins, I was worn out from crying all day long. Day and night you punished me, LORD; my strength was completely drained, as moisture is dried up by the summer heat. Then I confessed my sins to you; I did not conceal my wrongdoings. I decided to confess them to you, and you forgave all my sins. (GNT)

Psalm 25:17–18

Biblical Narratives

- Cain, depressed because of sin, Genesis 4:1–14
- Elijah, feeling all alone, 1 Kings 19:1–18
- Job, in great suffering, Job 19:7–29
- Jeremiah, in his persecution, 20:7–18

Practical Steps

- See your physician for a physical. Ask about blood tests for vitamin D, vitamin B-12, thyroid, testosterone, and so on.
- Study Ephesians 1:3 and list from Scripture as many spiritual blessings as you can—benefits of being a part of Christ's body. Review often with thanksgiving.
- Exercise frequently. Strenuous physical activity is a great reducer of stress. Plan for thirty minutes at least three times a week. Begin with walking.
- Recognize that our enemy has schemes for our destruction. Study carefully Ephesians 6:10–18.
- Make a list of lies you believe; contrast these with the truth of Scripture.
- Read daily Psalm 27; 37.
- Share struggles with strong believers who can provide objectivity.

Resources

- "Depression" in *Feelings and Faith: Cultivating Godly Emotions in the Christian Life*. Brian Borgman. Crossway.
- *Depression: Looking Up from the Stubborn Darkness*. Ed Welch. New Growth.
- *God as He Longs for You to See Him*. Chip Ingram. Baker.
- *Out of the Blues: Dealing with the Blues of Depression and Loneliness*. Wayne Mack. Focus.
- *When the Darkness Will Not Lift*. John Piper. Crossway.

Disappointment

See also Bitterness, Depression, Failure, Pride, Suffering, Trust

Disappointment is the feeling of loss or failure because our expectations, hopes, or dreams have not been met.

1. **Writers of the Psalms experienced disappointment and expressed it honestly to God.**

   Psalm 102:1–4 Hear my prayer, O LORD; let my cry come to you! Do not hide your face from me in the day of my distress! Incline your ear to me; answer me speedily in the day when I call! For my days pass away like smoke, and my bones burn like a furnace. My heart is struck down like grass and has withered; I forget to eat my bread. (ESV)
   Psalm 13; 22:1–2

2. **Even close and trusted friends may disappoint us.**

   Psalm 55:12–14 If an enemy were insulting me, I could endure it; if a foe were rising against me, I could hide. But it is you, a man like myself, my companion, my close friend, with whom I once enjoyed sweet fellowship at the house of God, as we walked about among the worshipers. (NIV)
   Jeremiah 20:10 For I hear many whispering. Terror is on every side! "Denounce him! Let us denounce him!" say all my close friends, watching for my fall. "Perhaps he will be deceived; then we can overcome him and take our revenge on him." (ESV)
   Psalm 41:9

3. **God's silence does not mean his absence. He knows and cares about our feelings.**

Psalm 56:8 You keep track of all my sorrows. You have collected all my tears in your bottle. You have recorded each one in your book. (NLT)

Job 23:8–10 Behold, I go forward but He is not there, and backward, but I cannot perceive Him; when He acts on the left, I cannot behold Him; He turns on the right, I cannot see Him. But He knows the way I take; when He has tried me, I shall come forth as gold. (NASB)

Psalm 34:18; 37:24

4. **God is in charge of the events of our lives and allows only what is for our ultimate good.**

Isaiah 25:1 LORD, you are my God; I will honor you and praise your name. You have done amazing things; you have faithfully carried out the plans you made long ago. (GNT)

James 1:2–5 My friends, consider yourselves fortunate when all kinds of trials come your way, for you know that when your faith succeeds in facing such trials, the result is the ability to endure. Make sure that your endurance carries you all the way without failing, so that you may be perfect and complete, lacking nothing. But if any of you lack wisdom, you should pray to God, who will give it to you; because God gives generously and graciously to all. (GNT)

Proverbs 19:21; Jeremiah 25:11–13

5. **Faith in the Lord Jesus will never disappoint. He was sent to save and set us free.**

Luke 4:17–18, 21 And the scroll of the prophet Isaiah was given to him. He unrolled the scroll and found the place where it was written, "The Spirit of the Lord is upon me, because he has anointed me to proclaim good news to the poor. He has sent me to proclaim liberty to the captives and recovering of sight to the blind, to set at liberty those who are oppressed. . . . And he began to say to them, "Today this Scripture has been fulfilled in your hearing." (ESV)

Romans 10:11 The scripture says, "Whoever believes in him will not be disappointed." (GNT)
Romans 5:1–5

6. **God will provide relief from disappointment. He sends deliverance, peace, and healing.**

Psalm 22:5 To You they cried out and were delivered; in You they trusted and were not disappointed. (NASB)
Isaiah 49:23 Then you will know that I am the LORD; no one who waits for my help will be disappointed. (GNT)
John 14:1, 27 Do not let your hearts be troubled. You believe in God; believe also in me. . . . Peace I leave with you; my peace I give you. I do not give to you as the world gives. Do not let your hearts be troubled and do not be afraid. (NIV)
Psalm 147:3; Ecclesiastes 3:11–12

7. **God encourages believers to bear one another's burdens. When we face disappointment, we should seek out support from fellow believers.**

Galatians 6:2 Carry each other's burdens, and in this way you will fulfill the law of Christ. (NIV)
Romans 15:1–2 We who are strong in the faith ought to help the weak to carry their burdens. We should not please ourselves. Instead, we should all please other believers for their own good, in order to build them up in the faith. (GNT)
James 5:16 Pray for one another. (NASB)

8. **Do not let Satan use disappointment to defeat you.**

1 Peter 5:7–9 Casting all your anxiety on Him, because He cares for you. Be of sober spirit, be on the alert. Your adversary, the devil, prowls around like a roaring lion, seeking someone to devour. But resist him, firm in your faith, knowing that the same experiences of suffering are being accomplished by your brethren who are in the world. (NASB)

9. **God can use our disappointments to help others who are hurting.**

> **2 Corinthians 1:3–4** Let us give thanks to the God and Father of our Lord Jesus Christ, the merciful Father, the God from whom all help comes! He helps us in all our troubles, so that we are able to help others who have all kinds of troubles, using the same help that we ourselves have received from God. (GNT)

Biblical Narratives

- Jeremiah, the persecuted prophet, Jeremiah 20:14–18
- Jesus, disappointed by Judas, John 13:2; Matthew 26:20–23
- Paul, disappointed in John Mark, Acts 13:13; 15:36–40

Practical Steps

- Research definitions for the attributes of God from the *Evangelical Dictionary of Theology*. List personal disappointments and compare what you have learned from the study.
- Commit to thanksgiving and thinking positively; write Philippians 4:6–9 on cards. Post close at hand in strategic locations—home, office, car.
- Memorize Psalm 34:18 and 147:3–5.
- Does pride make it difficult for you to be accepting when expectations are not met?

Resources

- *The Surprising Grace of Disappointment*. John Koessler. Moody.
- *Spiritual Depression: Its Causes and Cures*. Martin Lloyd-Jones. Eerdmans.
- *When Bad Things Happen* (booklet). William Smith. New Growth.
- *When Disappointment Deceives*. Jeff Olson. RBC Ministries.
- *When Your World Falls Apart*. David Jeremiah. Thomas Nelson.
- *When Will My Life Not Suck?* Ramon Presson. New Growth.

Divorce

See also Adultery, Forgiving Others, Grief, Marriage

The topic of divorce is controversial, especially the question of re-marriage. Bible scholars have different conclusions. No matter what the issues in the marriage, the goal must be first and foremost to seek reconciliation, to save the marriage. Divorce is not an optimal solution.

1. God created marriage to last.

Matthew 19:6 So they are no longer two, but one flesh. What therefore God has joined together, let no man separate. (NASB)
Genesis 2:22–25

2. God expects faithful commitment within marriage.

Malachi 2:14 You cry out, "Why doesn't the LORD accept my worship?" I'll tell you why! Because the LORD witnessed the vows you and your wife made when you were young. But you have been unfaithful to her, though she remained your faithful partner, the wife of your marriage vows. (NLT)
Matthew 5:27–28

3. Incompatibility can be changed and improved and is not a reason for divorce.

1 Corinthians 13:4–7 Love is patient and kind; it is not jealous or conceited or proud; love is not ill-mannered or selfish or irritable; love does not keep a record of wrongs; love is not happy with evil, but is happy with the truth. Love never gives up; and its faith, hope, and patience never fail. (GNT)
Philippians 2:2–7; 4:8, 13; 1 Peter 3:7

4. Having a spouse who is an unbeliever is not a reason for divorce.

> **1 Corinthians 7:12–13** But to the rest I say, not the Lord, that if any brother has a wife who is an unbeliever, and she consents to live with him, he must not divorce her. And a woman who has an unbelieving husband, and he consents to live with her, she must not send her husband away. (NASB)

5. Whatever the problems in a marriage, reconciliation and restoration are always the goal.

> **1 Corinthians 7:10–11** To the married I give this command (not I, but the Lord): A wife must not separate from her husband. But if she does, she must remain unmarried or else be reconciled to her husband. And a husband must not divorce his wife. (NIV)
> **Galatians 6:1–2; Hebrews 12:14–15**

6. God allowed divorce because of the hardness of Israel's heart.

> **Matthew 19:3–8** Some Pharisees came to him and tried to trap him by asking, "Does our Law allow a man to divorce his wife for whatever reason he wishes?" Jesus answered, "Haven't you read the scripture that says that in the beginning the Creator made people male and female? And God said, 'For this reason a man will leave his father and mother and unite with his wife, and the two will become one.' So they are no longer two, but one. No human being must separate, then, what God has joined together." The Pharisees asked him, "Why, then, did Moses give the law for a man to hand his wife a divorce notice and send her away?" Jesus answered, "Moses gave you permission to divorce your wives because you are so hard to teach. But it was not like that at the time of creation." (GNT)
> **Mark 10:3–5**

7. God allows divorce when there has been unfaithfulness and/or desertion by an unbelieving spouse. However, seeking reconciliation should be the goal.

> **Matthew 5:31–32** It has been said, "Anyone who divorces his wife must give her a certificate of divorce." But I tell you that anyone who divorces his wife, except for sexual immorality, makes

her the victim of adultery, and anyone who marries a divorced woman commits adultery. (NIV)

1 Corinthians 7:15 But if the unbeliever leaves, let it be so. The brother or the sister is not bound in such circumstances; God has called us to live in peace. (NIV)

8. **If divorce does happen, remarriage after divorce is biblically acceptable in three situations.**

IF THE DIVORCE TOOK PLACE BEFORE THE PERSON BECAME A BELIEVER

2 Corinthians 5:17 Therefore, if anyone is in Christ, he is a new creation; old things have passed away; behold, all things have become new. (NKJV)

IF THE DIVORCE HAPPENED BECAUSE OF THE UNREPENTANT UNFAITHFULNESS OF THE SPOUSE.

Matthew 19:9 I tell you that anyone who divorces his wife, except for sexual immorality, and marries another woman commits adultery. (NIV)

IF AN UNBELIEVING SPOUSE DESERTS A BELIEVING SPOUSE

1 Corinthians 7:15 But if the unbeliever leaves, let it be so. The brother or the sister is not bound in such circumstances; God has called us to live in peace. (NIV)

Practical Steps

- Commit on day one of your marriage that divorce will never be an option.
- Make sure you are seeking your wife's greatest good, living sacrificially for her, renewing your covenant with her often.
- Research the top reasons why people divorce. Construct a plan to prevent these in your marriage.
- If you are sinning against your wife, repent!

- If your wife is sinning, make sure you do not fall into the trap of anger, bitterness, ungodly living, gossip, lack of self-control, or hurtful speech. Whatever is happening, do not permit it to cause you to choose sin.

- Seek intensive, biblical counseling to reconcile and restore your marriage.

Resources

- *Divorce* (booklet). Charles Swindoll. Multnomah. (grace view)
- *Divorce—Before You Say I Don't* (booklet). Lou Priolo. P & R.
- *The Divorce Dilemma*. John MacArthur. Day One. (grace view)
- *The Divorce Myth*. J. Carl Laney. Bethany House. (restrictive view)
- *Divorce Recovery* (booklet). Winston T. Smith. New Growth.
- "Separating What God Has Joined Together: Divorce and Re-marriage" in *God, Marriage, and Family*. Andreas Kostenberger. Crossway.

Entertainment

See also Internet, Sexual Purity, Temptation

The activities we do for fun, enjoyment, or to give us a break from the tensions of life—movies, TV, games, athletics, music, reading, art—are an integral part of our culture. As with any other part of life, we must make choices in the entertainment arena that will help and not hinder us in experiencing the holy life God desires for us.

1. **Music, art, literature, theater, and sports are all creative, cultural expressions of the humanity the Creator has given us for our enjoyment and his glory. When God created mankind in his image, he included his creativity and love for beauty.**

   1 Chronicles 29:11 Yours, O LORD, is the greatness and the power and the glory and the victory and the majesty, for all that is in the heavens and in the earth is yours. Yours is the kingdom, O LORD, and you are exalted as head above all. (ESV)
   Revelation 4:11 Worthy are you, our Lord and God, to receive glory and honor and power, for you created all things, and by your will they existed and were created. (ESV)
   Genesis 1–2; Psalm 8

2. **As with everything God has created for good, Satan, through his worldly system, seeks to corrupt and degrade, replacing with counterfeits.**

   Ezekiel 28:17 Your heart was lifted up because of your beauty; you corrupted your wisdom by reason of your splendor. I cast you to the ground; I put you before kings, that they may see you. (NASB)

1 John 5:19 We know that we are of God, and that the whole world lies in the power of the evil one. (NASB)
John 8:44; 2 Corinthians 11:14

3. **As fallen, sinful people, we are naturally selfish and prone to follow the pathways of this world.**

Romans 7:18–20 For I know that nothing good dwells in me, that is, in my flesh. For I have the desire to do what is right, but not the ability to carry it out. For I do not do the good I want, but the evil I do not want is what I keep on doing. Now if I do what I do not want, it is no longer I who do it, but sin that dwells within me. (ESV)

James 1:14–15 But each person is tempted when he is lured and enticed by his own desire. Then desire when it has conceived gives birth to sin, and sin when it is fully grown brings forth death. (ESV)
Galatians 5:19–21

4. **With the Spirit's help, the Christian man must actively determine not to follow Satan's corruptions, rejecting what is vulgar, excessively violent, or immoral.**

Deuteronomy 7:26 Do not bring a detestable thing into your house or you, like it, will be set apart for destruction. Regard it as vile and utterly detest it, for it is set apart for destruction. (NIV)

Isaiah 5:20 Woe to those who call evil good and good evil, who put darkness for light and light for darkness, who put bitter for sweet and sweet for bitter. (NIV)

Ephesians 5:3–4 But among you there must not be even a hint of sexual immorality, or of any kind of impurity, or of greed, because these are improper for God's holy people. Nor should there be obscenity, foolish talk or coarse joking, which are out of place, but rather thanksgiving. (NIV)
Ephesians 4:30; Colossians 2:8; James 1:21

5. A godly man will also actively pursue what is right, making careful decisions that glorify God.

Psalm 101:2–4 I will be careful to live a blameless life—when will you come to help me? I will lead a life of integrity in my own home. I will refuse to look at anything vile and vulgar. I hate all who deal crookedly; I will have nothing to do with them. I will reject perverse ideas and stay away from every evil. (NLT)

Colossians 3:17 And whatever you do, whether in word or deed, do it all in the name of the Lord Jesus, giving thanks to God the Father through him. (NIV)

Romans 8:5–6; Galatians 5:16; 1 John 2:15–17; 3 John 1:11

6. We must be wise in our use of time. Any entertainment activity can be practiced excessively.

Psalm 90:12 So teach us to number our days, that we may present to You a heart of wisdom. (NASB)

Ephesians 5:15–17 Therefore be careful how you walk, not as unwise men but as wise, making the most of your time, because the days are evil. So then do not be foolish, but understand what the will of the Lord is. (NASB)

Titus 3:8

Practical Steps

- If computer sites are a problem, add accountability software or filters.

- Make sure your computer access password is kept away from children.

- Look over your movie and game library, evaluating what is God honoring. Remove what is not.

- Visit Christian websites to evaluate movies before viewing.

- Make meals a time for family interaction. Turn off the TV.

- Monitor time spent on entertainment. Keep a log so you can evaluate.

- Consider community offerings for art, museums, concerts, and theater. Choose the positive, godly presentations.

- Plan family-oriented activities in which all can be involved and enjoy.
- If you have moved into sinful activities, including viewing improper images, work on deleting these from the "hard drive" of your mind through saturation with Scripture.

Resources

- *Breaking the Addictive Cycle* (booklet). David Powlison. New Growth.
- *Hope and Help for Video Game, TV, and Internet Addiction* (booklet). Mark Shaw. Focus.
- "Life in the Real World" in *Age of Opportunity*. Paul Trip. P & R.
- *Living the Cross Centered Life*. C. J. Mahaney. Multnomah.

Failure/Success

See also Decision Making, Forgiving Others, Time Management, Trials, Trust, Work Ethic

1. **Knowing God through Christ in a personal way is the mark of a successful man. It's not our intellect, power, or money that count in the end.**

    Jeremiah 9:23–24 Thus says the LORD: "Let not the wise man boast in his wisdom, let not the mighty man boast in his might, let not the rich man boast in his riches, but let him who boasts boast in this, that he understands and knows me, that I am the LORD who practices steadfast love, justice, and righteousness in the earth. For in these things I delight, declares the LORD." (ESV)

    Galatians 6:14 But far be it from me to boast except in the cross of our Lord Jesus Christ, by which the world has been crucified to me, and I to the world. (ESV)

    Psalm 73:25–26

2. **Success is conditioned on knowing and obeying God's Word.**

    Joshua 1:8–9 This Book of the Law shall not depart from your mouth, but you shall meditate on it day and night, so that you may be careful to do according to all that is written in it. For then you will make your way prosperous, and then you will have good success. Have I not commanded you? Be strong and courageous. Do not be frightened, and do not be dismayed, for the LORD your God is with you wherever you go. (ESV)

    Deuteronomy 32:46–47

3. **We must give God the credit for whatever success we enjoy.**

    1 Corinthians 15:10 By the grace of God I am what I am, and his grace to me was not without effect. No, I worked harder than

115

all of them—yet not I, but the grace of God that was with me. (NIV)

James 4:13–15 Now listen, you who say, "Today or tomorrow we will go to this or that city, spend a year there, carry on business and make money." Why, you do not even know what will happen tomorrow. What is your life? You are a mist that appears for a little while and then vanishes. Instead, you ought to say, "If it is the Lord's will, we will live and do this or that." (NIV)

1 Corinthians 3:6–9

4. **When lack of success becomes a reality, God wants us to "keep on keeping on"—working, running, improving.**

1 Corinthians 9:24–25 Do you not know that in a race all the runners run, but only one gets the prize? Run in such a way as to get the prize. Everyone who competes in the games goes into strict training. They do it to get a crown that will not last, but we do it to get a crown that will last forever. (NIV)

Philippians 3:12–14 I keep striving to win the prize for which Christ Jesus has already won me to himself. Of course, my friends, I really do not think that I have already won it; the one thing I do, however, is to forget what is behind me and do my best to reach what is ahead. So I run straight toward the goal in order to win the prize, which is God's call through Christ Jesus to the life above. (GNT)

2 Timothy 1:6–7; Hebrews 12:1–2

5. **Though we sometimes fail, God will never fail us. Our trust needs to be strong in him.**

Habakkuk 3:17–19 Though the fig tree should not blossom, nor fruit be on the vines, the produce of the olive fail and the fields yield no food, the flock be cut off from the fold and there be no herd in the stalls, yet I will rejoice in the Lord; I will take joy in the God of my salvation. God, the LORD, is my strength; he makes my feet like the deer's; he makes me tread on my high places. (ESV)

Isaiah 58:11 And the LORD will guide you continually and satisfy your desire in scorched places and make your bones strong;

and you shall be like a watered garden, like a spring of water, whose waters do not fail. (ESV) (The context is helping others.)
Deuteronomy 31:6–8; Joshua 21:45; Psalm 34:4–7; 145:14–19; Lamentations 3:21–24; Matthew 7:7–11

6. **Our weakness is God's strength.**

2 Corinthians 12:9–10 He has said to me, "My grace is sufficient for you, for power is perfected in weakness." Most gladly, therefore, I will rather boast about my weaknesses, so that the power of Christ may dwell in me. Therefore I am well content with weaknesses, with insults, with distresses, with persecutions, with difficulties, for Christ's sake; for when I am weak, then I am strong. (NASB)
Isaiah 40:28–31

7. **If our failure involves personal sin, repentance and confession are necessary to get our lives back on track. See the topics Confession, Forgiveness from God.**

Biblical Narratives

- Peter, who failed but was restored to service, John 18:15–27; 21:15–19; Acts 2
- John Mark, who got a second chance, Acts 15:36–40; 2 Timothy 4:11
- Timothy, burned out, 2 Timothy 1–2
- Paul, pressing on, Philippians 3:8–14

Practical Steps

- Center your life on God's definition of success. (See number 1 above.)
- Contrast God's view with the world's view. Study 1 John 2:15–17 to understand what to avoid.

- Do not dwell on the past. Focus on blessings from God and what he will do in the future. Memorize Philippians 3:13–14 and 4:8; write the verses on a card and keep it close at hand.
- Talk to people—trusted, mature men in Christ. Open your heart to them. Get them praying for you and holding you accountable.

Resources

- *A Shelter in the Time of Storm*. Paul Tripp. Crossway.
- *Can God Be Trusted in Our Trials?* Tony Evans. Moody.
- *Finding God When You Need Him the Most*. Chip Ingram. Baker.
- *Where Is God When It Hurts?* Philip Yancey. Zondervan.
- *Trusting God: Even When Life Hurts*. Jerry Bridges. NavPress.

Faithfulness/Commitment

See also Integrity, Leadership, Peer Pressure

If integrity is standing for the right because it is the right thing to do, faithfulness is standing by your promises, doing what you say you will do. It is fulfilling responsibilities and following through with commitments made. For the follower of Jesus, it is loyalty to God and his Word.

1. God's faithfulness is the standard and hope for our faithfulness.

Deuteronomy 32:3–4 For I will proclaim the name of the LORD; ascribe greatness to our God! The Rock, his work is perfect, for all his ways are justice. A God of faithfulness and without iniquity, just and upright is he. (ESV)

Psalm 89:1–2 I will sing of the steadfast love of the LORD, forever; with my mouth I will make known your faithfulness to all generations. For I said, "Steadfast love will be built up forever; in the heavens you will establish your faithfulness." (ESV)

Deuteronomy 7:9; Lamentations 3:22–24; 1 Thessalonians 5:24; Hebrews 10:23; 1 Peter 4:19; Revelation 19:11

2. Past sins and failures do not preclude a life of faithful service to God.

1 Timothy 1:12–13, 15–16 I [Paul] give thanks to Christ Jesus our Lord, who has given me strength for my work. I thank him for considering me worthy and appointing me to serve him, even though in the past I spoke evil of him and persecuted and insulted him. . . . This is a true saying, to be completely accepted and believed: Christ Jesus came into the world to save sinners. I am the worst of them, but God was merciful to me in order that Christ Jesus might show his full patience in dealing with me, the worst of sinners, as an example for all those who would later believe in him and receive eternal life. (GNT)

3. Those to whom God has given responsibility must show themselves faithful.

> 1 Corinthians 4:1–2 This, then, is how you ought to regard us: as servants of Christ and as those entrusted with the mysteries God has revealed. Now it is required that those who have been given a trust must prove faithful. (NIV)

4. Faithfulness is one aspect of the fruit of the Spirit, the result of depending on the Spirit for daily living.

> Galatians 5:22–23 But the fruit of the Spirit is love, joy, peace, patience, kindness, goodness, faithfulness, gentleness, self-control; against such things there is no law. (ESV)

5. Faithfulness brings reward.

> Psalm 37:3–6 Trust in the LORD and do good; dwell in the land and cultivate faithfulness. Delight yourself in the LORD; and He will give you the desires of your heart. Commit your way to the LORD, trust also in Him, and He will do it. He will bring forth your righteousness as the light and your judgment as the noonday. (NASB)
>
> Matthew 25:23 The master said, "Well done, my good and faithful servant. You have been faithful in handling this small amount, so now I will give you many more responsibilities. Let's celebrate together!" (NLT)

6. Faithful men are needed to minister to others.

> 2 Timothy 2:2 The things which you have heard from me in the presence of many witnesses, entrust these to faithful men who will be able to teach others also. (NASB)

7. God remains faithful though we are sometimes faithless.

> 2 Timothy 2:13 If we are faithless, he remains faithful—for he cannot deny himself. (ESV)

8. Faithfulness equals obedience.

> Deuteronomy 10:12–13 And now, Israel, what does the LORD your God require of you, but to fear the LORD your God, to walk

in all his ways, to love him, to serve the LORD your God with all your heart and with all your soul, and to keep the commandments and statutes of the LORD, which I am commanding you today for your good? (ESV)

Biblical Narratives

- Abraham, found faithful, Nehemiah 9:6–8; Hebrews 11:8–10
- Joshua, choosing to be faithful in serving God, Joshua 24:15
- David, wanting faithful men as counselors, Psalm 101:6–7
- Paul, in his final testimony, 2 Timothy 4:7

Practical Steps

- Consider Psalm 119:30 as a starting point to a life of faithfulness. Keeping God's Word close before us is crucial. Also focus on Psalm 119:9, 11.
- If you have difficulty in following through with commitments, ask a godly, mature man to keep you accountable. When you make a commitment, inform this person and keep in contact with him.
- Don't let past times of lack of faithfulness drag you down. Confess these and move on. Ask others for forgiveness for hurting them or causing them harm or inconvenience.

Resources

- "Becoming a Faithful Man" in *The Measure of a Man*. Gene Getz. Regal.
- "The Faithfulness of God" in *God as He Longs for You to See Him*. Chip Ingram. Baker.
- *Joseph: Overcoming Obstacles through Faithfulness*. Gene Getz. B & H.
- *A Passion for Faithfulness: Wisdom from the Book of Nehemiah*. J. I. Packer. Crossway.

Fathering

See also Anxiety, Leadership, Prodigal Children, Single Father, Trust

1. **Children are God's gift and blessing.**

   Genesis 1:27–28 So God created man in his own image, in the image of God he created him; male and female he created them. And God blessed them. And God said to them, "Be fruitful and multiply and fill the earth . . ." (ESV)

   Psalm 127:3–5 Behold, children are a heritage from the LORD, the fruit of the womb a reward. Like arrows in the hand of a warrior are the children of one's youth. Blessed is the man who fills his quiver with them! He shall not be put to shame when he speaks with his enemies in the gate. (ESV)

   Psalm 128:3–4

2. **As our heavenly Father provides for his children, so will parents do their best to provide for the needs of their children.**

   Matthew 7:9–11 You parents—if your children ask for a loaf of bread, do you give them a stone instead? Or if they ask for a fish, do you give them a snake? Of course not! So if you sinful people know how to give good gifts to your children, how much more will your heavenly Father give good gifts to those who ask him. (NLT)

   Psalm 84:11; Romans 8:32

3. **Fathers are to be intentional and focused, imparting godly wisdom and instruction.**

   Deuteronomy 6:7–9 Repeat them [God's commands] again and again to your children. Talk about them when you are at home and when you are on the road, when you are going to bed and when you are getting up. Tie them to your hands and wear them on your forehead as reminders. Write them on the doorposts of your house and on your gates. (NLT)

Joshua 4:21–23 He said to the sons of Israel, "When your children ask their fathers in time to come, saying, 'What are these stones?' then you shall inform your children, saying, 'Israel crossed this Jordan on dry ground.' For the LORD your God dried up the waters of the Jordan before you . . ." (NASB)

Psalm 78:4–6 We will not hide these truths from our children; we will tell the next generation about the glorious deeds of the LORD, about his power and his mighty wonders. . . . He commanded our ancestors to teach them to their children, so the next generation might know them—even the children not yet born—and they in turn will teach their own children. (NLT) (See verses 1–8.)

Proverbs 4:3–5; 22:6; Isaiah 38:19; Ephesians 6:4; 1 Thessalonians 2:11–12

4. **Children must obey their parents. Fathers (and mothers) must lovingly and firmly establish parental authority.**

   Colossians 3:20 Children, obey your parents in everything, for this pleases the Lord. (ESV)

   Ephesians 6:1–3 Children, obey your parents in the Lord, for this is right. Honor your father and mother (this is the first commandment with a promise), "that it may go well with you and that you may live long in the land." (ESV)

   Deuteronomy 5:16

5. **Parents must use corrective discipline, firmly but lovingly and carefully applied.**

   Proverbs 3:11–12 My son, do not despise the LORD's discipline or be weary of his reproof, for the LORD reproves him whom he loves, as a father the son in whom he delights. (ESV)

   Proverbs 19:18 Discipline your children while there is hope. Otherwise you will ruin their lives. (NLT)

Hebrews 12:11 For the moment all discipline seems painful rather than pleasant, but later it yields the peaceful fruit of righteousness to those who have been trained by it. (ESV)
Proverbs 13:24; 29:17

6. **Fathers have specific instructions to have patience and understanding.**

   Ephesians 6:4 Fathers, do not provoke your children to anger, but bring them up in the discipline and instruction of the Lord. (NASB)
   Colossians 3:21 Fathers, do not exasperate your children, so that they will not lose heart. (NASB)

7. **Children will not always walk in God's ways. Note this principle of individual accountability. Children are responsible for their own decisions, good or bad.**

   Ezekiel 18:20 The soul who sins shall die. The son shall not suffer for the iniquity of the father, nor the father suffer for the iniquity of the son. The righteousness of the righteous shall be upon himself, and the wickedness of the wicked shall be upon himself. (ESV) (The context of chapter 18 is especially important.)
   Deuteronomy 24:16

8. **Scriptural concepts for good parenting.**

   LISTENING WELL BEFORE SPEAKING

   Proverbs 18:13 If one gives an answer before he hears, it is his folly and shame. (ESV)
   James 1:19

   SPEAKING SOFTLY AND CAREFULLY

   Proverbs 15:1, 4 A gentle answer deflects anger, but harsh words make tempers flare. . . . Gentle words are a tree of life; a deceitful tongue crushes the spirit. (NLT)
   Proverbs 12:18

LOVING WITH A HUMBLE, GENTLE, PATIENT ATTITUDE

Ephesians 4:2 Always be humble and gentle. Be patient with each other, making allowance for each other's faults because of your love. (NLT)

EVIDENCING THE FRUIT OF THE SPIRIT

Galatians 5:22–23 But the fruit of the Spirit is love, joy, peace, patience, kindness, goodness, faithfulness, gentleness, self-control; against such things there is no law. (NASB)

BUILDING UP WITH KINDNESS, COMPASSION, FORGIVENESS

Ephesians 4:29–32

EXPRESSING HUMILITY, SYMPATHY, LOVE

1 Peter 3:8–9 Finally, all of you, have unity of mind, sympathy, brotherly love, a tender heart, and a humble mind. Do not repay evil for evil or reviling for reviling, but on the contrary, bless, for to this you were called, that you may obtain a blessing. (ESV)

Biblical Narratives

- Abraham, who desired the best for his son Isaac, Genesis 24
- Joshua, determined that his family would choose to serve God, Joshua 24
- Israel, failing to communicate God's truth to the next generation, Judges 2:10
- Hophni and Phinehas, who rebelled against God and their father, 1 Samuel 2:22–25
- Samuel's sons, who did not live honestly and justly, 1 Samuel 8:1–3
- Joseph, listening to God's instructions for protecting his family, Matthew 2:13–15
- Joseph and Mary, doing their best for their son, Jesus, Luke 2:39–52

Practical Steps

- Model godliness always. Make sure you are growing and abiding in Christ.

- Spending time with your children is the best investment you can make. Evaluate that amount of time; most likely it needs to be increased.

- Plan activities with your children they will enjoy. Think about their age and development when deciding what they would like to do.

- When you leave work, leave work behind. Turn off your work cell phone at home.

- Recognize that our culture's view of child discipline is vastly different from Scripture. Resist pop-culture pressures advocating permissiveness and overindulgence.

- Never discipline when you are angry. Reacting too quickly is usually overreacting. Discuss with your spouse specific measures for specific offenses. Have a plan in place.

- Always keep in mind that one of your parenting goals is to prepare children to move out and be on their own when they become adults. Avoid smothering and overprotecting.

Resources

- *Family Shepherds: Calling and Equipping Men to Lead Their Homes*. Voddie Baucham. Crossway.

- *Fathering like the Father: Becoming the Dad God Wants You to Be*. Kenneth Gangel. Baker.

- *Hope and Help for Husbands and Fathers* (booklet). Mark Shaw. Focus.

- *Preparing Your Daughter for Every Woman's Battle*. Shannon Ethridge. WaterBrook.

- *Preparing Your Son for Every Man's Battle*. Stephen Arterburn. WaterBrook.

- *You Never Stop Being a Parent: Thriving in Relationship with Your Adult Children*. Jim Newheiser and Elyse Fitzpatrick. P & R.

Fear

See also Anxiety, Disappointment, Suffering, Trust

Fear is the anticipation of what could go wrong, of what might or might not happen. It is brought about by circumstances of danger or unforeseen events in our lives. Fear is a part of everyone's life; how it is handled biblically is the key.

Causes of Fear

These are a selection of many causes. See the context of each passage.

1. Sin

> Genesis 3:10 And he said, "I heard the sound of you in the garden, and I was afraid, because I was naked, and I hid myself." (ESV)

2. Lack of faith

> Genesis 18:14–15 "Is anything too hard for the LORD? At the appointed time I will return to you, about this time next year, and Sarah shall have a son." But Sarah denied it, saying, "I did not laugh," for she was afraid. He said, "No, but you did laugh." (ESV)

3. Lack of love

> 1 John 4:18 There is no fear in love, but perfect love casts out fear. For fear has to do with punishment, and whoever fears has not been perfected in love. (ESV)

4. Physical danger

Genesis 26:7 When the men of the place asked him about his wife, he said, "She is my sister," for he feared to say, "My wife," thinking, "lest the men of the place should kill me because of Rebekah," because she was attractive in appearance. (ESV)

5. National enemies

Deuteronomy 31:6 Be strong and courageous. Do not fear or be in dread of them, for it is the LORD your God who goes with you. He will not leave you or forsake you. (ESV)

6. Words of an enemy

2 Kings 19:5–6 When the servants of King Hezekiah came to Isaiah, Isaiah said to them, "Say to your master, 'Thus says the LORD: Do not be afraid because of the words that you have heard.'" (ESV)

7. Storms of life

Matthew 8:25–26 And they went and woke him, saying, "Save us, Lord; we are perishing." And he said to them, "Why are you afraid, O you of little faith?" Then he rose and rebuked the winds and the sea, and there was a great calm. (ESV)

8. The unknown

Mark 6:48–50 He meant to pass by them, but when they saw him walking on the sea they thought it was a ghost, and cried out, for they all saw him and were terrified. (ESV)

9. Spiritual danger

2 Corinthians 11:3 I am afraid that as the serpent deceived Eve by his cunning, your thoughts will be led astray from a sincere and pure devotion to Christ. (ESV)

Our Heavenly Father Is Greater than Any Fear

1. His presence with us in every situation leaves no reason to fear.

Isaiah 41:10 Fear not, for I am with you; be not dismayed, for I am your God; I will strengthen you, I will help you, I will uphold you with my righteous right hand. (ESV)

Isaiah 41:13 For I, the LORD your God, hold your right hand; it is I who say to you, "Fear not, I am the one who helps you." (ESV)

Joshua 1:9; Psalm 73:23–24; Isaiah 43:1–2; Haggai 2:4; Hebrews 13:5

2. He is our defense and more powerful than any forces against us.

Psalm 61:1–4 Hear my cry, O God, listen to my prayer; from the end of the earth I call to you when my heart is faint. Lead me to the rock that is higher than I, for you have been my refuge, a strong tower against the enemy. Let me dwell in your tent forever! Let me take refuge under the shelter of your wings! (ESV)

Romans 8:31–32 What then shall we say to these things? If God is for us, who can be against us? He who did not spare his own Son but gave him up for us all, how will he not also with him graciously give us all things? (ESV)

Psalm 27:1–3; 91:4

What Our Response Should Be

1. Centering our hearts and minds on God is vital. We must focus on what is real and true.

Psalm 34:4 I prayed to the LORD, and he answered me. He freed me from all my fears. (NLT)

Psalm 33:13–14, 18–19 The LORD looks down from heaven and sees the whole human race. From his throne he observes all who live on the earth. . . . But the LORD watches over those who fear him, those who rely on his unfailing love. He rescues them from death and keeps them alive in times of famine. (NLT)

Philippians 4:8–9 And now, dear brothers and sisters, one final thing. Fix your thoughts on what is true, and honorable, and right, and pure, and lovely, and admirable. Think about things that are excellent and worthy of praise. Keep putting into practice all you learned and received from me—everything you heard from me and saw me doing. Then the God of peace will be with you. (NLT)

2. **Neither the past nor the future should be cause for fear.**

Isaiah 43:18–19 Remember not the former things, nor consider the things of old. Behold, I am doing a new thing; now it springs forth, do you not perceive it? (ESV)

Jeremiah 29:11 "For I know the plans that I have for you," declares the LORD, "plans for welfare and not for calamity to give you a future and a hope." (NASB)

Proverbs 3:5–6

3. **We must trust God to know and provide what we need for daily life.**

Matthew 6:31–34 So do not start worrying: "Where will my food come from? or my drink? or my clothes?" (These are the things the pagans are always concerned about.) Your Father in heaven knows that you need all these things. Instead, be concerned above everything else with the Kingdom of God and with what he requires of you, and he will provide you with all these other things. So do not worry about tomorrow; it will have enough worries of its own. There is no need to add to the troubles each day brings. (GNT)

Philippians 4:19 And my God will supply all your needs according to His riches in glory in Christ Jesus. (NASB)

4. **We must trust God completely even though we don't always understand what is happening.**

Habakkuk 3:16–18 I hear all this, and I tremble; my lips quiver with fear. My body goes limp, and my feet stumble beneath me. I will quietly wait for the time to come when God will punish those who attack us. Even though the fig trees have no fruit and no grapes grow on the vines, even though the olive crop fails and the fields produce no grain, even though the sheep all die and the cattle stalls are empty, I will still be joyful and glad, because the Lord God is my savior. (GNT)

Practical Steps

- Compare David's discouragement in 1 Samuel 27:1 with his total trust in God in Psalm 27.
- Memorize and meditate on Isaiah 43:1–2. Copy and post close at hand.
- Study the list of causes of fear above. Consider the context of each passage and determine the outcome of the situation. What can be learned, good or bad, from each? List personal applications.

Resources

- "Fear, Anxiety, and Worry" in *Feelings and Faith: Cultivating Godly Emotions in the Christian Life*. Brian Borgman. Crossway.
- *Fear Factor: What Satan Doesn't Want You to Know*. Wayne Mack. Hensley.
- *Fear: Breaking Its Grip*. Lou Priolo. P & R.
- "Fear" in *The Strength of a Man: 50 Devotionals to Help Men Find Their Strength in God*. David Roper. Discovery House.
- "When You Are Gripped by Fear" in *Finding God When You Need Him the Most*. Chip Ingram. Baker.

Finances/Money

See also Anxiety, Compassion, Contentment, Jealousy, Materialism, Purpose for Living

We get a paycheck and cash it or bank it. What's next? Is there an order of priorities a godly man should establish? Suggestions are given here for a financial priority framework. Helping others should always be in our plans, whether little or much, depending on our financial standing.

Priority Grid

1. **God must be first. Part of what we earn should be given back to God. Grace giving can include the tithing standard of the Old Testament. Those laws help us understand God's mind and heart about giving. See the topic Spiritual Disciplines.**

   Proverbs 3:9–10 Honor the LORD with your wealth and with the best part of everything you produce. Then he will fill your barns with grain, and your vats will overflow with good wine. (NLT)

   2 Corinthians 9:7 You must each decide in your heart how much to give. And don't give reluctantly or in response to pressure. "For God loves a person who gives cheerfully." (NLT)

   Leviticus 27:30–33; Malachi 3:8; Romans 6:14–15

2. **Taxes. We all have responsibility for paying required taxes.**

   Romans 13:1, 6–7 Let everyone be subject to the governing authorities, for there is no authority except that which God has established. The authorities that exist have been established by God. . . . This is also why you pay taxes, for the authorities are God's servants, who give their full time to governing. Give to everyone what you owe them: If you owe taxes, pay taxes; if revenue, then revenue; if respect, then respect; if honor, then honor. (NIV)

Matthew 22:17–21 (on paying taxes)

3. **Bills. Never be late in paying these monthly missives. Be careful of borrowing more than you can pay back.**

Romans 13:8 Let no debt remain outstanding, except the continuing debt to love one another, for whoever loves others has fulfilled the law. (NIV)

4. **Saving. Planning for future needs, "paying the pig," is a mark of a wise man.**

Proverbs 6:6–8 Take a lesson from the ants, you lazybones. Learn from their ways and become wise! Though they have no prince or governor or ruler to make them work, they labor hard all summer, gathering food for the winter. (NLT)

Proverbs 10:5

5. **Others. Those who are able should share financially with others.**

Proverbs 11:25 The generous will prosper; those who refresh others will themselves be refreshed. (NLT)

1 Timothy 6:17–18 As for the rich in this present age, charge them not to be haughty, nor to set their hopes on the uncertainty of riches, but on God, who richly provides us with everything to enjoy. They are to do good, to be rich in good works, to be generous and ready to share. (ESV)

Psalm 41:1; Proverbs 19:17

Additional Scriptural Standards

1. **Beware of taking on someone else's debt.**

Proverbs 6:1–3 My child, if you have put up security for a friend's debt or agreed to guarantee the debt of a stranger—if you have trapped yourself by your agreement and are caught by what you said—follow my advice and save yourself, for you have placed yourself at your friend's mercy. Now swallow your pride; go and beg to have your name erased. (NLT)

2. **God expects us to work for what we acquire.**

1 Thessalonians 4:11–12 Make it your goal to live a quiet life, minding your own business and working with your hands, just as we instructed you before. Then people who are not Christians will respect the way you live, and you will not need to depend on others. (NLT)

3. **Maintaining a good reputation, financially and otherwise, is critical.**

1 Timothy 3:7 He should be a man who is respected by the people outside the church, so that he will not be disgraced and fall into the Devil's trap. (GNT)

4. **Asking God for wisdom is important in every area of life, including finances.**

James 1:5 But if any of you lack wisdom, you should pray to God, who will give it to you; because God gives generously and graciously to all. (GNT)

5. **Getting counsel and advice can be crucial to success.**

Proverbs 11:14 Where there is no guidance, a people falls, but in an abundance of counselors there is safety. (ESV)
Proverbs 15:22

6. **We must guard our hearts against greed and covetousness. Loving money is not to be a part of our lives.**

Exodus 20:17 You shall not covet your neighbor's house. You shall not covet your neighbor's wife, or his male or female servant, his ox or donkey, or anything that belongs to your neighbor. (NIV)
1 Timothy 6:9–10 Those who want to get rich fall into temptation and a trap and into many foolish and harmful desires that plunge people into ruin and destruction. For the love of money

is a root of all kinds of evil. Some people, eager for money, have wandered from the faith and pierced themselves with many griefs. (NIV)

Matthew 6:19–21 Do not store up for yourselves treasures on earth, where moth and rust destroy, and where thieves break in and steal. But store up for yourselves treasures in heaven, where neither moth nor rust destroys, and where thieves do not break in or steal; for where your treasure is, there your heart will be also. (NASB)

Psalm 49:16–20; Hebrews 13:5

7. **Ultimately, everything belongs to God. It is only by his provision we have anything.**

1 Chronicles 29:11–12 Yours, O LORD, is the greatness and the power and the glory and the victory and the majesty, for all that is in the heavens and in the earth is yours. Yours is the kingdom, O LORD, and you are exalted as head above all. Both riches and honor come from you, and you rule over all. In your hand are power and might, and in your hand it is to make great and to give strength to all. (ESV)

Deuteronomy 8:18 And you shall remember the LORD your God, for it is He who gives you power to get wealth, that He may establish His covenant which He swore to your fathers, as it is this day. (NKJV)

Psalm 50:12; Proverbs 10:22; Haggai 2:8

8. **God wants us to enjoy the blessings he provides.**

Ecclesiastes 2:24–26 A person can do nothing better than to eat and drink and find satisfaction in their own toil. This too, I see, is from the hand of God, for without him, who can eat or find enjoyment? To the person who pleases him, God gives wisdom, knowledge and happiness. (NIV)

1 Timothy 6:17 Command those who are rich in this present world not to be arrogant nor to put their hope in wealth, which is so uncertain, but to put their hope in God, who richly provides us with everything for our enjoyment. (NIV)

John 10:9–10

Biblical Narratives

- Ananias and Sapphira, Acts 5:1–11
- Paul, Philippians 4:10–13

Practical Steps

- Seriously consider the benefits of living on just one income.
- Maintain a budget plan with financial goals. If necessary, seek accountability with another man so you can stick to it.
- If credit card use is out of control—stop using, pay off, or destroy.
- Sign up for a Financial Peace University course or check out Crown Financial Ministries.

Resources

- *Counterfeit Gods: The Empty Promises of Money, Sex, and Power.* Timothy Keller. Dutton.
- "Financial Dealings" in *Character Counts.* Rod Handley. Cross Training.
- *Help, I'm Drowning in Debt* (booklet). John Temple. Day One.
- *Money, Possessions, and Eternity.* Randy Alcorn. Tyndale.
- *Sex and Money: Pleasures That Leave You Empty and Grace That Satisfies.* Paul Tripp. Crossway.
- *The Total Money Makeover* (audio book available). Dave Ramsey. Thomas Nelson.

Flirting

See also Integrity, Marriage, Reputation, Sexual Purity, Temptation, Workplace

Defined as showing an interest in someone of the opposite sex, but without serious intent, flirting is seen by many as an innocent activity. Yet in our sexually charged, promiscuous culture, it can have serious repercussions for the Christian man who needs to maintain a godly commitment to his wife (if married), purity, and a good reputation with others.

1. **Married men must be single-minded in their devotion to the one woman God has given them. Associations with other women must be pure and responsible, never provocative.**

   1 Timothy 3:2 Therefore an overseer must be above reproach, the husband of one wife. (ESV) ("Husband of one wife" in original language is "one-woman man"—she is to be the only source of satisfaction for his masculine needs. The context is church leadership, but application can be made to every man.)

   Matthew 12:36–37 I tell you, on the day of judgment people will give account for every careless word they speak, for by your words you will be justified, and by your words you will be condemned. (ESV)

   Proverbs 21:23; Malachi 2:14–15

2. **Single men must also be pure and above reproach in their relationship with women.**

   1 Timothy 5:2 Treat older women as you would your mother, and treat younger women with all purity as you would your own sisters. (NLT)

   Ephesians 5:4 Let there be no filthiness nor foolish talk nor crude joking. (ESV)

   1 Corinthians 10:12; 1 Thessalonians 5:22

3. A good testimony and reputation that encourage others is the goal.

Matthew 5:16 In the same way, let your light shine before others, so that they may see your good works and give glory to your Father who is in heaven. (ESV)

1 Peter 2:11–12 Dear friends, I warn you as "temporary residents and foreigners" to keep away from worldly desires that wage war against your very souls. Be careful to live properly among your unbelieving neighbors. Then even if they accuse you of doing wrong, they will see your honorable behavior, and they will give honor to God when he judges the world. (NLT)

Proverbs 10:11

4. Flirtatious and provocative speech and actions are to be avoided.

2 Peter 2:18 They brag about themselves with empty, foolish boasting. With an appeal to twisted sexual desires, they lure back into sin those who have barely escaped from a lifestyle of deception. (NLT)

Proverbs 10:10 Whoever winks the eye causes trouble, and a babbling fool will come to ruin. (ESV)

Isaiah 3:16–17 Moreover, the LORD said, "Because the daughters of Zion are proud and walk with heads held high and seductive eyes, and go along with mincing steps and tinkle the bangles on their feet, therefore the LORD will afflict the scalp of the daughters of Zion with scabs, and the LORD will make their foreheads bare." (NASB) (These statements apply equally to men for their similar words and actions.)

Proverbs 2:16–17

5. Flirting could have disastrous results, causing a fall into sin.

Matthew 18:7 Woe to the world because of the things that cause people to stumble! Such things must come, but woe to the person through whom they come! (NIV)

Romans 14:13, 21 Therefore let us stop passing judgment on one another. Instead, make up your mind not to put any stumbling block or obstacle in the way of a brother or sister. . . . It is better not to eat meat or drink wine or to do anything else that will cause your brother or sister to fall. (NIV)

Luke 17:1; 2 Corinthians 6:3

6. Such irresponsible behavior could open our lives to Satan's attacks.

1 Peter 5:8 Be sober-minded; be watchful. Your adversary the devil prowls around like a roaring lion, seeking someone to devour. (ESV)

2 Corinthians 11:3 But I am afraid that just as Eve was deceived by the serpent's cunning, your minds may somehow be led astray from your sincere and pure devotion to Christ. (NIV)

Proverbs 9:13–18; Ephesians 6:11–13

Biblical Narrative

- Women to avoid, Proverbs 5:1–14; 7:10–27

Practical Steps

- Set boundaries for relationships with women—at work, socially, at church.
- Avoid being alone with a woman who is not your wife (other than family members or the elderly).
- Read Proverbs 5 and in your own words describe flirting from God's point of view.
- List flirtatious actions on one side of a paper; on the other side list opposite actions. Compare and contrast. Commit to nonflirtatious behavior.
- Be cautious about touching or hugging women. Use wisdom in greeting; be an example of purity. If others are "touchy" with you, communicate kindly that this is not acceptable.

Resources

- "Character" in *Disciplines of a Godly Man*. Kent Hughes. Crossway.
- *Not Even a Hint: Guarding Your Heart*. Shannon and Joshua Harris. Multnomah.
- *Respectable Sins*. Jerry Bridges. NavPress.

Forgiveness from God

See also Confession, Forgiving Others, Guilt, Hope, Past Memories

1. There is no sin so great that God will not forgive.

Psalm 86:5 For you, O Lord, are good and forgiving, abounding in steadfast love to all who call upon you. (ESV)

Daniel 9:9 The Lord our God is merciful and forgiving, even though we have rebelled against him. (NIV)

Romans 8:1–2 There is therefore now no condemnation for those who are in Christ Jesus. For the law of the Spirit of life has set you free in Christ Jesus from the law of sin and death. (ESV)

Psalm 130:3–4; Lamentations 3:22

2. Receiving forgiveness must begin with repentance and confession.

1 John 1:9 If we confess our sins, he is faithful and just to forgive us our sins and to cleanse us from all unrighteousness. (ESV)

Proverbs 28:13 Whoever conceals their sins does not prosper, but the one who confesses and renounces them finds mercy. (NIV)

Psalm 32:5 Then I acknowledged my sin to you and did not cover up my iniquity. I said, "I will confess my transgressions to the LORD." And you forgave the guilt of my sin. (NIV)

Psalm 51:1–2 Have mercy on me, O God, according to your unfailing love; according to your great compassion blot out my transgressions. Wash away all my iniquity and cleanse me from my sin. (NIV)

Psalm 25:7; 38:18; 66:18–19; Isaiah 55:6–7; Acts 3:19

3. Note these word pictures from the Old Testament as to how God views our sins once they have been forgiven—the results of what Christ's death on the cross has accomplished.

Isaiah 43:25 I—yes, I alone—will blot out your sins for my own sake and will never think of them again. (NLT)

Isaiah 44:22 I have wiped out your transgressions like a thick cloud and your sins like a heavy mist. (NASB)

Isaiah 38:17 Behold, it was for my welfare that I had great bitterness; but in love you have delivered my life from the pit of destruction, for you have cast all my sins behind your back. (ESV)

Micah 7:19 He will again have compassion on us; he will tread our iniquities underfoot. You will cast all our sins into the depths of the sea. (ESV)

Psalm 32:1; 51:7; 103:12; Isaiah 1:18; Hebrews 8:12

4. God will supply complete restoration.

Colossians 1:13–14 For he has rescued us from the kingdom of darkness and transferred us into the Kingdom of his dear Son, who purchased our freedom and forgave our sins. (NLT)

Romans 8:1–2 There is therefore now no condemnation for those who are in Christ Jesus. For the law of the Spirit of life has set you free in Christ Jesus from the law of sin and death. (ESV)

Psalm 51:12; 103:10–11; 130:7; 2 Corinthians 5:17

5. Nowhere in Scripture is it taught that we are to forgive ourselves. We must accept what we have done and take steps to make it right, but our sin was against God. Christ paid the price for all our sins and offers forgiveness.

Biblical Narratives

- God, who forgave Israel in the wilderness, Nehemiah 9:16–21
- David, his great sins, 2 Samuel 12, Psalm 51
- Christ's crucifixion—he paid it all; he says, "I forgive!" Luke 23:26–49

- Paul, who committed heinous sins against the church yet experienced total forgiveness, Acts 26:9–18; Galatians 1:13; 1 Timothy 1:13.

Practical Steps

- Spend much time in prayer and reflection on Psalms 32 and 51.
- How did Christ forgive? Read the crucifixion account in all four Gospels. Write down details, and reflect on how he forgave us.
- Complete a word study on *redemption* in the New Testament. Center on the concept of freedom.
- Write out on a card what God does with forgiven sin (see number 4 above). Keep it close as a reminder.
- Honor God by believing the truth of his forgiveness. When doubts arise, realize they come from the enemy.
- Pray the Lord's Prayer out loud daily.

Resources

- *Accepting God's Forgiveness* (booklet). C. John Miller. New Growth.
- *After You've Blown It: Reconnecting with God and Others*. Erwin Lutzer. Multnomah.
- "The Faithfulness of God" in *God as He Longs for You to See Him*. Chip Ingram. Baker.
- *Forgiveness*. Robert Jones. P & R.
- *Free at Last: Experiencing True Freedom through Your Identity with Christ*. Tony Evans. Moody.
- *The Knowledge of the Holy*. A. W. Tozer. Harper Collins.
- *What's So Amazing about Grace?* Philip Yancey. Zondervan.

Forgiving Others

See also Bitterness, Confession, Disappointment, Forgiveness from God, Guilt, Past Memories

1. **Our model for forgiving others is God himself. It is a part of his character to forgive.**

   Nehemiah 9:17–19 But you are a God ready to forgive, gracious and merciful, slow to anger and abounding in steadfast love, and did not forsake them. Even when they had made for themselves a golden calf and said, "This is your God who brought you up out of Egypt," and had committed great blasphemies, you in your great mercies did not forsake them in the wilderness. (ESV)

   Micah 7:18–19 Who is a God like you, pardoning iniquity and passing over transgression for the remnant of his inheritance? He does not retain his anger forever, because he delights in steadfast love. He will again have compassion on us; he will tread our iniquities underfoot. You will cast all our sins into the depths of the sea. (ESV)

   Psalm 30:5; 130:3–4; Romans 8:1–2

2. **Though often it is difficult to forgive others, there is no option. It is a step of obedience to God.**

   Ephesians 4:32 Be kind and compassionate to one another, forgiving each other, just as in Christ God forgave you. (NIV)

   Matthew 5:23–24 So if you are offering your gift at the altar and there remember that your brother has something against you, leave your gift there before the altar and go. First be reconciled to your brother, and then come and offer your gift. (ESV)

   Matthew 6:9–15; Luke 23:34; Colossians 3:13–14

3. Revenge is not an acceptable option. We must leave the matter to God.

> **Romans 12:17–19** Repay no one evil for evil, but give thought to do what is honorable in the sight of all. If possible, so far as it depends on you, live peaceably with all. Beloved, never avenge yourselves, but leave it to the wrath of God. (ESV)
>
> **Proverbs 20:22** Do not say, "I will repay evil"; wait for the LORD, and he will deliver you. (ESV)
>
> **Proverbs 24:29; 1 Thessalonians 5:15–16**

4. There is no need to keep a record of how many times you have forgiven.

> **Luke 17:3–4** Pay attention to yourselves! If your brother sins, rebuke him, and if he repents, forgive him, and if he sins against you seven times in the day, and turns to you seven times, saying, "I repent," you must forgive him. (ESV)
>
> **Matthew 18:21–22**

Biblical Narratives

- Joseph, his gracious attitude, Genesis 50:15–21
- Parable of the unforgiving servant, Matthew 18:23–35
- Jesus, on the cross, Luke 23:34
- Stephen, who forgave his attackers, Acts 7:60
- Philemon, whom Paul instructed to forgive

Practical Steps

- Contemplate: what would it be like if God did not forgive me? Does that change my heart for forgiving others?
- Write these statements on cards and post them: 1. Forgiveness is not a feeling but an action. 2. Forgiveness is a choice of obedience to God. 3. Forgiveness does not mean the other person was right, but forgiving provides freedom.

- Every time a past wrong is remembered, no longer hold it to the offender's account. You have forgiven them.
- Study Genesis 50:15–21 and write out principles of application.

Resources

- *Forgiving Others: Joining Wisdom and Love.* Timothy Lane. New Growth.
- *From Forgiving to Forgiven.* Jay Adams. Calvary Press.
- *Freedom from Resentment: Stopping Hurts from Turning Bitter* (booklet). Robert Jones. CCEF.
- *Help, I Can't Forgive* (booklet). Jim Newcomer. Day One.
- *Unpacking Forgiveness.* Chris Brauns. Crossway.

Friendship

See also **Boundaries, Commitment, Peer Pressure**

The dictionary defines a friend as one attached to another by mutual affection and esteem, a preferred companion. In Scripture, friendship is close companionship, the experience of mutual kindness, devotion, or affection, often raised to a spiritual level. It is close in meaning to "brotherly love." Jesus refers to those who obediently follow him as friends in John 15:14–15.

1. **Reasons for having good friends:**

   WE ALL NEED SOMEONE WHO "HAS OUR BACK," PROVIDING STRENGTH AND SUPPORT.

   Ecclesiastes 4:9–10 Two people are better off than one, for they can help each other succeed. If one person falls, the other can reach out and help. But someone who falls alone is in real trouble. (NLT)

   Ecclesiastes 4:12 A person standing alone can be attacked and defeated, but two can stand back-to-back and conquer. Three are even better, for a triple-braided cord is not easily broken. (NLT)

   WE NEED THOSE WHO WILL HELP US WALK WISELY.

   Proverbs 13:20 Walk with the wise and become wise; associate with fools and get in trouble. (NLT)

   WE NEED MUTUAL ENCOURAGEMENT AND ACCOUNTABILITY.

   1 Thessalonians 5:11 Therefore encourage one another and build up one another, just as you also are doing. (NASB)

   Hebrews 10:24

GOOD FRIENDS WILL KEEP US SHARP AND "ON THE CUTTING EDGE."

Proverbs 27:17 As iron sharpens iron, so a friend sharpens a friend. (NLT)
Ecclesiastes 10:10

2. **Our choice in friends is critical. We must avoid:**

THOSE WHO USE OTHERS FOR PERSONAL ADVANCEMENT OR GAIN

Proverbs 19:4–7 Wealth adds many friends, but a poor man is separated from his friend. A false witness will not go unpunished, and he who tells lies will not escape. Many will seek the favor of a generous man, and every man is a friend to him who gives gifts. All the brothers of a poor man hate him; how much more do his friends abandon him! He pursues them with words, but they are gone. (NASB)
Proverbs 14:20

THOSE WHO ARE PRONE TO ANGER AND RAGE

Proverbs 22:24–25 Do not make friends with a hot-tempered person, do not associate with one easily angered, or you may learn their ways and get yourself ensnared. (NIV)

THOSE WHO WOULD LEAD US INTO SIN

Proverbs 12:26 The righteous choose their friends carefully, but the way of the wicked leads them astray. (NIV)
Exodus 23:2

THOSE WHO DRINK AND EAT TOO MUCH

Proverbs 23:20 Don't associate with people who drink too much wine or stuff themselves with food. (GNT)

3. **Marks of a good friend include:**

LOYALTY

Psalm 15:1–3 O LORD, who shall sojourn in your tent? Who shall dwell on your holy hill? He who walks blamelessly and does what is right and speaks truth in his heart; who does not slander with his tongue and does no evil to his neighbor, nor takes up a reproach against his friend. (ESV)

Proverbs 18:24 There are "friends" who destroy each other, but a real friend sticks closer than a brother. (NLT)

Romans 12:10

SUBMITTING TO GOD IN OBEDIENCE

Psalm 119:63 I am a friend to anyone who fears you—anyone who obeys your commandments. (NLT)

GIVING ONE'S LIFE FOR ANOTHER

John 15:13 Greater love has no one than this: to lay down one's life for one's friends. (NIV)

OBEDIENCE TO CHRIST, A PART OF WHICH IS LOVE FOR OTHERS

John 15:12, 14 My command is this: Love each other as I have loved you. . . . You are my friends if you do what I command. (NIV)

MUTUAL ACCEPTANCE

Romans 15:7 Therefore, accept one another, just as Christ also accepted us to the glory of God. (NASB)

MUTUAL BURDEN BEARING

Galatians 6:2 Bear one another's burdens, and thereby fulfill the law of Christ. (NASB)

4. **There are times when earthly friends will fail us, but our heavenly Father will not.**

Psalm 55:12–14 For it is not an enemy who reproaches me, then I could bear it; nor is it one who hates me who has exalted himself against me, then I could hide myself from him. But it is you, a man my equal, my companion and my familiar friend; we who had sweet fellowship together walked in the house of God in the throng. (NASB)

Psalm 41:9 Even my close friend in whom I trusted, who ate my bread, has lifted his heel against me. (ESV)

Jeremiah 20:10 For I hear many whispering. Terror is on every side! "Denounce him! Let us denounce him!" say all my close friends, watching for my fall. (ESV)

Deuteronomy 31:6; Joshua 1:9; 21:45

5. **We need to work at maintaining and, if necessary, restoring our friendships.**

   Romans 12:18 If possible, so far as it depends on you, be at peace with all men. (NASB)

   Proverbs 19:11 Good sense makes one slow to anger, and it is his glory to overlook an offense. (ESV)

   Ephesians 4:3 Make every effort to keep the unity of the Spirit through the bond of peace. (NIV)

   Matthew 5:23–24; Ephesians 4:32; Philippians 2:1–2

Biblical Narratives

- Job, his friends/critics, Job 2:11; 12:4; 16:20; 19:14
- God and Abraham, their friendship, 2 Chronicles 20:7; James 2:23
- Jonathan, his sacrificial efforts for David, 1 Samuel 18–20
- Paul and Timothy, their friendship

Practical Steps

- Be proactive about being a good friend. Show interest in the interests of others. Keep up on current happenings in the things your friend enjoys, such as sports teams, hunting and fishing, investments.
- Seek out older, mature Christians as friends. Seek advice in mutual need areas. Be praying for each other.
- Develop relationships by participating in a men's Bible study.

- Think through and write a list of qualities you look for in friends. Do you have these qualities?
- Take the initiative to befriend someone who seems to have few friends. Getting to know him could be a positive adventure.

Resources

- "The Discipline of Friendship" in *Disciplines of a Godly Man*. Kent Hughes. Crossway.
- "Friendship" in *The Four Loves*. C. S. Lewis. Mariner.
- "Loneliness" in *The Strength of a Man: 50 Devotionals to Help Men Find Their Strength in God*. David Roper. Discovery House.
- "Relationships" (booklet). Paul Tripp. CCEF.
- *The Peacemaker: A Biblical Guide to Resolving Conflicts*. Ken Sande. Baker.
- "Wanted: Male Bonding" in *The Secrets Men Keep*. Stephen Arterburn. Thomas Nelson.

Gambling

See also Contentment, Entertainment, Materialism, Money, Temptation

Gambling for monetary gain is the emphasis here. However, even casual gambling can lead to greater temptation or loss of reputation and testimony for Christ. The reader should consider principles from Romans 14:1–23; 1 Corinthians 6:12.

1. **We must exercise care to avoid traps set by Satan.**

   Ephesians 6:11–12 Put on the whole armor of God, that you may be able to stand against the schemes of the devil. For we do not wrestle against flesh and blood, but against the rulers, against the authorities, against the cosmic powers over this present darkness, against the spiritual forces of evil in the heavenly places. (ESV)

   Romans 16:18 Such people are not serving Christ our Lord; they are serving their own personal interests. By smooth talk and glowing words they deceive innocent people. (NLT)

   Psalm 64:2, 5; 2 Corinthians 11:3; 1 John 2:15–17

2. **Getting rich is not the goal. Being content with what we have is required.**

   Proverbs 30:7–9 Two things I ask of you, LORD; do not refuse me before I die: Keep falsehood and lies far from me; give me neither poverty nor riches, but give me only my daily bread. Otherwise, I may have too much and disown you and say, "Who is the Lord?" Or I may become poor and steal, and so dishonor the name of my God. (NIV)

   1 Timothy 6:6 Godliness with contentment is great gain. (ESV) (See verses 6–11.)

   Ephesians 4:22

3. **Gambling is not good stewardship.**

Luke 12:42–44 The Lord answered, "Who then is the faithful and wise manager, whom the master puts in charge of his servants to give them their food allowance at the proper time? It will be good for that servant whom the master finds doing so when he returns. Truly I tell you, he will put him in charge of all his possessions. (NIV)

1 Corinthians 4:1–2 This, then, is how you ought to regard us: as servants of Christ and as those entrusted with the mysteries God has revealed. Now it is required that those who have been given a trust must prove faithful. (NIV)

1 Peter 4:10

4. **God can and will supply all our needs financially.**

Philippians 4:19 And this same God who takes care of me will supply all your needs from his glorious riches, which have been given to us in Christ Jesus. (NLT)

Matthew 6:33–34 Seek the Kingdom of God above all else, and live righteously, and he will give you everything you need. So don't worry about tomorrow, for tomorrow will bring its own worries. Today's trouble is enough for today. (NLT)

Jeremiah 32:27

Biblical Narrative

- Paul's contentment, Philippians 4

Practical Steps

- Instead of buying lottery tickets, use that money to give to the poor, to someone who has been through a tornado, or to your church missions program.
- Commit to staying out of gambling pools at work. Don't be smug about it; just quietly keep away.

- To help relieve the pressure when tempted to buy lottery tickets, say, "That's one tax I don't have to pay!"
- If married, ask your wife to keep you accountable. Together make wise choices for spending.

Resources

- *Counterfeit Gods: The Empty Promises of Money, Sex, and Power*. Timothy Keller. Dutton.
- *Tony Evans Speaks Out on Gambling and the Lottery*. Tony Evans. Moody.
- *Hope and Help for Gambling* (booklet). Mark Shaw. Focus.
- "Gambling: Is It a Good Bet?" in *Seven Snares of the Enemy*. Erwin Lutzer. Moody.
- *Sex and Money: Pleasures That Leave You Empty and Grace That Satisfies*. Paul Tripp. Crossway.

Grief/Sorrow

See also Death, Disappointment, Forgiveness from God, Hope, Past Memories, Suffering, Trust

Grief is a deep emotion of distress caused by great loss or difficulty. Sorrow is the sadness and regret that accompany that loss. The words "if only" are often repeated. Martha and Mary both said these words to Jesus after Lazarus died: "if only you had been here" (John 11:21, 32 NLT).

1. **Inevitably, sadness and sorrow are part of our present human experience in this fallen world.**

   Job 14:1–2 Man who is born of a woman is few of days and full of trouble. He comes out like a flower and withers; he flees like a shadow and continues not. (ESV)

   Psalm 31:9–10 Be gracious to me, O LORD, for I am in distress; my eye is wasted away from grief, my soul and my body also. For my life is spent with sorrow and my years with sighing; my strength has failed because of my iniquity, and my body has wasted away. (NASB)

   Genesis 3:16–19; Job 5:7; Psalm 6:6–7; 90:10

2. **We are not alone when grief overwhelms. God in his goodness is our refuge, our strength, our rock, and our joy!**

   Psalm 31:19 Oh, how abundant is your goodness, which you have stored up for those who fear you and worked for those who take refuge in you, in the sight of the children of mankind! (ESV)

   Psalm 28:7 The LORD is my strength and my shield; my heart trusted in Him, and I am helped; therefore my heart greatly rejoices, and with my song I will praise Him. (NKJV)

   Isaiah 43:2 When you pass through the waters, I will be with you; and through the rivers, they shall not overflow you. When you walk through the fire, you shall not be burned, nor shall the flame scorch you. (NKJV)

Psalm 30:5; 31:1–3; 55:22; 107:28–31; Nehemiah 8:10

3. **When loss of a loved one is the cause of our grief, knowing God is in control of future events brings comfort.**

   Psalm 116:15 Precious in the sight of the LORD is the death of his saints. (ESV)

   1 Thessalonians 4:13, 18 But we do not want you to be uninformed, brothers, about those who are asleep, that you may not grieve as others do who have no hope. . . . Therefore encourage one another with these words. (ESV)

   Isaiah 25:8; Revelation 21:3–4

4. **God understands our tears and gives strength.**

   Psalm 56:8 You have kept count of my tossings; put my tears in your bottle. Are they not in your book? (ESV)

   Psalm 126:5–6 Those who sow in tears shall reap with shouts of joy! He who goes out weeping, bearing the seed for sowing, shall come home with shouts of joy, bringing his sheaves with him. (ESV)

   Psalm 6:8; 119:28; Isaiah 40:28–29

5. **Knowing that our sin brings sorrow to God is an encouragement to live in obedience to his Word.**

   Ephesians 4:30–31 Do not bring sorrow to God's Holy Spirit by the way you live. Remember, he has identified you as his own, guaranteeing that you will be saved on the day of redemption. Get rid of all bitterness, rage, anger, harsh words, and slander, as well as all types of evil behavior. (NLT)

   Mark 3:5

Biblical Narratives

- Isaac and Rebekah, sorrow over Esau, Genesis 26:35
- Jacob, in his supposed loss of Joseph, Genesis 37:31–35

- Israel's sorrow will turn to joy upon the return to the land, Jeremiah 31:13
- Builders of the second temple, Ezra 3:12–13; Haggai 2
- Disciples, sorrow over Jesus's departure, John 16:16–22
- Paul, grief for unrepentant Israel, Romans 9:1–3

Practical Steps

- Journal your grief. Get on your knees with your writing before you. Know that God is right there reading along with you. Plead your case with him.
- Communicating with trusted friends is crucial. Keeping thoughts inside does nothing to alleviate your grief and only makes it more intense. Tell your story and then tell it again. Get it out in the open.
- Be aware of the time of day when grief is the most intense. Find others who can support you during this time.
- Spend consistent time in the Psalms, especially 32; 34; 37; 42; 46; 91; 107; 145.
- Exercise daily; practice healthy eating. Both are strong assets for emotional health.

Resources

- *A Grief Observed*. C. S. Lewis. Crosswicks.
- *Comforting Those Who Grieve*. Paul Tautges. DayOne.
- *Every Day Is a New Shade of Blue: Comfort for Dark Days from Psalm 23*. David Roper. Discovery House.
- *Through a Season of Grief* (devotionals). Bill Dunn. Thomas Nelson.
- *What Grievers Can Expect* (booklet). Wally Stephenson. RBP.
- "The Sovereignty of God" and "The Wisdom of God" in *God as He Longs for You to See Him*. Chip Ingram. Baker.

Guilt/Shame

See also Confession, Forgiveness from God, The Gospel, Hope, Past Memories

True guilt results from disobedience to God. False guilt can occur when we think we did something wrong (having received bad advice or mistaken information or even a misinterpretation of Scripture), but it wasn't really wrong. Also feelings of guilt and shame can linger when we fail to take God at his word for forgiveness and feel we must do something to earn removal of guilt.

1. **True guilt is the result of sin and continues until confession occurs. We need to agree with God about our sin.**

    Psalm 32:3–5 When I kept silent about my sin, my body wasted away through my groaning all day long. For day and night Your hand was heavy upon me; my vitality was drained away as with the fever heat of summer. I acknowledged my sin to You, and my iniquity I did not hide; I said, "I will confess my transgressions to the LORD"; and You forgave the guilt of my sin. (NASB)
    Psalm 69:5

2. **We need to admit our sin and seek forgiveness, turning and going in the opposite direction of that sin.**

    1 John 1:8–10 If we say that we have no sin, we are deceiving ourselves and the truth is not in us. If we confess our sins, He is faithful and righteous to forgive us our sins and to cleanse us from all unrighteousness. If we say that we have not sinned, we make Him a liar and His word is not in us. (NASB)
    Hebrews 10:22 Let us draw near to God with a sincere heart and with the full assurance that faith brings, having our hearts

sprinkled to cleanse us from a guilty conscience and having our bodies washed with pure water. (NIV)

Zechariah 1:3

3. **Writers of the Psalms expressed their desire to God for relief from shame.**

Psalm 31:17 Do not let me be ashamed, O LORD, for I have called upon You; let the wicked be ashamed; let them be silent in the grave. (NKJV)

Psalm 71:1–3 In You, O LORD, I put my trust; let me never be put to shame. Deliver me in Your righteousness, and cause me to escape; incline Your ear to me, and save me. Be my strong refuge, to which I may resort continually. (NKJV)

Psalm 69:19

4. **Christ died to remove our guilt and intercedes for us from heaven.**

Romans 8:33–35 Who dares accuse us whom God has chosen for his own? No one—for God himself has given us right standing with himself. Who then will condemn us? No one—for Christ Jesus died for us and was raised to life for us, and he is sitting in the place of honor at God's right hand, pleading for us. Can anything ever separate us from Christ's love? Does it mean he no longer loves us if we have trouble or calamity, or are persecuted, or hungry, or destitute, or in danger, or threatened with death? (NLT)

Isaiah 61:1; Hebrews 7:24–25; 9:24

5. **Freedom from guilt must not be based on feelings, but on the fact that once forgiven, our sins have been completely discarded from the mind of God.**

Micah 7:18–19 Who is a God like You, who pardons iniquity and passes over the rebellious act of the remnant of His possession? He does not retain His anger forever, because He delights in unchanging love. He will again have compassion on us; He will tread our iniquities under foot. Yes, You will cast all their sins into the depths of the sea. (NASB)

Psalm 103:12; Isaiah 1:18; 38:17; 43:25 (must see)

6. We need to reprogram our minds, asking God to change our thinking from guilt to freedom.

> **Psalm 30:5** For his anger lasts only a moment, but his favor lasts a lifetime! Weeping may last through the night, but joy comes with the morning. (NLT)
>
> **Philippians 4:8** And now, dear brothers and sisters, one final thing. Fix your thoughts on what is true, and honorable, and right, and pure, and lovely, and admirable. Think about things that are excellent and worthy of praise. (NLT)
>
> **John 8:31–32; Romans 12:2**

Biblical Narratives

- David, after his great sins, Psalm 32; 51
- Peter, who blew it and was restored, Matthew 26:69–75 with John 21:15–17

Practical Steps

- Recognize that if you feel guilty after confessing and repenting, that feeling does not come from God. You must accept and apply the truth of his Word.
- Write the verses from number 5 above on cards. Keep close at hand; review constantly.
- Practice "keeping short accounts with God"; that is, confess sin immediately when it occurs.

Resources

- *Free at Last: Experiencing True Freedom through Your Identity in Christ.* Tony Evans. Moody.
- *Freedom from Guilt* (booklet). Timothy Lane. New Growth.
- *The Gospel for Real Life.* Jerry Bridges. NavPress.
- "Putting Your Past Behind You" in *Winning the Inner War.* Erwin Lutzer. Victor.
- *Shame Interrupted.* Ed Welch. New Growth.

Health/Illness

See also **Aging, Anxiety, Disease, Fear, Grief, Suffering, Trust**

1. **Health problems are a part of our humanity, our present life on earth.**

   Job 14:1–2, 5 How frail is humanity! How short is life, how full of trouble! We blossom like a flower and then wither. Like a passing shadow, we quickly disappear. . . . You have decided the length of our lives. You know how many months we will live, and we are not given a minute longer. (NLT)

   Psalm 103:15–17 The life of mortals is like grass, they flourish like a flower of the field; the wind blows over it and it is gone, and its place remembers it no more. But from everlasting to everlasting the LORD's love is with those who fear him, and his righteousness with their children's children. (NIV)

   Romans 8:22–23; 2 Corinthians 5:4

2. **Health problems build character, helping us grow as Christians. Ability to help others can also result.**

   Job 23:8–10 Behold, I go forward but He is not there, and backward, but I cannot perceive Him; when He acts on the left, I cannot behold Him; He turns on the right, I cannot see Him. But He knows the way I take; when He has tried me, I shall come forth as gold. (NASB)

   2 Corinthians 1:3–4 Blessed be the God and Father of our Lord Jesus Christ, the Father of mercies and God of all comfort, who comforts us in all our affliction, so that we may be able to comfort those who are in any affliction, with the comfort with which we ourselves are comforted by God. (ESV)

   Psalm 119:71; James 1:2–4

3. Whatever the outcome of our health problems, God will be glorified.

1 Peter 1:6–7 So be truly glad. There is wonderful joy ahead, even though you have to endure many trials for a little while. These trials will show that your faith is genuine. It is being tested as fire tests and purifies gold—though your faith is far more precious than mere gold. So when your faith remains strong through many trials, it will bring you much praise and glory and honor on the day when Jesus Christ is revealed to the whole world. (NLT)
2 Corinthians 12:9–10

4. We never face health problems alone; God's presence with us is promised.

Deuteronomy 31:6 Be strong and courageous. Do not be afraid or terrified because of them, for the LORD your God goes with you; he will never leave you nor forsake you. (NIV)
Isaiah 43:1–2 But now, this is what the LORD says—he who created you, Jacob, he who formed you, Israel: "Do not fear, for I have redeemed you; I have summoned you by name; you are mine. When you pass through the waters, I will be with you; and when you pass through the rivers, they will not sweep over you. When you walk through the fire, you will not be burned; the flames will not set you ablaze." (NIV)
Joshua 1:7–9; Isaiah 41:10–13

5. Though we experience great weakness, our all-powerful God gives strength.

2 Samuel 22:33 This God is my strong refuge and has made my way blameless. (ESV)
Psalm 31:24 Be strong, and let your heart take courage, all you who wait for the LORD! (ESV)
2 Corinthians 4:16 So we do not lose heart. Though our outer self is wasting away, our inner self is being renewed day by day. (ESV)
Isaiah 40:30–31 Even youths shall faint and be weary, and young men shall fall exhausted; but they who wait for the LORD

shall renew their strength; they shall mount up with wings like eagles; they shall run and not be weary; they shall walk and not faint. (ESV)

Psalm 73:26; 91:4; 2 Corinthians 4:7–10

6. **God can and does heal, in his time, according to his will. God is the one who does the healing.**

Psalm 30:2–3 LORD my God, I called to you for help, and you healed me. You, LORD, brought me up from the realm of the dead; you spared me from going down to the pit. (NIV)

James 5:14–16 Is anyone among you sick? Let them call the elders of the church to pray over them and anoint them with oil in the name of the Lord. And the prayer offered in faith will make the sick person well; the Lord will raise them up. If they have sinned, they will be forgiven. Therefore confess your sins to each other and pray for each other so that you may be healed. The prayer of a righteous person is powerful and effective. (NIV)

2 Kings 20:1–11; Psalm 103:2–5

7. **Ultimately, heaven awaits us with freedom from pain and illness.**

Revelation 21:4 And He will wipe away every tear from their eyes; and there will no longer be any death; there will no longer be any mourning, or crying, or pain; the first things have passed away. (NASB)

Philippians 3:20–21 But our citizenship is in heaven, and from it we await a Savior, the Lord Jesus Christ, who will transform our lowly body to be like his glorious body, by the power that enables him even to subject all things to himself. (ESV)

1 Corinthians 15:51–55; Revelation 22:1–2

Biblical Narratives

- Job, a strong faith even though greatly afflicted, Job 1:21; 10
- Hezekiah, gravely ill, prays for healing, Isaiah 38:1–5
- Naaman, when healed gave glory to God, 2 Kings 5:1–15
- Paul's thorn in his flesh, 2 Corinthians 12:7–10

Practical Steps

- If possible, keep on exercising—walk, swim, etc.
- Be checked for levels of vitamins D and B-12 and testosterone.
- Keep all your records and progress reports. Obtain copies of all tests. Do research; educate yourself so you are knowledgeable about treatments, risks, natural alternatives, and nutrition.
- Memorize Isaiah 43:1–2 and review often. Post verses about God's care around your home. Read them often.
- If confined to home or bed, write notes to encourage others. Memorize Scripture; pray for missionaries; invite visitors who can encourage you as you encourage them.
- Have others pray with you and for you. Prayer is our lifeline!

Resources

- *Chronic Pain: Living by Faith When Your Body Hurts* (booklet). Michael Emlet. CCEF.
- *Making Sense of Suffering* (pamphlet). Joni Eareckson Tada. Rose.
- *Pain: The Plight of Fallen Man.* James Halla. Timeless Texts.
- *The Problem of Pain.* C. S. Lewis. Macmillan.

Homosexuality

See also Forgiveness from God, Sexual Purity, Temptation

Homosexuality is an issue for which conservative Christians are facing great opposition from a decadent secular culture. The consequences of taking the scriptural view will become decidedly more pronounced as the years pass. As Paul teaches, "in the last days there will come times of difficulty" (2 Timothy 3:1 ESV). Taking a strong stand for God's truth must never be compromised—no equivocation! Yet showing God's love for those who struggle must always remain constant.

1. **In the beginning God created male and female; sex was God's idea. Woman was created to be with a man; man was created to be with a woman. God has established these natural boundaries for sexual expression. Any other expression is sin.**

   Genesis 1:27 God created man in His own image, in the image of God He created him; male and female He created them. (NASB)
   Genesis 2:21–24 Then the LORD God made the man fall into a deep sleep, and while he was sleeping, he took out one of the man's ribs and closed up the flesh. He formed a woman out of the rib and brought her to him. Then the man said, "At last, here is one of my own kind—bone taken from my bone, and flesh from my flesh. 'Woman' is her name because she was taken out of man." That is why a man leaves his father and mother and is united with his wife, and they become one. (GNT)
   1 Corinthians 7:2–3

2. **Homosexual activity is sinful, unnatural, indecent, degrading, and detestable. What more does God need to tell us?**

   Romans 1:24–27 Therefore God gave them over in the lusts of their hearts to impurity, so that their bodies would be dishonored among them. For they exchanged the truth of God for a lie, and worshiped and served the creature rather than the Creator, who is blessed forever. Amen. For this reason God gave them over to degrading passions; for their women exchanged the natural function for that which is unnatural, and in the same way also the men abandoned the natural function of the woman and burned in their desire toward one another, men with men committing indecent acts and receiving in their own persons the due penalty of their error. (NASB)

Leviticus 18:22; 20:13; Romans 8:5–8; Galatians 5:19–21; Jude 1:7

3. **As with any sexual sin, homosexuality does not satisfy the cravings of the human heart (love, joy, peace, contentment, true intimacy, wellness of body and soul)—only God can do that.**

Jeremiah 2:13 For My people have committed two evils: they have forsaken Me, the fountain of living waters, to hew for themselves cisterns, broken cisterns that can hold no water. (NASB)

Isaiah 55:1–2 Come, everyone who thirsts, come to the waters; and he who has no money, come, buy and eat! Come, buy wine and milk without money and without price. Why do you spend your money for that which is not bread, and your labor for that which does not satisfy? Listen diligently to me, and eat what is good, and delight yourselves in rich food. (ESV)

John 10:10

4. **We must recognize as Christians that our bodies are a temple of the Holy Spirit and that we must run from sexual sin.**

1 Corinthians 6:18–20 Flee from sexual immorality. Every other sin a person commits is outside the body, but the sexually immoral person sins against his own body. Or do you not know that your body is a temple of the Holy Spirit within you, whom you have from God? You are not your own, for you were bought with a price. So glorify God in your body. (ESV)

Ephesians 5:11–12

5. As with any sin, complete forgiveness is available.

1 Corinthians 6:9–11 Do you not know that the unrighteous will not inherit the kingdom of God? Do not be deceived: neither the sexually immoral, nor idolaters, nor adulterers, nor men who practice homosexuality, nor thieves, nor the greedy, nor drunkards, nor revilers, nor swindlers will inherit the kingdom of God. And such were some of you. But you were washed, you were sanctified, you were justified in the name of the Lord Jesus Christ and by the Spirit of our God. (ESV)

Micah 7:18–19 Who is a God like you, who pardons iniquity and passes over the rebellious act of the remnant of His possession? He does not retain His anger forever, because He delights in unchanging love. He will again have compassion on us; He will tread our iniquities under foot. Yes, you will cast all their sins into the depths of the sea. (NASB)

Isaiah 43:25; 1 John 1:9

6. God's help for the homosexual to change is available and genuine.

2 Corinthians 5:17 Therefore, if anyone is in Christ, he is a new creation. The old has passed away; behold, the new has come. (ESV)

John 8:36 So if the Son sets you free, you will be free indeed. (ESV)

1 Corinthians 10:13 No temptation has overtaken you that is not common to man. God is faithful, and he will not let you be tempted beyond your ability, but with the temptation he will also provide the way of escape, that you may be able to endure it. (ESV)

Romans 7:23–25; Galatians 5:16–17

7. Moral choices must be made.

Romans 6:6, 11–14, 19 For we know that our old self was crucified with him so that the body ruled by sin might be done away with, that we should no longer be slaves to sin. . . . In the same way, count yourselves dead to sin but alive to God in Christ Jesus. Therefore do not let sin reign in your mortal body so that you obey its evil desires. Do not offer any part of yourself to sin as an instrument of wickedness, but rather offer yourselves to God as those who have been brought from death to life; and offer every part of yourself to him as an instrument of righteousness. For sin shall no longer be your master, because you are not under the law, but under grace. . . . I am using an example from everyday life because of your human limitations. Just as you used to offer yourselves as slaves to impurity and to ever-increasing wickedness, so now offer yourselves as slaves to righteousness leading to holiness. (NIV) (Note the "know," "count," "offer" sequence for action steps.)

Psalm 141:4; Ephesians 4:17–24; 1 Thessalonians 4:3–7; 2 Timothy 2:22

8. Use wisdom in avoiding evil situations.

Proverbs 2:11–15 Wise choices will watch over you. Understanding will keep you safe. Wisdom will save you from evil people, from those whose words are twisted. These men turn from the right way to walk down dark paths. They take pleasure in doing wrong, and they enjoy the twisted ways of evil. Their actions are crooked, and their ways are wrong. (NLT)

Proverbs 1:10; 4:14–16, 25–27

9. It is our responsibility to show kindness and God's love to those who struggle.

Galatians 6:1–2 Brothers, if anyone is caught in any transgression, you who are spiritual should restore him in a spirit of gentleness. Keep watch on yourself, lest you too be tempted. Bear one another's burdens, and so fulfill the law of Christ. (ESV)

Matthew 9:36 When he saw the crowds, he had compassion for them, because they were harassed and helpless, like sheep without a shepherd. (ESV)

Colossians 3:12

Biblical Narrative

• Events in Sodom, Genesis 19:1–13; Jude 1:7

Practical Steps

- Know that just because you have a thought, it does not mean the thought is true. We are constantly hammered by the homosexual agenda in public schools and the media in the attempt to lead young men toward sinful thoughts and to question their sexuality.

- Be wise in your lifestyle choices—associations, friends, dress, games, music, Internet, movies, and so on. Stay away from the openly sinful.

- If you have children, carefully monitor who they spend time with and any overnight stays. Parents today should take no chances.

- Support "one man–one woman" causes. Vote, get involved.

- Churches and individuals must commit to showing Christ's love. Violence or verbal abuse is never acceptable. In this age of grace, leading sinners to Christ is the rule. Befriend and reach out—open the door to help.

- Reach out to parents and family members who have children who struggle—listen, encourage, assist.

Resources

- "Abandoning Natural Relations: The Biblical Verdict on Homosexuality" in *God, Marriage, and Family*. Andreas Kostenberger. Crossway.

- *Homosexuality* (booklet). Ed Welch. P & R.

- *When Homosexuality Hits Home*. Joe Dallas. Harvest House.

- *Leaving Homosexuality: A Practical Guide for Men and Women Looking For a Way Out*. Alan Chambers. Harvest House.

- "Homosexuality" in *Counseling the Hard Cases*. Stuart Scott. B & H Academic.

- *You Can Change: God's Transforming Power for Our Sinful Behavior and Negative Emotions*. Tim Chester. Crossway.

Hope

See also Depression, Forgiveness from God, Purpose for Living, Trials

A universal principle for helping others is that we must above all else give hope that comes from God to the person going through a difficult time.

1. **Hope is the anticipation that there are answers or solutions to our problems, that our needs will be met.**

    Psalm 39:7 What, then, can I hope for, Lord? I put my hope in you. (GNT)

    Romans 15:13 May God, the source of hope, fill you with all joy and peace by means of your faith in him, so that your hope will continue to grow by the power of the Holy Spirit. (GNT)

2. **Going through difficult times does not mean that God has forsaken us or that we have no hope.**

    Psalm 43:5 Why are you cast down, O my soul, and why are you in turmoil within me? Hope in God; for I shall again praise him, my salvation and my God. (ESV)

    Psalm 145:14, 18–19 The LORD sustains all who fall and raises up all who are bowed down. . . . The LORD is near to all who call upon Him, to all who call upon Him in truth. He will fulfill the desire of those who fear Him; He will also hear their cry and will save them. (NASB)

    Psalm 42:5–6; Jeremiah 29:11–14; Romans 5:3–5; 1 Peter 4:12–13

3. Despair can come when sin is part of the problem. As a sinning and captive Israel was given hope for their future, so can we have hope for forgiveness and restoration regarding our sins.

Jeremiah 31:16–17 Thus says the LORD: "Keep your voice from weeping, and your eyes from tears, for there is a reward for your work, declares the LORD, and they shall come back from the land of the enemy. There is hope for your future, declares the LORD, and your children shall come back to their own country." (ESV)

Daniel 9:9 The Lord our God is merciful and forgiving, even though we have rebelled against him. (NIV)

1 John 1:9

4. Our only true source of hope is God himself, our rock of strength and refuge, our very present help in trouble.

2 Chronicles 32:7–8 "Be strong and courageous, do not fear or be dismayed because of the king of Assyria nor because of all the horde that is with him; for the one with us is greater than the one with him. With him is only an arm of flesh, but with us is the LORD our God to help us and to fight our battles." And the people relied on the words of Hezekiah king of Judah. (NASB)

Psalm 62:5–8 My soul, wait in silence for God only, for my hope is from Him. He only is my rock and my salvation, my stronghold; I shall not be shaken. On God my salvation and my glory rest; the rock of my strength, my refuge is in God. Trust in Him at all times, O people; pour out your heart before Him; God is a refuge for us. (NASB)

Haggai 2:4–5 But now don't be discouraged, any of you. Do the work, for I am with you. When you came out of Egypt, I promised that I would always be with you. I am still with you, so do not be afraid. (GNT)

Psalm 25:5; 39:7; 71:5–6; Lamentations 3:21–24; 1 Timothy 4:10; Hebrews 12:1–2; 13:5

5. Men who rely on God for wisdom, strength, and resources will find him to be their secure anchor and hope.

Jeremiah 9:23–24 Thus says the LORD: "Let not the wise man boast in his wisdom, let not the mighty man boast in his might, let not the rich man boast in his riches, but let him who boasts boast in this, that he understands and knows me, that I am the LORD who practices steadfast love, justice, and righteousness in the earth. For in these things I delight, declares the LORD." (ESV)

Hebrews 6:18–20 By two unchangeable things in which it is impossible for God to lie, we who have taken refuge would have strong encouragement to take hold of the hope set before us. This hope we have as an anchor of the soul, a hope both sure and steadfast and one which enters within the veil, where Jesus has entered as a forerunner for us. (NASB)

Zechariah 4:6

6. **Walking closely with the Lord is required for blessing, hope, and success.**

   Deuteronomy 10:12–13, 20 What does the LORD your God require of you? He requires only that you fear the LORD your God, and live in a way that pleases him, and love him and serve him with all your heart and soul. And you must always obey the LORD's commands and decrees that I am giving you today for your own good. . . . You must fear the LORD your God and worship him and cling to him. (NLT)

   John 15:4–5 Abide in me, and I in you. As the branch cannot bear fruit by itself, unless it abides in the vine, neither can you, unless you abide in me. I am the vine; you are the branches. Whoever abides in me and I in him, he it is that bears much fruit, for apart from me you can do nothing. (ESV)

   Proverbs 10:28; 1 John 3:3

7. **As believers in Jesus, we have a guaranteed hope that our future in heaven is secure.**

   Job 19:25–27 But as for me, I know that my Redeemer lives, and he will stand upon the earth at last. And after my body has decayed, yet in my body I will see God! I will see him for myself. Yes, I will see him with my own eyes. I am overwhelmed at the thought! (NLT)

   1 Peter 1:3, 13 Blessed be the God and Father of our Lord Jesus Christ! According to his great mercy, he has caused us to be born

again to a living hope through the resurrection of Jesus Christ from the dead. . . . Therefore, preparing your minds for action, and being sober-minded, set your hope fully on the grace that will be brought to you at the revelation of Jesus Christ. (ESV)
1 Thessalonians 5:8–9; Titus 3:5–7

8. For further study, see the benefits of hope in the following:

Isaiah 57:10; Romans 8:24–25; 12:12; Philippians 1:20; Colossians 1:4–5; 1 Thessalonians 1:3; 4:13; 1 Timothy 4:10; Hebrews 7:19; 1 John 3:3

Biblical Narratives

- Job's great statement of hope, Job 13:15
- Israelites sinned but were not without hope, Ezra 10:2
- Sons of Korah, musicians, Psalm 42

Practical Steps

- Memorize Romans 15:13. Write it on a card and keep it close at hand—in your wallet, on a nightstand or office desk, for example.
- Participate in men's Bible study. Fellowship with other men and the discipline in the Word are crucial when hope is needed.
- Study Romans 5:1–8. Complete a word study on the word *hope*.

Resources

- *A Shelter in the Time of Storm: Meditations on God and Trouble*. Paul Tripp. Crossway.
- *Finding God When You Need Him the Most*. Chip Ingram. Baker.
- *From Despair to Hope*. Peter Williams. Day One.
- *Gaining a Hopeful Spirit* (booklet). Joni Eareckson Tada. Rose.
- *Hope Again*. Charles Swindoll. Thomas Nelson.
- *Never Beyond Hope*. J. I. Packer. IVP.

Integrity/Character

See also Peer Pressure, Self-Control, Temptation, Work Ethic

Concepts related to integrity and character are honesty, sincerity, accountability, responsibility, faithfulness, justice. All of these qualities connect and interact. They are vital for men who would please God, be successful in life, and engage their culture for Christ.

1. **Integrity is standing for what is right because it is the right thing to do.**

   Psalm 15:1–2 O LORD, who may abide in Your tent? Who may dwell on Your holy hill? He who walks with integrity, and works righteousness, and speaks truth in his heart. (NASB)

   Micah 6:8 The LORD has told you what is good, and this is what he requires of you: to do what is right, to love mercy, and to walk humbly with your God. (NLT)

   Psalm 24:3–5; Isaiah 33:15–16; Jeremiah 22:3

2. **Maintaining integrity requires a strong commitment, even sacrifice.**

   Proverbs 28:6 Better is a poor man who walks in his integrity than a rich man who is crooked in his ways. (ESV)

   Titus 2:6–8 In the same way, encourage the young men to live wisely. And you yourself must be an example to them by doing good works of every kind. Let everything you do reflect the integrity and seriousness of your teaching. Teach the truth so that your teaching can't be criticized. Then those who oppose us will be ashamed and have nothing bad to say about us. (NLT)

   Philippians 1:9–11

3. **Practicing integrity is always pleasing to God and brings his blessing.**

Matthew 5:6–8 Blessed are those who hunger and thirst for righteousness, for they shall be filled. Blessed are the merciful, for they shall obtain mercy. Blessed are the pure in heart, for they shall see God. (NKJV)

1 Kings 9:4–5 As for you, if you will follow me with integrity and godliness, as David your father did, obeying all my commands, decrees, and regulations, then I will establish the throne of your dynasty over Israel forever. (NLT)

Psalm 25:21 May integrity and honesty protect me, for I put my hope in you. (NLT)

Proverbs 2:7 He grants a treasure of common sense to the honest. He is a shield to those who walk with integrity. (NLT)

1 Chronicles 29:17–18; Psalm 37:3–4; 41:12; 119:1–3; Proverbs 10:9; 11:3; 13:6

4. **Practicing integrity can bring persecution.**

Matthew 5:10–11 Blessed are those who are persecuted for righteousness' sake, for theirs is the kingdom of heaven. Blessed are you when they revile and persecute you, and say all kinds of evil against you falsely for My sake. (NKJV)

Proverbs 29:10 The bloodthirsty hate a person of integrity and seek to kill the upright. (NIV)

Amos 5:10 There are those who hate the one who upholds justice in court and detest the one who tells the truth. (NIV)

1 Peter 3:13–15

Biblical Narratives

- Job held fast his integrity, Job 2:3, 9–10
- Joseph resisted great temptation, Genesis 39:8–10
- David, as shepherd of Israel, Psalm 78:70–72 (though he sinned grievously, he sought forgiveness from God, Psalm 32; 51)
- Jehoshaphat appointed judges of integrity, 2 Chronicles 19:4–7

- Paul, a model of integrity, 2 Corinthians 1:12; 2:17; 1 Thessalonians 2:3–10; 2 Thessalonians 3:7–9

Practical Steps

- Use a concordance to do a word study of *integrity*. The NASB has twenty-seven entries for the word. Note lack of integrity in some instances, as well as positive examples.
- When making decisions that will reflect on your integrity, pray for strength and wisdom, while making a solid commitment to stand for the right. Seek accountability from others.
- Make a list of men in your life who have demonstrated integrity. If possible, talk to each about their standards, decision making, and commitment.

Resources

- *Character Counts—Who's Counting Yours?* Rod Handley. Cross Training.
- "Discipline of Integrity" in *Disciplines of a Godly Man*. Kent Hughes. Crossway.
- *Men of Character* (series, biblical characters). Gene Getz. B & H.
- *Men of Honor* (four-week study). Mike Cleveland. Focus.
- *The Quest for Character*. John MacArthur. Thomas Nelson.
- *The Resolution for Men*. Stephen Kendrick. B & H.
- *Three Steps Forward, Two Steps Back*. Charles Swindoll. Thomas Nelson.

Internet/Social Networking

See also Entertainment, Flirting, Integrity, Laziness, Pornography, Sexual Purity, Spiritual Warfare, Time Management, Work Ethic

The Internet has added great benefit to the quality of our lives. Much of what we need to do has been made easier and more efficient by this technology. Yet there are observable cautions for its use—the issue of time and the issue of temptation.

Issue of Time

1. **As with anything innovative, attractive, and fun to use, wasting time is a threat. Set limits and stick to them.**

   Ephesians 5:15–17 Look carefully then how you walk, not as unwise but as wise, making the best use of the time, because the days are evil. Therefore do not be foolish, but understand what the will of the Lord is. (ESV)
   Psalm 90:12 So teach us to number our days, that we may gain a heart of wisdom. (NKJV)

2. **Married men must be cautious in their use of the Internet, guarding time with family as a priority.**

   Ephesians 5:25, 28 For husbands, this means love your wives, just as Christ loved the church. He gave up his life for her. . . . In the same way, husbands ought to love their wives as they love their own bodies. For a man who loves his wife actually shows love for himself. (NLT)
   1 Peter 3:7

3. Temptations to use the Internet at work for socializing or enter-tainment purposes must be avoided.

Colossians 3:22–23 Slaves, obey your earthly masters in every-thing; and do it, not only when their eye is on you and to curry their favor, but with sincerity of heart and reverence for the Lord. Whatever you do, work at it with all your heart, as working for the Lord, not for human masters. (NIV) (In today's context it would be employee and employer.)
Ephesians 4:28

Issue of Temptation

1. Godly men will carefully maintain biblical standards, carefully choosing to walk in God's pathways.

Joshua 24:15 Choose this day whom you will serve, whether the gods your fathers served in the region beyond the River, or the gods of the Amorites in whose land you dwell. But as for me and my house, we will serve the LORD. (ESV)
Ephesians 4:22–24 Put off your old self, which belongs to your former manner of life and is corrupt through deceitful desires, and to be renewed in the spirit of your minds, and to put on the new self, created after the likeness of God in true righteousness and holiness. (ESV)
Jeremiah 6:16; 1 John 2:15–16; Ephesians 4:1; James 1:27

2. Satan's plan is to corrupt and destroy, turning what is good into opportunities for sinning. We must be aware of his schemes and our own weaknesses, having plans in place to resist the temptations.

John 8:44 You [Pharisees] are of your father the devil, and you want to do the desires of your father. He was a murderer from the beginning, and does not stand in the truth because there is no truth in him. Whenever he speaks a lie, he speaks from his own nature, for he is a liar and the father of lies. (NASB)
Ephesians 6:10–11 Finally, be strong in the Lord and in the strength of His might. Put on the full armor of God, so that

177

you will be able to stand firm against the schemes of the devil. (NASB)

1 Peter 5:8–9 Be alert, be on watch! Your enemy, the Devil, roams around like a roaring lion, looking for someone to devour. Be firm in your faith and resist him. (GNT)

Psalm 37:27; 2 Corinthians 11:3; Galatians 5:16; James 4:7; 1 John 5:21

3. **Sexual temptation to look and lust is powerful. Images are imprinted on your mind in a flash but they do not disappear as easily. Be protected and pure.**

Matthew 6:22–23 The eye is the lamp of the body. If your eyes are healthy, your whole body will be full of light. But if your eyes are unhealthy, your whole body will be full of darkness. If then the light within you is darkness, how great is that darkness! (NIV)

Psalm 101:3–4 I will not look with approval on anything that is vile. I hate what faithless people do; I will have no part in it. The perverse of heart shall be far from me; I will have nothing to do with what is evil. (NIV)

Psalm 119:37; James 1:27

4. **Temptation for material things can also be a problem with the Internet. Having more stuff doesn't satisfy; wisdom is needed for restraint. Contentment is commanded.**

Ecclesiastes 2:10–11 All that my eyes desired I did not refuse them. I did not withhold my heart from any pleasure, for my heart was pleased because of all my labor and this was my reward for all my labor. Thus I considered all my activities which my hands had done and the labor which I had exerted, and behold all was vanity and striving after wind and there was no profit under the sun. (NASB)

James 1:5 But if any of you lacks wisdom, let him ask of God, who gives to all generously and without reproach, and it will be given to him. (NASB)

Psalm 73; Matthew 6:19–34; 1 Timothy 6:6–17

Practical Steps

- For one week, write down daily how much time you spend on the computer. Total these hours and consider what you have accomplished with this time.
- Use the Internet to serve you; don't let it obsess you. Set time limits.
- If married, guard against building relationships with the opposite sex online. Or, if single, guard against building relationships with married women. The danger is emotional adultery and destruction of marriages.
- Are there responsibilities you are neglecting because of the Internet? Are you neglecting time with God, with family, in church?
- Be open to others about your use of the Internet; be accountable to someone who is disciplined.
- Place firewalls and safety guards on your computer for areas in which you struggle. Give the passwords to a trusted friend.

Resources

- *Hope and Help for Video Game, TV, and Internet "Addiction."* (booklet). Mark Shaw. Focus.
- *Changing Your Thought Patterns* (booklet). George Sanchez. NavPress.

Jealousy/Envy

See also Attitude, Bitterness, Contentment

Note the texts below and the progression into deeper sin—envy leads to jealousy to coveting to stealing and so on. At the very least, jealousy can move us toward making ill-advised decisions.

1. Jealousy is a dangerous emotion.

> **Proverbs 27:4** Anger is cruel, and wrath is like a flood, but jealousy is even more dangerous. (NLT)
> **Proverbs 6:34** For jealousy makes a man furious, and he will not spare when he takes revenge. (ESV)
> **Proverbs 14:30; Acts 5:17; 1 John 3:12**

2. Envious desires lead to coveting and even more sin.

> **Deuteronomy 5:21** And you shall not covet your neighbor's wife. And you shall not desire your neighbor's house, his field, or his male servant, or his female servant, his ox, or his donkey, or anything that is your neighbor's. (ESV)
> **Psalm 10:3** For the wicked boasts of the desires of his soul, and the one greedy for gain curses and renounces the LORD. (ESV)
> **James 3:14–16** But if you are bitterly jealous and there is selfish ambition in your heart, don't cover up the truth with boasting and lying. For jealousy and selfishness are not God's kind of wisdom. Such things are earthly, unspiritual, and demonic. For wherever there is jealousy and selfish ambition, there you will find disorder and evil of every kind. (NLT)
> **1 Corinthians 3:3; Galatians 5:25–26; 1 Peter 2:1**

3. Loving others and putting them first are crucial to overcoming the sin of jealousy.

Romans 13:9–10 For the commandments say, "You must not commit adultery. You must not murder. You must not steal. You must not covet." These—and other such commandments—are summed up in this one commandment: "Love your neighbor as yourself." Love does no wrong to others, so love fulfills the requirements of God's law. (NLT)

John 13:34–35 So now I am giving you a new commandment: Love each other. Just as I have loved you, you should love each other. Your love for one another will prove to the world that you are my disciples. (NLT)

1 Corinthians 13:3–4; 1 Peter 1:22

4. Having a heart desire for God is the solution; he will provide for us and satisfy.

Psalm 37:1–4 Fret not yourself because of evildoers; be not envious of wrongdoers! For they will soon fade like the grass and wither like the green herb. Trust in the LORD, and do good; dwell in the land and befriend faithfulness. Delight yourself in the LORD, and he will give you the desires of your heart. (ESV)

Proverbs 23:17 Let not your heart envy sinners, but continue in the fear of the LORD all the day. (ESV)

Matthew 6:19–34; Philippians 4:11–19; Hebrews 13:5

Biblical Narratives

- Cain, whose jealousy led to murder, Genesis 4
- Ahab and Jezebel, who stole from Naboth, 1 Kings 21
- Asaph, who felt he didn't have enough money, Psalm 73
- David, who brings his needs to God, Psalm 37

Practical Steps

- Contentment is key to overcoming jealousy. Ask God to give you a thankful spirit. When you pray, express thanksgiving as you begin, before asking for anything.
- Do a careful heart search as to reasons for your jealousy. Ask God's forgiveness, praying over each item, asking God to change your mind and heart about it.
- Monitor your thinking carefully. Quickly stop jealous thoughts as they enter your mind. Memorize Philippians 4:8.
- Seek accountability with a mature brother in Christ.

Resources

- "Envy, Jealousy" in *Respectable Sins*. Jerry Bridges. NavPress.
- *Real Prosperity: Biblical Principles of Material Possessions*. Gene Getz. Moody.

Laziness

See also Entertainment, Failure, Purpose for Living, Work Ethic

There are two trends in present culture that encourage laziness. Some today see leisure time as the goal and work as something to simply endure until the weekend or retirement. There is also the extensive availability of entertainment options that can take far too much of our time and keep us on the couch. Rest and relaxation are components for a healthy life, but excess is always a danger.

1. Laziness is always seen in a negative light in Scripture.

Proverbs 19:15 Laziness brings on deep sleep, and the shiftless go hungry. (NIV)
Ecclesiastes 10:18 Because of laziness the building decays, and through idleness of hands the house leaks. (NKJV)
Proverbs 10:4; 12:24; 20:4

2. Laziness can result in poverty.

Proverbs 24:30–34 I walked by the field of a lazy person, the vineyard of one with no common sense. I saw that it was overgrown with nettles. It was covered with weeds, and its walls were broken down. Then, as I looked and thought about it, I learned this lesson: A little extra sleep, a little more slumber, a little folding of the hands to rest—then poverty will pounce on you like a bandit; scarcity will attack you like an armed robber. (NLT)
Proverbs 6:6–11; 13:4; 20:4; 26:13–14

3. Too much sleep can be a detriment to success.

Proverbs 6:9–11 But you, lazybones, how long will you sleep? When will you wake up? A little extra sleep, a little more slumber,

a little folding of the hands to rest—then poverty will pounce on you like a bandit; scarcity will attack you like an armed robber. (NLT)
Proverbs 10:5; 20:13; Mark 14:37–38

4. **Hard work was a part of God's plan even before the fall. The positive nature of work is a recurring theme of Scripture.**

Genesis 2:15–16 The LORD God took the man and put him in the garden of Eden to work it and keep it. (ESV)

2 Thessalonians 3:10–12 For even when we were with you, we would give you this command: If anyone is not willing to work, let him not eat. For we hear that some among you walk in idleness, not busy at work, but busybodies. Now such persons we command and encourage in the Lord Jesus Christ to do their work quietly and to earn their own living. (ESV)

Ecclesiastes 9:10; Hebrews 6:12 (NIV)

5. **God honors enthusiastic work accomplished for his glory.**

Romans 12:11 Never be lazy, but work hard and serve the Lord enthusiastically. (NLT)

1 Corinthians 10:31 So whether you eat or drink, or whatever you do, do it all for the glory of God. (NLT)

1 Corinthians 15:58; Galatians 6:9

6. **Time is a gift from God to be used wisely.**

Psalm 39:4 O LORD, make me know my end and what is the measure of my days; let me know how fleeting I am! (ESV)

Ephesians 5:15–17 Look carefully then how you walk, not as unwise but as wise, making the best use of the time, because the days are evil. Therefore do not be foolish, but understand what the will of the Lord is. (ESV)

Job 16:22; Psalm 90:12

7. **Self-discipline is a character trait that gets things accomplished.**

1 Corinthians 9:24–27 Do you not know that in a race all the runners run, but only one receives the prize? So run that you may obtain it. Every athlete exercises self-control in all things. They do it to receive a perishable wreath, but we an imperishable. So I do not run aimlessly; I do not box as one beating the air. But I discipline my body and keep it under control, lest after preaching to others I myself should be disqualified. (ESV)

8. Paul offers a model for hard work.

2 Thessalonians 3:7–9 For you yourselves know how you ought to imitate us, because we were not idle when we were with you, nor did we eat anyone's bread without paying for it, but with toil and labor we worked night and day, that we might not be a burden to any of you. It was not because we do not have that right, but to give you in ourselves an example to imitate. (ESV)
Acts 18:3; 1 Thessalonians 2:5–12

Biblical Narratives

- Adam, working in the garden, Genesis 2:15–20
- Jacob, working for Rachel, Genesis 29:20
- Procrastination in rebuilding the temple, Haggai 1
- Israel, having "a mind to work," Nehemiah 4:6

Practical Steps

- Make God and others your focus, not yourself.
- Once you have a task ahead of you, just get started. Overcoming initial inertia is the biggest obstacle to completion.
- Record your activity for each hour of the day for a full week. Review and evaluate your wise or unwise use of time.
- If you own your own home, make sure you are taking the leadership to do home maintenance and repairs. Make lists if necessary. Plan specific times to do the work. You will be a hero to your wife.
- Evaluate your laziness. Lack of motivation could result from physical causes. See your family physician.

Resources

- *Balancing Life's Demands*. Chip Ingram. Living on the Edge.
- *Help, I Can't Get Motivated* (booklet). Adam Embry. DayOne.
- *Procrastination: First Steps to Change* (booklet). Walter Henegar. P & R.
- *Work Matters: Connecting Sunday Worship to Monday Morning*. Tom Nelson. Crossway.

Leadership/Influence

See also the many topics in this book that reflect on the qualities of good leadership. To avoid repetition, the approach to this topic is somewhat different, sampling good and bad examples of leadership/influence from biblical characters.

1. Positive examples:

    Genesis 11:27–12:8 Abraham believed God, leading his family into a new land of blessing.

    Exodus 3; 4 Moses accepted God's call to lead Israel out of Egypt, in spite of his many doubts.

    Exodus 18:13–27; Deuteronomy 1:12–18 Moses accepted good advice to delegate leadership responsibilities to qualified others.

    Joshua 24:14–15 Joshua led his family in his choice to serve God alone.

    2 Kings 18–19; 22–23 Hezekiah and Josiah were godly reformers, builders and defenders of Israel.

    Haggai 1–2 Haggai calls Israel to complete work on the temple.

    Nehemiah 2:11–16 Nehemiah assessed the situation with the wall of Jerusalem.

    John 1:40–42; 6:8–9; 12:20–22 Andrew led others into contact with Jesus.

    John 18:26–27; 21:15–17; Acts 2 Peter became a great leader of the early church, though he failed Jesus at his trial.

    Acts 8:1–3; Galatians 1:13 Paul became a great leader of the early church, though he was a persecutor early on.

    Acts 9:27; 11:22–26; 12:25; 13:1–3 Barnabas helped develop leaders through strong encouragement.

2. Negative examples:

    Genesis 9:20–27 Noah allowed himself in his drunkenness to get into a compromising situation with his sons.

Genesis 12:10–20; 26:6–11 Abraham and Isaac with lack of leadership brought their wives into danger.

Genesis 13:11–13; 14:12; 19:1–38 Lot led his family into disaster.

Genesis 32 Aaron caved in to pressure to build the golden calf.

1 Samuel 13–15 Saul lacked conviction and courage to obey God.

2 Samuel 11–20 David failed to resist temptation, leading to personal and national problems.

1 Kings 11–12 Solomon compromised with idolatry leading his nation into sin and eventual division.

3. **As God searched for leaders in the past, so today there is the need for strong male leadership.**

Ezekiel 22:30 I searched for a man among them who would build up the wall and stand in the gap before Me for the land, so that I would not destroy it; but I found no one. (NASB)

2 Chronicles 16:9 For the eyes of the LORD move to and fro throughout the earth that He may strongly support those whose heart is completely His. (NASB)

Psalm 106:23; Isaiah 6:8; Romans 12:6–8

Practical Steps

- As God places you in responsible positions of leadership—head of your home, in your church, at work, etc.—determine, with his help, to serve to the best of your ability.

- Ask your pastor to help you in finding Scripture-based leadership training courses. Commit to one and follow through in completing it.

- Read and study thoroughly *Hand Me Another Brick* listed below.

Resources

- *Hand Me Another Brick* (leadership principles from Nehemiah). Charles Swindoll. Thomas Nelson.
- "Give Your Heart" in *Quest for Character*. Charles Swindoll. Multnomah.
- *Spiritual Leadership*. J. Oswald Sanders. Moody.
- *The Ten Top Mistakes Leaders Make*. Hans Finzel. Cook.

Loneliness

See also Depression, Hope, Purpose for Living, Single Father, Singleness, Trust

Loneliness is the feeling of being without meaningful human contact or community because of circumstances (or choice). The actuality may be that the person has contact with others yet still experiences the emotion. Loneliness is often accompanied by feelings of sadness, depression, or hopelessness.

1. **Men of Scripture experienced devastating loneliness, a heavy burden for anyone to bear.**

    Psalm 102:7 I lie awake, I have become like a lonely bird on a housetop. (NASB)
    Psalm 142:4 I look for someone to come and help me, but no one gives me a passing thought! No one will help me; no one cares a bit what happens to me. (NLT)
    Job 19:13–14 He has put my brothers far from me, and those who knew me are wholly estranged from me. My relatives have failed me, my close friends have forgotten me. (ESV)
    Psalm 38:9–11

2. **Feeling as if we are separated from God increases our loneliness.**

    Job 23:8–9 Behold, I go forward but He is not there, and backward, but I cannot perceive Him; when He acts on the left, I cannot behold Him; He turns on the right, I cannot see Him. (NASB)
    Psalm 13:1 How long, O LORD? Will You forget me forever? How long will You hide Your face from me? (NASB)

3. **David finds in God his refuge, rock, fortress, and protector.**

    Psalm 25:16 Turn to me and be gracious to me, for I am lonely and afflicted. (NASB)

Psalm 143:8–10 Remind me each morning of your constant love, for I put my trust in you. My prayers go up to you; show me the way I should go. I go to you for protection, LORD; rescue me from my enemies. You are my God; teach me to do your will. Be good to me, and guide me on a safe path. (GNT)

Psalm 62:5–8

4. God's presence with us guarantees that we can never be truly alone. He will supply our emotional and spiritual needs.

Deuteronomy 31:6 Be strong and of good courage, do not fear nor be afraid of them; for the LORD your God, He is the One who goes with you. He will not leave you nor forsake you. (NKJV)

Hebrews 13:5 Keep your life free from love of money, and be content with what you have, for he has said, "I will never leave you nor forsake you." (ESV)

Joshua 1:9; John 16:32

5. God's comfort and help is promised when we are lonely.

Zephaniah 3:17 The LORD your God in your midst, the Mighty One, will save; He will rejoice over you with gladness, He will quiet you with His love, He will rejoice over you with singing. (NKJV)

Psalm 68:5–6 A father of the fatherless and a judge for the widows, is God in His holy habitation. God makes a home for the lonely; He leads out the prisoners into prosperity, only the rebellious dwell in a parched land. (NASB)

Psalm 73:25–26

6. Note Paul's testimony when he was facing death and felt very alone.

2 Timothy 4:16–18 At my first defense no one came to stand by me, but all deserted me. May it not be charged against them! But the Lord stood by me and strengthened me, so that through me the message might be fully proclaimed and all the Gentiles might hear it. So I was rescued from the lion's mouth. The Lord will rescue me from every evil deed and bring me safely into his heavenly kingdom. To him be the glory forever and ever. Amen. (ESV)

Biblical Narratives

- Adam, alone in the garden, Genesis 2:18–23
- Elijah, who believed he alone was left to serve God, 1 Kings 19:10
- Jesus, on the cross, Matthew 27:46

Practical Steps

- Study the metaphors of the Old Testament that describe God's presence and strength—*rock, refuge, high tower, fortress.* Begin with the Psalms. Expand to Isaiah with a study of *highway, road through the wilderness,* etc.
- Use the Notes app on your cell phone to record special verses, such as Deuteronomy 31:6 or Philippians 4:13, 19. Better yet, add the Bible app to your phone.
- Get away from social media and spend time face-to-face with people. Get more involved in your church or volunteer services. Become relational instead of isolated.
- Find others who are alone. Connect with them through Bible study, in prayer, through serving others.
- Take the initiative to invite others over, go out to sporting events, concerts, eating out. Set a goal of doing this at least twice a month.

Resources

- *Alone: Finding Connection in a Lonely World.* Andy Braner. NavPress.
- *God as He Longs for You to See Him.* Chip Ingram. Baker.
- *God: Do You Really Care? Finding Strength When He Seems Distant.* Tony Evans. Multnomah.
- "Living a Balanced Life" and "Overcoming Self-Centeredness" in *Measure of a Man.* Gene Getz. Regal.
- "Loneliness" in *The Strength of a Man: 50 Devotionals to Help Men Find Their Strength in God.* David Roper. Discovery House.

Lust

See also Boundaries, Pornography, Sexual Purity, Thought Life

Lust, in a sinful sense, is craving for that which is prohibited or restricted by God, a desire for gratification outside his will. For most men it involves sex, but materialism or lust for power could also be included.

1. **Lust begins with a look, then a thought, continues with repeated thoughts, and moves into desire for the forbidden.**

    Joshua 7:20–21 And Achan answered Joshua, "Truly I have sinned against the LORD God of Israel, and this is what I did: when I saw among the spoil a beautiful cloak from Shinar, and 200 shekels of silver, and a bar of gold weighing 50 shekels, then I coveted them and took them. And see, they are hidden in the earth inside my tent, with the silver underneath." (ESV)
    Genesis 3:6; Ecclesiastes 2:10–11

2. **We need a commitment to not look, or to look away.**

    Job 31:1 I made a covenant with my eyes not to look with lust at a young woman. (NLT)
    Proverbs 4:25–27 Let your eyes look straight ahead; fix your gaze directly before you. Give careful thought to the paths for your feet and be steadfast in all your ways. Do not turn to the right or the left; keep your foot from evil. (NIV)
    Psalm 101:3

3. **The Word of God is given to us to keep us on his righteous path. We ignore it to our peril.**

    Psalm 119:9–11 How can a young man keep his way pure? By guarding it according to your word. With my whole heart I seek you; let me not wander from your commandments! I have stored up your word in my heart, that I might not sin against you. (ESV)

Jeremiah 6:16 Stand by the roads, and look, and ask for the ancient paths, where the good way is; and walk in it, and find rest for your souls. But they said, "We will not walk in it." (ESV)

Mark 4:19; 2 Timothy 4:3–4

4. **Lust has serious consequences, creating a downward spiral of sin upon sin.**

James 1:14–15 But each person is tempted when he is lured and enticed by his own desire. Then desire when it has conceived gives birth to sin, and sin when it is fully grown brings forth death. (ESV)

James 4:1–4

5. **Lust is a part of Satan's plan and attack, using the world system he controls.**

1 John 5:19 We know that we are from God, and the whole world lies in the power of the evil one. (ESV)

1 John 2:16–17 For all that is in the world, the lust of the flesh and the lust of the eyes and the boastful pride of life, is not from the Father, but is from the world. The world is passing away, and also its lusts; but the one who does the will of God lives forever. (NASB)

2 Peter 1:4

6. **God provides us with the strength to resist lust and live obediently.**

Psalm 46:1 God is our refuge and strength, a very present help in trouble. (ESV)

Ephesians 6:10–11 Finally, be strong in the Lord and in the strength of his might. Put on the whole armor of God, that you may be able to stand against the schemes of the devil. (ESV)

1 Peter 4:1–2

7. Each man must be on guard for what is his own individual area of sinful desires.

Proverbs 4:23 Above all else, guard your heart, for everything you do flows from it. (NIV)

1 Thessalonians 4:3–5 For this is the will of God, your sanctification; that is, that you abstain from sexual immorality; that each of you know how to possess his own vessel in sanctification and honor, not in lustful passion, like the Gentiles who do not know God. (NASB)

8. With God's help, it is possible to remove lustful thoughts.

1 Corinthians 10:13 No temptation has overtaken you that is not common to man. God is faithful, and he will not let you be tempted beyond your ability, but with the temptation he will also provide the way of escape, that you may be able to endure it. (ESV)

Romans 6:12–13 Therefore do not let sin reign in your mortal body so that you obey its lusts, and do not go on presenting the members of your body to sin as instruments of unrighteousness; but present yourselves to God as those alive from the dead, and your members as instruments of righteousness to God. (NASB)

2 Timothy 2:22; Titus 2:12

Biblical Narratives

- Eve, who looked and desired, Genesis 3
- Lot, who moved closer and closer to sin, Genesis 13; 18–19
- Achan's confession, Joshua 7:20–21

Practical Steps

- Since lusting begins with looking, ask God to help you control your eyes. Looking continues with thinking; ask God to help you control your thoughts.

- Accountability is crucial; get someone on your team to confide in and challenge you.

- Indentify triggers (for example, movies, reading material, music, time of day, places) and work toward minimizing and eliminating them.

- Research the meaning of *idol*, and locate ten scriptural texts dealing with idolatry, for example Judges 2:12.

- Memorize 2 Timothy 2:22 and 1 Corinthians 10:13. Review each day.

Resources

- "A Powerful Response to Temptation" in *The Hand of God: Finding His Care in all Circumstances.* Alistair Begg. Moody.

- *Counterfeit Gods: The Empty Promises of Money, Sex, and Power.* Timothy Keller. Dutton.

- *Sex Is Not the Problem (Lust Is).* Joshua Harris. Multnomah.

- *Sexual Addiction* (booklet). David Powlison. New Growth.

- *Winning the Inner War: How to Say No to a Stubborn Habit.* Erwin Lutzer. Cook.

Lying

See also Communication, Forgiveness from God, Integrity, Temptation

Once a person begins to lie, there is often no end to lie upon lie. Consequences multiply with devastating effects to family and friends. This behavior must be stopped, reversed, and corrected. Firm scriptural admonishment must be given to those entangled in this sin.

1. **Lying is sin. It is always wrong and detestable to God.**

    Exodus 20:16 You shall not bear false witness against your neighbor. (NKJV)

    Leviticus 19:11–12 You shall not steal, nor deal falsely, nor lie to one another. And you shall not swear by My name falsely, nor shall you profane the name of your God: I am the LORD. (NKJV)

    Proverbs 6:16–19 These six things the LORD hates, yes, seven are an abomination to Him: a proud look, a lying tongue, hands that shed innocent blood, a heart that devises wicked plans, feet that are swift in running to evil, a false witness who speaks lies, and one who sows discord among brethren. (NKJV)

    Zechariah 8:17 Don't scheme against each other. Stop your love of telling lies that you swear are the truth. I hate all these things, says the LORD. (NLT)

    Exodus 23:1–2; Psalm 5:6; 34:13; Proverbs 24:28; James 3:14–15

2. **Lying is a component of our sin nature and always a struggle through life.**

    Psalm 51:5 For I was born a sinner—yes, from the moment my mother conceived me. (NLT)

Matthew 15:19 For from the heart come evil thoughts, murder, adultery, all sexual immorality, theft, lying, and slander. (NLT)
Psalm 58:3; Romans 3:13

3. **Lying has many sad consequences.**

Proverbs 19:5 A false witness will not go unpunished, and he who speaks lies will not escape. (NKJV)

Proverbs 25:18 Telling lies about others is as harmful as hitting them with an ax, wounding them with a sword, or shooting them with a sharp arrow. (NLT)

Revelation 21:8 But the cowardly, unbelieving, abominable, murderers, sexually immoral, sorcerers, idolaters, and all liars shall have their part in the lake which burns with fire and brimstone, which is the second death. (NKJV)
Deuteronomy 19:16–19; Psalm 5:6; 31:18; 63:11; Proverbs 12:13; James 1:26

4. **Truth telling brings great blessing.**

Psalm 15:1–2 Who may worship in your sanctuary, LORD? Who may enter your presence on your holy hill? Those who lead blameless lives and do what is right, speaking the truth from sincere hearts. (NLT)

Proverbs 12:22 Lying lips are an abomination to the LORD, but those who deal truthfully are His delight. (NKJV)
Psalm 24:3–5; Proverbs 12:19

5. **Truth telling is possible through our new life in Christ.**

Ephesians 4:22–25 Throw off your old sinful nature and your former way of life, which is corrupted by lust and deception. Instead, let the Spirit renew your thoughts and attitudes. Put on your new nature, created to be like God—truly righteous and holy. So stop telling lies. Let us tell our neighbors the truth, for we are all parts of the same body. (NLT)

Colossians 3:9–10 Do not lie to one another, since you have put off the old man with his deeds, and have put on the new man who is renewed in knowledge according to the image of Him who created him. (NKJV)
Romans 6:12–13; Galatians 2:20; 1 John 2:21

Biblical Narratives

- Abraham lied about Sarai being his wife, Genesis 12:1–20
- Jacob lied to his father, Genesis 27
- Ananias and Sapphira lied to God, Acts 5:1–11
- Potiphar's wife, whose lies caused Joseph great trial, Genesis 39:7–18

Practical Steps

- Repentance, confession, and restoration are required when you have not been truthful.
- Talk with someone to whom you are accountable. Share your desire to obey God's requirement of truth. Permit this person to evaluate your progress often.
- Consider those situations where you lied. Evaluate the reasons—was it fear of others, fear of being exposed, fear of losing friends, fear of rejection? Was it pride? Recognize your need to see lying as God sees it.
- Are you believing lies in your mind? Compare untruthful thoughts to Philippians 4:8.

Resources

- *Deception: Letting Go of Lying* (booklet). Lou Priolo. P & R.
- "Half Truths and Outright Lies" in *Character Counts*. Rod Handley. Cross Training.
- *Pursuit of Holiness*. Jerry Bridges. NavPress.
- "The Truth Matters" in *Pathway to Freedom: How God's Laws Guide Our Lives*. Alistair Begg. Moody.
- "Your Struggle with Truth" in *The 10 Greatest Struggles of Your Life*. Colin S. Smith. Moody.

Marriage

See also Boundaries, Commitment, Divorce, Integrity, Sex Life, Sexual Purity, Unbelieving Spouse

You got married! Has reality set in yet? Two fallen, sinful people (hopefully both redeemed by the blood of Christ, a new creation in him) together for life, with a road ahead that won't always be easy. The benefits are fantastic, but how do you love and serve this wonderful creature for the rest of your life? What's the plan? How is this supposed to work?

1. **Know for certain that this marriage concept is not something that caught on somewhere back in any primeval history. Marriage was God's idea, design, and plan, a part of his creation from the beginning.**

   Genesis 2:21–25 So the LORD God caused a deep sleep to fall upon the man, and while he slept took one of his ribs and closed up its place with flesh. And the rib that the LORD God had taken from the man he made into a woman and brought her to the man. Then the man said, "This at last is bone of my bones and flesh of my flesh; she shall be called Woman, because she was taken out of Man." Therefore a man shall leave his father and his mother and hold fast to his wife, and they shall become one flesh. And the man and his wife were both naked and were not ashamed. (ESV)
   Genesis 1:27; Matthew 19:4–6

2. **God created marriage to last, a permanent covenant/commitment for life.**

   Mark 10:7–9 "For this reason a man shall leave his father and mother and be joined to his wife, and the two shall become one

flesh"; so then they are no longer two, but one flesh. Therefore what God has joined together, let not man separate. (NKJV)
Malachi 2:14–16

3. Living together before marriage is never in the will of God. There must be a covenantal, promissory relationship.

COVENANT RELATIONSHIP REQUIRED AND NOT TO BE IGNORED

Malachi 2:14 It is because the LORD is the witness between you and the wife of your youth. You have been unfaithful to her, though she is your partner, the wife of your marriage covenant. (NIV)

Proverbs 2:17 [A sinful woman is one] who has left the partner of her youth and ignored the covenant she made before God. (NIV)

SEX ONLY WITH ONE'S WIFE

Proverbs 5:15–18 Drink water from your own cistern, running water from your own well. Should your springs overflow in the streets, your streams of water in the public squares? Let them be yours alone, never to be shared with strangers. May your fountain be blessed, and may you rejoice in the wife of your youth. (NIV)
1 Corinthians 7:2; 1 Thessalonians 4:3–7

4. Safe arrival at the destination is desired. Marriage functions best when God's road map is followed.

HUSBAND—LOVING LEADER

Colossians 3:19 Husbands, love your wives, and do not be harsh with them. (ESV)

Ephesians 5:25–29 Husbands, love your wives, just as Christ also loved the church and gave Himself for her, that He might sanctify and cleanse her with the washing of water by the word, that He might present her to Himself a glorious church, not having spot or wrinkle or any such thing, but that she should be holy and without blemish. So husbands ought to love their own wives as their own bodies; he who loves his wife loves himself.

For no one ever hated his own flesh, but nourishes and cherishes it, just as the Lord does the church. (NKJV)

WIFE—RESPECTFUL COMPLETER

Ephesians 5:22–24 Wives, submit to your own husbands, as to the Lord. For the husband is head of the wife, as also Christ is head of the church; and He is the Savior of the body. Therefore, just as the church is subject to Christ, so let the wives be to their own husbands in everything. (NKJV)

Genesis 2:18–25; Proverbs 19:13–14; 31:10–11; 1 Peter 3:5–6

5. **Scriptural concepts that promote intimacy and longevity in marriage:**

KNOWING WHAT LOVE IS AND IS NOT

1 Corinthians 13:4–7 Love is patient and kind; love does not envy or boast; it is not arrogant or rude. It does not insist on its own way; it is not irritable or resentful; it does not rejoice at wrongdoing, but rejoices with the truth. Love bears all things, believes all things, hopes all things, endures all things. (ESV)

REALIZING THAT IT'S NOT ALL ABOUT YOU

Philippians 2:3–4 Do nothing out of selfish ambition or vain conceit. Rather, in humility value others above yourselves, not looking to your own interests but each of you to the interests of the others. (NIV)

Romans 15:2–3

LISTENING WELL BEFORE SPEAKING

Proverbs 18:13 If one gives an answer before he hears, it is his folly and shame. (ESV)

James 1:19

SPEAKING SOFTLY AND CAREFULLY

Proverbs 15:1, 4 A gentle answer deflects anger, but harsh words make tempers flare. . . . Gentle words are a tree of life; a deceitful tongue crushes the spirit. (NLT)

Proverbs 12:18

SPEAKING INTIMATELY AND EXPRESSIVELY

Song of Solomon 7:1–8

EXPERIENCING THE FRUIT OF THE SPIRIT IN ONE'S LIFE

Galatians 5:22–23 The fruit of the Spirit is love, joy, peace, patience, kindness, goodness, faithfulness, gentleness, self-control; against such things there is no law. (ESV)

UNDERSTANDING THE DIFFERENCES BETWEEN A MAN AND A WOMAN

1 Peter 3:7 Likewise, husbands, live with your wives in an understanding way, showing honor to the woman as the weaker vessel, since they are heirs with you of the grace of life, so that your prayers may not be hindered. (ESV)

Practical Steps

- Make sure you and your wife are both practicing the "leaving your parents" concept and making your new home your priority.
- You and your wife together must understand biblical submission. Study Wayne Mack's list of what submission is, and is not, in *Strengthening Your Marriage*. Submission is for all believers.
- Establish goals for your marriage and family. What do you want to see accomplished in each life? Break these down into basic steps, with specifics to implement in a reasonable time frame.
- Get away for an occasional weekend without children. Plan "dates" throughout your marriage.
- Pray and read your Bible with your spouse on a daily basis.
- Always work on communication. Don't permit conflicts to build—handle them biblically. Men especially need to develop the art of careful, interested listening. Discuss fears, hopes, and dreams.
- Tell your wife she is precious every day; tell her often that you love her.

- Always kiss her goodnight. Show affection by loving touches—holding hands, arm around, etc. At the end of the day, share your happiest and saddest moments.

Resources

- *A Husband after God's Own Heart*. Jim George. Harvest House.
- *Can We Talk? The Art of Relationship Building* (booklet). Rob Green. New Growth.
- *Every Man's Marriage: An Every Man's Guide to Winning the Heart of a Woman*. Steve Arterburn. WaterBrook.
- *Lasting Love*. Alistair Begg. Moody.
- *Living Together: A Guide to Counseling Unmarried Couples*. Jeff VanGoethem. Regal.
- *Love, Sex, and Lasting Relationships*. Chip Ingram. Baker.
- *The Meaning of Marriage*. Timothy Keller. Hodder and Stoughton.
- *Real Marriage: The Truth about Sex, Friendship, and Life Together*. Mark and Grace Driscoll. Thomas Nelson.
- *Song of Solomon: God's Best for Love, Marriage, Sex, and Romance* (4-DVD series). Tommy Nelson.

Masturbation

See also Marriage, Sexual Purity, Temptation, Thought Life

1. While there is no direct mention of masturbation in Scripture, certain truths do apply.

SELFISHNESS

Romans 13:14 But put on the Lord Jesus Christ, and make no provision for the flesh in regard to its lusts. (NASB)

James 1:14–15 But each one is tempted when he is carried away and enticed by his own lust. Then when lust has conceived, it gives birth to sin; and when sin is accomplished, it brings forth death. (NASB)

Exodus 20:3–4; Colossians 3:5

MENTAL IMAGES

Ephesians 5:3 But sexual immorality and all impurity or covetousness must not even be named among you, as is proper among saints. (ESV)

Matthew 5:28 But I say to you that everyone who looks at a woman with lustful intent has already committed adultery with her in his heart. (ESV)

2 Corinthians 10:5

HEART ISSUES

Psalm 51:10 Create in me a pure heart, O God, and renew a steadfast spirit within me. (NIV)

Psalm 19:14; Mark 7:20–23

2. Jesus clearly rebuked looking or visualizing that leads to sexual fantasies.

> Matthew 5:27–28 You have heard the commandment that says, "You must not commit adultery." But I say, anyone who even looks at a woman with lust has already committed adultery with her in his heart. (NLT)

3. When a man is married, his sexual satisfaction must come from his wife. Self-relief is not sex as God planned.

> 1 Corinthians 7:3–4 The husband should fulfill his wife's sexual needs, and the wife should fulfill her husband's needs. The wife gives authority over her body to her husband, and the husband gives authority over his body to his wife. (NLT)

4. Secret activity and isolation are to be avoided.

> Ephesians 5:11–12 Take no part in the unfruitful works of darkness, but instead expose them. For it is shameful even to speak of the things that they do in secret. (ESV)
> Ecclesiastes 12:13–14

5. God offers escape from sin and helps us to be holy.

> 1 Corinthians 10:13 The temptations in your life are no different from what others experience. And God is faithful. He will not allow the temptation to be more than you can stand. When you are tempted, he will show you a way out so that you can endure. (NLT)
> 2 Corinthians 7:1–2

6. One reason that God designed marriage was to alleviate problems of lust. Despite the difficulties, a man must save his body for the wife God will give him. (This is not applicable if a man has the gift of singleness.)

> 1 Corinthians 7:1–2, 9 Now for the matters you wrote about: "It is good for a man not to have sexual relations with a woman." But since sexual immorality is occurring, each man should have sexual relations with his own wife, and each woman with her

own husband. . . . If they cannot control themselves, they should marry, for it is better to marry than to burn with passion. (NIV)
Genesis 2:21–25

Practical Steps

- If you are married, seek accountability with your wife and always let her know if you have failed in this area of masturbation.
- For help in resisting the temptation, communicate with your wife in a timely manner your readiness for sex, even planning ahead with a specific day and time.
- Study these passages for instruction—Romans 13:14; 1 Corinthians 6:13; Galatians 5:16; Colossians 3:17; 1 Timothy 4:12; 2 Timothy 2:22; James 1:13–15; 1 John 2:15–17.
- Study Galatians 5:22–25 on the fruit of the Spirit. What does it mean to be self-controlled?

Resources

- *At the Altar of Sexual Idolatry.* Steve Gallagher. Pure Life Ministry.
- *Hope and Help for Sexual Temptation* (booklet). Mark Shaw. Focus.
- *It's All about Me* (booklet). Winston Smith. CCEF.
- "Self-Centered Sex" in *Sex Is Not the Problem (Lust Is).* Joshua Harris. Multnomah.
- *Winning the Inner War: How to Say No to a Stubborn Habit.* Erwin Lutzer. Cook.

Materialism

See also Contentment, Finances, Jealousy, Pride

Maybe you've seen the bumper sticker: "He who has the most toys wins!" More realistic is, "Gravity wins in the end!" In other words, death is the great equalizer and it doesn't matter at all in the end how much stuff we have accumulated. Fact—two topics Jesus talked about most—hell and *possessions*!

1. Riches in heaven are much to be preferred to riches on earth.

Matthew 6:19–21 Do not store up for yourselves treasures on earth, where moth and rust destroy, and where thieves break in and steal. But store up for yourselves treasures in heaven, where neither moth nor rust destroys, and where thieves do not break in or steal; for where your treasure is, there your heart will be also. (NASB)

1 Corinthians 3:11–15

2. The desire for more possessions can be a trap leading to ruin.

Proverbs 23:4–5 Don't wear yourself out trying to get rich. Be wise enough to know when to quit. In the blink of an eye wealth disappears, for it will sprout wings and fly away like an eagle. (NLT)

1 Timothy 6:6–9 Yet true godliness with contentment is itself great wealth. After all, we brought nothing with us when we came into the world, and we can't take anything with us when we leave it. So if we have enough food and clothing, let us be content. But people who long to be rich fall into temptation and are trapped by many foolish and harmful desires that plunge them into ruin and destruction. (NLT)

Psalm 73:2–3; Proverbs 28:25; James 5:1–5

3. **Godly men prioritize! We must ask which has become more important—riches or our walk with God?**

Proverbs 30:8–9 Keep deception and lies far from me, give me neither poverty nor riches; feed me with the food that is my portion, that I not be full and deny You and say, "Who is the LORD?" Or that I not be in want and steal, and profane the name of my God. (NASB)

1 Timothy 6:10 For the love of money is a root of all kinds of evil, for which some have strayed from the faith in their greediness, and pierced themselves through with many sorrows. (NKJV)

1 John 2:15–17

4. **Material possessions do not provide the security we desire.**

Jeremiah 9:23–24 Thus says the LORD: "Let not the wise man glory in his wisdom, let not the mighty man glory in his might, nor let the rich man glory in his riches; but let him who glories glory in this, that he understands and knows Me, that I am the LORD, exercising lovingkindness, judgment, and righteousness in the earth. For in these I delight," says the LORD. (NKJV)

Luke 12:15 And he said to them, "Take care, and be on your guard against all covetousness, for one's life does not consist in the abundance of his possessions." (ESV)

Psalm 39:4–6; 49:16–20; Isaiah 58:11; Proverbs 28:6; 1 Timothy 6:17; Hebrews 13:5

5. **Giving willingly to God's work, for to help those less fortunate is a blessing for the giver as well as the receiver.**

Proverbs 31:8–9 Speak up for those who cannot speak for themselves, for the rights of all who are destitute. Speak up and judge fairly; defend the rights of the poor and needy. (NIV)

1 Timothy 6:18–19 They are to do good, to be rich in good works, to be generous and ready to share, thus storing up treasure for themselves as a good foundation for the future, so that they may take hold of that which is truly life. (ESV)

2 Corinthians 9:6–8

6. Solutions for avoiding materialism:

> **1 Timothy 6:11** But you, O man of God, flee these things [love of money] and pursue righteousness, godliness, faith, love, patience, gentleness. (NKJV)
>
> **Philippians 4:11–13** And I am not saying this because I feel neglected, for I have learned to be satisfied with what I have. I know what it is to be in need and what it is to have more than enough. I have learned this secret, so that anywhere, at any time, I am content, whether I am full or hungry, whether I have too much or too little. I have the strength to face all conditions by the power that Christ gives me. (GNT)
>
> **Colossians 3:1–2** You have been raised to life with Christ, so set your hearts on the things that are in heaven, where Christ sits on his throne at the right side of God. Keep your minds fixed on things there, not on things here on earth. (GNT)

7. Never forget that the source of everything we have is God.

> **Deuteronomy 8:11–14** Take care lest you forget the LORD your God by not keeping his commandments and his rules and his statutes, which I command you today, lest, when you have eaten and are full and have built good houses and live in them, and when your herds and flocks multiply and your silver and gold is multiplied and all that you have is multiplied, then your heart be lifted up, and you forget the LORD your God, who brought you out of the land of Egypt, out of the house of slavery. (ESV)

Biblical Narratives

- Kings, who planned together to "go for the gold" without seeking God's will, 1 Kings 22:48; 2 Chronicles 20:35–37

- Rich man, who made plans but didn't take God into account, Luke 12:18–21

- Ananias and Sapphira, who lied to God about their resources, Acts 5:1–11

Practical Steps

- If "things" are your gods, repent, confess, pray for renewal. Commit to a lifestyle change. Seek accountability from a wiser, more mature believer.

- If you are married, work at living on one income. If you have children at home, know that your wife's home responsibilities are her full-time job and more valuable than any employment outside the home.

- Evaluate purchases, prayerfully taking time to consider what you should buy. For major purchases, never buy the first time you look. Have a cooling off period. Evaluate real needs versus wants.

- Ask for wisdom for electronic update purchases. Do you really need all those bells and whistles? Do you really need that latest and greatest cell phone?

- Follow a budget; have a plan and goal; set limits. Make giving to God the first check you write each pay period.

Resources

- *Real Prosperity: Biblical Principles of Material Possessions*. Gene Getz. Moody.

- *When Money Runs Out* (booklet). James Petty. New Growth.

- *Gospel Treason: Betraying the Gospel with Hidden Idols*. Brad Bigney. P & R.

- *Counterfeit Gods: The Empty Promises of Money, Sex, and Power*. Timothy Keller. Dutton.

- *Money, Possessions, and Eternity*. Randy Alcorn. Tyndale.

Maturity/Manhood

See also Aging, Entertainment, Leadership, Priorities

For whatever reasons, some men are reluctant to accept adulthood with its responsibilities. Others would like to grow up, but find it difficult to do so. Growth and maturity in Christ are critical concepts as well. Here are some scriptural thoughts and standards.

1. **Younger men sometimes need to work hard to establish themselves as responsible, godly, mature adults.**

   1 Timothy 4:12 Let no one look down on your youthfulness, but rather in speech, conduct, love, faith and purity, show yourself an example of those who believe. (NASB)
   1 Corinthians 16:10–11

2. **Paul uses coming of age as an illustration of events at Christ's return. This is how becoming a man should work.**

   1 Corinthians 13:11 When I was a child, I used to speak like a child, think like a child, reason like a child; when I became a man, I did away with childish things. (NASB)

3. **God assures the young man Jeremiah that he will provide necessary resources as Jeremiah accepts his adult calling.**

   Jeremiah 1:7–8 But the LORD said to me, "Do not say that you are too young, but go to the people I send you to, and tell them everything I command you to say. Do not be afraid of them, for I will be with you to protect you. I, the LORD, have spoken!" (GNT)

4. A young Solomon makes a mature request for wisdom to govern God's people.

> 1 Kings 3:9 So give me the wisdom I need to rule your people with justice and to know the difference between good and evil. Otherwise, how would I ever be able to rule this great people of yours? (GNT)

5. Jesus matured in the four standard areas of growth—intellectual, physical, spiritual, and social. This is the normal, expected pattern.

> Luke 2:52 Jesus increased in wisdom and in stature and in favor with God and man. (ESV)

6. Note the marks of mature Christian men as Paul lists the qualifications for elders.

> 1 Timothy 3:1–7; Titus 1:6–9

7. Growth to maturity as a Christian is vital to living the life that God wants for us.

> Ephesians 4:15 Rather, speaking the truth in love, we are to grow up in every way into him who is the head, into Christ. (ESV) (See verses 11–16.)
>
> Philippians 1:9; Colossians 1:9–14; 2 Thessalonians 1:3; 1 Peter 2:2–3

Biblical Narratives

- A young David shows his growth to maturity, 1 Samuel 17
- Daniel matures, Daniel 1
- John Mark becomes useful to Paul after a slow start, Acts 15:35–40; 2 Timothy 4:11
- Timothy's growth as a believer, 2 Timothy 1:3; 3:14–15

Practical Steps

- What "childish things" are you still hanging onto that need to be put aside?

- Do you have a proper balance in the use of time spent on games, sports, TV, movies, and so on?

- Evaluate: am I neglecting responsibilities at work or with family for excessive involvement in entertainment activities?

- Evaluate: why am I behind in accepting the obligations of adulthood? If you find it difficult to make this assessment, ask others who know you well to help you.

- Interview four or five men you admire for their strong character. Evaluate godly steps they have taken and use them for your own growth.

Resources

- *Broken-Down House: Living Productively in a World Gone Bad*. Paul Tripp. Shepherd.

- *Disciplines of a Godly Man*. Kent Hughes. Crossway.

- *The Mark of a Man: Following Christ's Example of Masculinity*. Elisabeth Elliot. Revell.

- "True Stories" and "Becoming a Faithful Man" in *The Measure of a Man*. Gene Getz. Regal.

Natural Disasters/Disease

See also Fear, Health, Suffering, Trust

Why is our natural world so conflicted—nature out of control—with cataclysmic storms and ravaging diseases? Why so much pain and suffering? The biblical worldview does supply answers.

1. **Because of Adam and Eve's sin in Eden, every aspect of creation has been brought to a state of change and decay.**

   Genesis 3:17–18 And to Adam he said, "Because you have listened to the voice of your wife and have eaten of the tree of which I commanded you, 'You shall not eat of it,' cursed is the ground because of you; in pain you shall eat of it all the days of your life; thorns and thistles it shall bring forth for you; and you shall eat the plants of the field." (ESV)
   Romans 8:20–22

2. **Yet God has given us hope in his promise, as a part of his complete redemptive plan, to remove this curse of decay from all of creation.**

   Romans 8:21 That the creation itself will be set free from its bondage to corruption and obtain the freedom of the glory of the children of God. (ESV)
   Isaiah 25:8 He will swallow up death forever; and the Lord GOD will wipe away tears from all faces, and the reproach of his people he will take away from all the earth, for the LORD has spoken. (ESV)
   Revelation 21:4–5; 22:3

3. **God is in control.** He remains sovereign over all his creation.

> **Psalm 33:11** But the LORD's plans stand firm forever; his intentions can never be shaken. (NLT)
> Job 9:4–10; Daniel 7:13–14; Jeremiah 10:12–13

4. **Scripture shows that the blessings of heaven and eternity far outweigh the present frustrations of physical suffering.**

> **2 Corinthians 4:16–18** So we do not lose heart. Though our outer self is wasting away, our inner self is being renewed day by day. For this slight momentary affliction is preparing for us an eternal weight of glory beyond all comparison, as we look not to the things that are seen but to the things that are unseen. For the things that are seen are transient, but the things that are unseen are eternal. (ESV)
> John 16:33; 2 Corinthians 5:1–4

Biblical Narrative

- Locusts, Joel 1

Practical Steps

- Show compassion to people who have been through a natural disaster; reach out to them and help them physically or financially.
- Take time to listen to their stories. If you have had a similar experience, identify with them and express to them how God has helped you.
- Study Psalm 91; memorize 91:1–2. Note and study the four different names for God in these two verses. Study key words—*shelter, refuge, rest, fortress*.
- Memorize and keep close at hand Isaiah 43:1–2.

Resources

- *An Act of God?: Answers to Tough Questions about God's Role in Natural Disasters*. Erwin Lutzer. Tyndale.
- *Bible Knowledge Commentary*. New Testament ed. See pages 471–72 for explanation as to nature being cursed and renewed in the future (begins at the Romans 8:18–27 section). Roy Zuck, ed. Victor.
- "God's Power over Nature" in *Trusting God: Even When Life Hurts*. Jerry Bridges. NavPress.
- *Not the Way It's Supposed to Be*. Cornelius Plantinga. Eerdmans.
- "The Stained Planet" in *Where Is God When It Hurts?* Philip Yancey. Zondervan.
- *Ultimate Questions*. John Blanchard. Faith Resources.

Past Memories

See also Bitterness, Forgiveness from God, Forgiving Others, Grief, Guilt, Thought Life

We all have a history, events of the past—gains or losses, victory or defeat, high points and low, exciting things or those deeply disturbing. How we handle these memories affects every aspect of our lives.

1. **A constant review of past accomplishments or failures and losses can trap us into negative thinking that limits our ability to be successful in the present or future.**

   Ezra 3:12 But many of the priests and Levites and heads of fathers' houses, old men who had seen the first house, wept with a loud voice when they saw the foundation of this house being laid, though many shouted aloud for joy. (ESV) (See verses 8–13 for context of the story and Haggai 1–2.)

   Psalm 42:3–4 Day and night I cry, and tears are my only food; all the time my enemies ask me, "Where is your God?" My heart breaks when I remember the past, when I went with the crowds to the house of God and led them as they walked along, a happy crowd, singing and shouting praise to God. (GNT)

2. **If past memories involve sin, we can be assured that, once full confession has taken place, Christ will enable us to move beyond to a life that pleases him.**

   1 John 1:9 If we confess our sins, he is faithful and just to forgive us our sins and to cleanse us from all unrighteousness. (ESV)

   Hebrews 12:1–2 Therefore, since we are surrounded by so great a cloud of witnesses, let us also lay aside every weight, and sin which clings so closely, and let us run with endurance the race that is set before us, looking to Jesus, the founder and perfecter of our faith, who for the joy that was set before him endured the cross, despising the shame, and is seated at the right hand of the throne of God. (ESV)

2 Corinthians 5:17; 1 Peter 4:1–3

3. **Dealing with past memories is a challenge to our thinking processes.**

Psalm 13:2 How long must I wrestle with my thoughts and day after day have sorrow in my heart? How long will my enemy triumph over me? (NIV)

Isaiah 26:3–4 You will keep in perfect peace all who trust in you, all whose thoughts are fixed on you! Trust in the LORD always, for the LORD GOD is the eternal Rock. (NLT)

2 Corinthians 10:4–5

4. **We choose to move beyond the past by changing how we think.**

Psalm 63:6–8 On my bed I remember you; I think of you through the watches of the night. Because you are my help, I sing in the shadow of your wings. I cling to you; your right hand upholds me. (NIV)

Romans 12:2 Don't copy the behavior and customs of this world, but let God transform you into a new person by changing the way you think. Then you will learn to know God's will for you, which is good and pleasing and perfect. (NLT)

Ephesians 4:22–24; Philippians 4:6–8

5. **Our need is to focus on all God has done for us, his provision in the past. Will he not do the same now?**

Deuteronomy 8:2 And you shall remember the whole way that the LORD your God has led you these forty years in the wilderness. (ESV) (The context is a test for obedience, but the principle applies.)

Joshua 21:45 Not one word of all the good promises that the LORD had made to the house of Israel had failed; all came to pass. (ESV)

Psalm 34:4; 77:11; 143:5–6

6. **Concentrate on what God is doing right now and will do in the future.**

Isaiah 43:18–19 Remember not the former things, nor consider the things of old. Behold, I am doing a new thing; now it springs forth, do you not perceive it? I will make a way in the wilderness and rivers in the desert. (ESV)

Philippians 3:13–14 No, dear brothers and sisters, I have not achieved it, but I focus on this one thing: Forgetting the past and looking forward to what lies ahead, I press on to reach the end of the race and receive the heavenly prize for which God, through Christ Jesus, is calling us. (NLT)

Biblical Narratives

- Joseph, able to forget, Genesis 41:51
- Ruth and Naomi, as God helps them move beyond their past, Ruth 1–4
- Israelites after the captivity, sad over the memory of the former temple, Ezra 3:10–13

Practical Steps

- Seek out mature believers who can encourage you. Share your memories and seek their counsel.
- Make a record of God's goodness, provision, and providence. Continue to focus on this throughout life with gratitude and thanksgiving.
- If others have sinned against you, make sure you have forgiven them.
- Prayerfully examine your heart. Consider what past memories are coming to your mind repeatedly. Journal what you value as you dwell on these memories. What do you fear? What do you worship?

Resources

- *God Is Up to Something Great: Turning Your Yesterdays into Better Tomorrows*. Tony Evans. Multnomah.
- *The Hand of God: Finding His Care in All Circumstances* (the life of Joseph). Alistair Begg. Moody.
- *Putting the Past behind You*. Erwin Lutzer. Moody.
- *Putting the Past in Its Place*. Steve Viars. Harvest House.
- "PTSD: Healing for Bad Memories" (booklet). Timothy Land. New Growth.
- "Redeeming the Bad Memories of Your Past Sins" in *Journal of Biblical Counseling*. Robert Jones. Fall, 2003.

Peer Pressure

See also Boundaries, Decision Making, Friendship, Temptation, Workplace

Peer pressure can be a good thing if it keeps us on the straight and narrow (for example, not jumping ahead in a line of traffic and maintaining our social skills). But if the pressure is to make poor decisions or to join others in sin, it becomes a problem.

1. **We must take a stand for what is right, not permitting others to pressure us to do what is wrong or what we know would be a bad choice.**

    Proverbs 1:10 My son, if sinners entice you, do not consent. (ESV)

    Proverbs 24:1–2 Be not envious of evil men, nor desire to be with them, for their hearts devise violence, and their lips talk of trouble. (ESV)

    Habakkuk 2:15–16 Woe to him who gives drink to his neighbors, pouring it from the wineskin till they are drunk, so that he can gaze on their naked bodies! You will be filled with shame instead of glory. (NIV)

    1 Corinthians 15:33 Do not be deceived: "Bad company ruins good morals." (ESV)

    Isaiah 51:7; Ephesians 5:3–17; 2 Peter 2:18–19

2. **Moving away from what is wrong is a good start, but we must also choose to set an example by doing what is right. Associating with other strong believers is crucial.**

    2 Timothy 2:22 So flee youthful passions and pursue righteousness, faith, love, and peace, along with those who call on the Lord from a pure heart. (ESV)

1 Timothy 4:12 Let no one despise you for your youth, but set the believers an example in speech, in conduct, in love, in faith, in purity. (ESV)
Joshua 24:14–16; James 4:17

Biblical Narratives

- Aaron, pressured to construct the golden calf, Exodus 32
- Herod Antipas, pressured to kill John the Baptist, Matthew 14:1–12
- Peter, pressured to compromise, Galatians 2:11–14

Practical Steps

- If someone is pressuring you to do something you know you should not do, be firm in your no. Or if they won't accept that, tell them you need time to think things through (which is true—thinking about how better to say no).

- Knowing the kinds of pressures others have placed on you in the past, keep a list of why those decisions would be wrong for you. Be prepared with your no.

- Share with other men at church the pressures you are facing. They probably face the same things.

Resources

- "Demonstrating Wisdom" in *The Measure of a Man*. Gene Getz. Regal.
- *When People Are Big and God Is Small*. Ed Welch. P & R.
- *Peer Pressure* (booklet). Paul Tripp. New Growth.

Pornography

See also Hope, Integrity, Lust, Selfishness, Sexual Purity, Temptation

The sin of pornography has become a plague of epic proportions in today's society. Sinning has never been easier; our moral slide as a nation is ongoing. It's sad that Christian men are involved to an alarming degree. Helping men toward repentance, confession, and restoration must be a priority of those who counsel others.

1. **Pornography is a part of Satan's destructive counterfeit of lies.**

   John 8:44 You [Pharisees] are of your father the devil, and your will is to do your father's desires. He was a murderer from the beginning, and does not stand in the truth, because there is no truth in him. When he lies, he speaks out of his own character, for he is a liar and the father of lies. (ESV)

   Ephesians 6:12 For we do not wrestle against flesh and blood, but against the rulers, against the authorities, against the cosmic powers over this present darkness, against the spiritual forces of evil in the heavenly places. (ESV)

   1 John 2:16 For all that is in the world— the desires of the flesh and the desires of the eyes and pride of life—is not from the Father but is from the world. (ESV)

   1 Peter 5:8; 1 John 5:19

2. **Viewing pornography will affect every aspect of our lives.**

   Luke 11:34–36 Your eye is the lamp of your body. When your eye is healthy, your whole body is full of light, but when it is bad, your body is full of darkness. Therefore be careful lest the light in you be darkness. If then your whole body is full of light, having no part dark, it will be wholly bright, as when a lamp with its rays gives you light. (ESV)

James 1:14–15

3. **God sees everything; nothing we do is hidden from him.**

Psalm 90:8 You have set our iniquities before you, our secret sins in the light of your presence. (ESV)

Psalm 139:7–12 Where shall I go from your Spirit? Or where shall I flee from your presence? If I ascend to heaven, you are there! If I make my bed in Sheol, you are there! If I take the wings of the morning and dwell in the uttermost parts of the sea, even there your hand shall lead me, and your right hand shall hold me. If I say, "Surely the darkness shall cover me, and the light about me be night," even the darkness is not dark to you; the night is bright as the day, for darkness is as light with you. (ESV)

Proverbs 15:3 The eyes of the LORD are in every place, keeping watch on the evil and the good. (ESV)

Proverbs 5:21; Jeremiah 23:23–24

4. **Scripture clearly states that our eyes are not to be used for sinning.**

Job 31:1 I made a covenant with my eyes not to look with lust at a young woman. (NLT)

Psalm 101:3–4 I will not look with approval on anything that is vile. I hate what faithless people do; I will have no part in it. The perverse of heart shall be far from me; I will have nothing to do with what is evil. (NIV)

Isaiah 1:16; Matthew 5:28

5. **It is vital to turn from this sin and remove pornography entirely from one's life. Radical measures are necessary.**

Psalm 32:3–5 When I kept silent about my sin, my body wasted away through my groaning all day long. For day and night Your hand was heavy upon me; my vitality was drained away as with the fever heat of summer. I acknowledged my sin to You, and my iniquity I did not hide; I said, "I will confess my transgressions to the LORD"; and You forgave the guilt of my sin. (NASB)

Psalm 119:37 Turn my eyes from worthless things, and give me life through your word. (NLT)

Matthew 5:29 If your right eye causes you to sin, tear it out and throw it away. For it is better that you lose one of your members than that your whole body be thrown into hell. (See context; Jesus is speaking metaphorically.) (ESV)

Psalm 139:23–24; Romans 13:14; 1 Peter 2:24

6. **There is hope for freedom from this sin. God supports us as we make godly choices.**

2 Chronicles 16:9 For the eyes of the Lord run to and fro throughout the whole earth, to give strong support to those whose heart is blameless toward him. (ESV)

Romans 6:12–14 Let not sin therefore reign in your mortal body, to make you obey its passions. Do not present your members to sin as instruments for unrighteousness, but present yourselves to God as those who have been brought from death to life, and your members to God as instruments for righteousness. For sin will have no dominion over you, since you are not under law but under grace. (ESV)

Galatians 5:16 But I say, walk by [depend on] the Spirit, and you will not gratify the desires of the flesh. (ESV) (See verses 16–25.)

1 Corinthians 6:9–11; 2 Corinthians 5:17

7. **God hears and answers our cries for help.**

Psalm 33:18–20 Behold, the eye of the Lord is on those who fear Him, on those who hope for His lovingkindness, to deliver their soul from death and to keep them alive in famine. Our soul waits for the Lord; He is our help and our shield. (NASB)

Psalm 34:14–15 Depart from evil and do good; seek peace and pursue it. The eyes of the Lord are toward the righteous and His ears are open to their cry. (NASB) (See entire psalm.)

8. **Mature believers can help us. We should seek out godly people for accountability.**

2 Timothy 2:21–22 Therefore, if anyone cleanses himself from what is dishonorable, he will be a vessel for honorable use, set apart as holy, useful to the master of the house, ready for every good work. So flee youthful passions and pursue righteousness, faith, love, and peace, along with those who call on the Lord from a pure heart. (ESV)

Galatians 6:1 Brothers, if anyone is caught in any transgression, you who are spiritual should restore him in a spirit of gentleness. (ESV)

Practical Steps

- For use of home and work computers, be accountable to others—wife, friends, co-workers. Install the necessary access blocks. Locate your computer in an open area.

- Avoid looking at magazine racks in drug stores or supermarkets.

- Be alert for catalogs that are selling their product by using the female body. Either stop them from coming or throw them away without looking.

- Find someone trustworthy to confess to and pray with when you struggle.

- Stop making excuses. Ask God the Spirit to break you and move you to the place you need to be—conquest and freedom.

- Have options in place for when you are tempted—call a friend, read a good book, exercise.

- Keep the phrase "Be a Joseph" on a card above your computer or in your pocket. See Genesis 39:9.

Resources

- *Closing the Window: Steps to Living Porn Free.* Tim Chester. IVP.

- *Every Man's Battle: Winning the War on Sexual Temptation One Victory at a Time* (workbook available). Stephen Arterburn. Water-Brook.

- *Pornography: Slaying the Dragon.* David Powlison. P & R.

- *The Way of Purity.* Mike Cleveland. Focus.

- *Think before You Look*. Daniel Henderson. Living Ink.
- *Winning the Inner War: How to Say No to a Stubborn Habit*. Erwin Lutzer. Cook.
- *You Can Change: God's Transforming Power for Our Sinful Behavior and Negative Emotions*. Tim Chester. Crossway.

Pride/Humility

See also Attitude, Complaining, Self-Worth, Subjectivity

Sinful pride is not giving God the credit for who we are, what we have, what we can do. The classic '60s song, "I Did It My Way!" is reflective of this attitude. Godly Christian men must give God the credit and the glory. We have no other choice; that is God's way.

1. **Humility is pleasing to God; sinful pride he clearly hates.**

   Proverbs 8:13 The fear of the LORD is hatred of evil. Pride and arrogance and the way of evil and perverted speech I hate. (ESV)
   Psalm 138:6 Though the LORD is great, he cares for the humble, but he keeps his distance from the proud. (NLT)
   James 4:6 But he gives more grace. Therefore it says, "God opposes the proud, but gives grace to the humble." (ESV)
   Psalm 18:27; Proverbs 3:34; 16:19; 21:4; 26:12

2. **Sinful pride produces only negative outcomes.**

   Proverbs 13:10 Pride leads to conflict; those who take advice are wise. (NLT)
   Proverbs 16:18 Pride goes before destruction, and haughtiness before a fall. (NLT)
   Isaiah 2:11 Human pride will be brought down, and human arrogance will be humbled. Only the LORD will be exalted on that day of judgment. (NLT)
   Mark 7:20–23

3. **Consider boasting that pleases God!**

   Psalm 44:8 In God we have boasted continually, and we will give thanks to your name forever. (ESV)

Galatians 6:14 But far be it from me to boast except in the cross of our Lord Jesus Christ, by which the world has been crucified to me, and I to the world. (ESV)

Jeremiah 9:23–24

4. We must recognize that God is the source of whatever we possess and all of our abilities.

1 Corinthians 15:10 By the grace of God I am what I am, and his grace to me was not without effect. No, I worked harder than all of them—yet not I, but the grace of God that was with me. (NIV)

1 Timothy 6:17 As for the rich in this present age, charge them not to be haughty, nor to set their hopes on the uncertainty of riches, but on God, who richly provides us with everything to enjoy. (ESV)

Deuteronomy 8:11–14; John 15:5; 1 Corinthians 3:1–9

5. Note Jesus's thoughts on the issue of pride versus humility.

Matthew 18:1–4 At that time the disciples came to Jesus and said, "Who then is greatest in the kingdom of heaven?" And He called a child to Himself and set him before them, and said, "Truly I say to you, unless you are converted and become like children, you will not enter the kingdom of heaven. Whoever then humbles himself as this child, he is the greatest in the kingdom of heaven." (NASB)

Luke 14:11 For everyone who exalts himself will be humbled, and he who humbles himself will be exalted. (NASB)

Matthew 20:25–28; John 13:12–14

6. Pride must be replaced by humility.

Philippians 2:3 Do nothing from selfishness or empty conceit, but with humility of mind regard one another as more important than yourselves. (NASB)

Romans 12:3 For by the grace given to me I say to everyone among you not to think of himself more highly than he ought to think, but to think with sober judgment, each according to the measure of faith that God has assigned. (ESV)

1 Peter 5:5; 1 John 2:15–17

7. God's plan for the humble.

Micah 6:8 He has told you, O man, what is good; and what does the LORD require of you but to do justice, and to love kindness, and to walk humbly with your God? (ESV)

Psalm 10:17 O LORD, You have heard the desire of the humble; You will strengthen their heart, You will incline Your ear. (NASB)

2 Chronicles 7:14

Biblical Narratives

Negative

- Joseph, revealing his dreams to parents and brothers, Genesis 37:5–8
- Nebuchadnezzar, in his accomplishments, Daniel 4:28–37
- Satan, in his pride, Isaiah 14:13–14
- Edomites, in their might, Obadiah 1:3–4
- James and John, wanting to rule, Mark 10:35–45

Positive

- Jesus, in his humility, John 13; Philippians 2:5–8
- Paul's good attitude, 2 Corinthians 12:1–10; Philippians 3:4–8

Practical Steps

- Make it a point to always begin your prayers with several areas of thanksgiving. Acknowledge God as the ultimate provider. Give credit to him.
- Make a list of accomplishments and possessions of which you could be proud. Then, going through each item, write down why each of these comes from the hand of God. Turn this list into one of praise and thanksgiving for his grace to you!

- Memorize Jeremiah 9:23–24. Write it on a card and keep it handy for a reminder.
- Memorize Philippians 2:3–4. Review these verses often when you are tempted to feel you are always right, or better than others.

Resources

- "Pride" in *Respectable Sins*. Jerry Bridges. NavPress.
- *Humility: The Forgotten Virtue* (booklet). Wayne Mack. P & R.
- *Humility: The True Greatness*. C. J. Mahaney. Multnomah.
- *From Pride to Humility*. Stuart Scott. Focus.

Priorities

See also Fathering, Marriage, Purpose for Living, Selfishness, Time Management

What do we think about the most? What do we spend the most time doing? Answering these two questions provides a good assessment of priorities. Loving, serving, and obeying God must always come first and after that, spouse and children. Beyond these, our priorities will vary at different times in our lives and depending on what responsibilities God brings our way. Placing God first is always necessary.

1. **Our Creator expects us to give him the first and most important place in our lives.**

    Matthew 22:35–38 And one of them, a lawyer, asked him [Jesus] a question to test him. "Teacher, which is the great commandment in the Law?" And he said to him, "You shall love the Lord your God with all your heart and with all your soul and with all your mind. This is the great and first commandment." (ESV)

    Matthew 6:31–33 Therefore do not be anxious, saying, "What shall we eat?" or "What shall we drink?" or "What shall we wear?" For the Gentiles seek after all these things, and your heavenly Father knows that you need them all. But seek first the kingdom of God and his righteousness, and all these things will be added to you. (ESV)

    Deuteronomy 6:4–5; 10:20–21

2. **Family—wife and children—must be our next priority.**

    Ephesians 5:25, 28 Husbands, love your wives, as Christ loved the church and gave himself up for her. . . . In the same way husbands should love their wives as their own bodies. He who loves his wife loves himself. (ESV)

Ephesians 6:4 Fathers, do not provoke your children to anger, but bring them up in the discipline and instruction of the Lord. (ESV)

Deuteronomy 6:6–7; Psalm 127:1–3; 1 Thessalonians 2:10–12

3. Placing others ahead of ourselves must be high on our list. Loving and serving must be priorities!

Matthew 22:39–40 And a second [after the first commandment—loving God] is like it: You shall love your neighbor as yourself. On these two commandments depend all the Law and the Prophets. (ESV)

Galatians 5:13–14 For you were called to freedom, brothers. Only do not use your freedom as an opportunity for the flesh, but through love serve one another. For the whole law is fulfilled in one word: "You shall love your neighbor as yourself." (ESV)

Philippians 2:3–4 Do nothing from selfish ambition or conceit, but in humility count others more significant than yourselves. Let each of you look not only to his own interests, but also to the interests of others. (ESV)

4. Other priority areas where decisions must be made include Church Involvement, Career/Employment, Finances/Money (topics in this book).

Practical Steps

- Evaluate carefully where your priorities lie. What is really first? What do you think about the most? Is selfishness a problem? Ask God to convict you and change your heart.

- Are you a workaholic? Practice leaving work behind when you come home to your family.

- Realize that heavy involvement in church does not necessarily mean that God is first in your life. There are other priorities that God wants us to establish. Too much time spent in church could mean you are neglecting your family.

- Commit to a consistent time each day spent in Bible reading and prayer.

Resources

- *Balancing Life's Demands: Biblical Priorities for a Busy Life.* DVD series. Chip Ingram. Living on the Edge Ministries.
- *Priorities: Mastering Time Management* (booklet). James Petty. P & R.

Prodigal Children

See also Anxiety, Disappointment, Fathering, Forgiving Others, Hope, Trust

Of all the struggles Christian parents face, having an unbelieving child or one who as a teen or adult is walking away from the Lord is among the most heartbreaking. Guilt, blame, fear, conflict, and other emotions are all part of the pain. The "if only we had done this" thoughts never seem to go away. Yet, as always, knowing and applying God's Word is critical as we deal with the many issues involved.

1. Parents who face this crisis must be careful to maintain a loving, understanding relationship with each other—no blame game or heaping guilt on the other.

   Proverbs 19:13 A foolish child is a father's ruin, and a quarrelsome wife is like the constant dripping of a leaky roof. (NIV) (The same would apply as the genders are reversed.)
   Psalm 19:14; Ephesians 5:25, 28; 1 Peter 3:7; James 3:2–12

2. Children will not always walk in God's ways. Yet they are responsible for their own decisions, good or bad. Note this principle of individual accountability.

   Ezekiel 18:20 The son shall not suffer for the iniquity of the father, nor the father suffer for the iniquity of the son. The righteousness of the righteous shall be upon himself, and the wickedness of the wicked shall be upon himself. (ESV) (The context of chapter 18 is especially important.)
   Deuteronomy 24:16

3. It hurts severely to have a child who is not walking with God.

Proverbs 17:25 Foolish children bring grief to their father and bitterness to the one who gave them birth. (NLT)

Proverbs 10:1 A wise son makes a glad father, but a foolish son is the grief of his mother. (NKJV)

Isaiah 65:2

4. God understands wayward children and the grief they bring. (The context is his nation, Israel.)

Jeremiah 3:22 "My wayward children," says the LORD, "come back to me, and I will heal your wayward hearts." (NLT)

Isaiah 1:2 Listen, O heavens! Pay attention, earth! This is what the LORD says: "The children I raised and cared for have rebelled against me." (NLT)

Jeremiah 6:16

5. There are consequences for turning one's back on God.

Proverbs 6:27–28 Can a man carry fire next to his chest and his clothes not be burned? Or can one walk on hot coals and his feet not be scorched? (ESV) (See context.)

Galatians 6:7 Do not be deceived: God is not mocked, for whatever one sows, that will he also reap. (ESV)

Proverbs 11:21

6. The battle with the enemy must be turned over to God.

2 Chronicles 20:15 And he said, "Listen, all Judah and inhabitants of Jerusalem and King Jehoshaphat: Thus says the LORD to you, 'Do not be afraid and do not be dismayed at this great horde, for the battle is not yours but God's.'" (ESV)

Proverbs 21:31 The horse is prepared for the day of battle, but deliverance is of the LORD. (NKJV)

John 16:33 These things I have spoken to you, that in Me you may have peace. In the world you will have tribulation; but be of good cheer, I have overcome the world. (NKJV)

2 Chronicles 14:11; Psalm 62:11–12; Isaiah 49:25

7. As you deal with this pain, make sure your own walk with the Lord remains vital and fresh. Do not lose your confidence in God. Live out your faith before your child.

James 1:2–5 Consider it all joy, my brethren, when you encounter various trials, knowing that the testing of your faith produces endurance. And let endurance have its perfect result, so that you may be perfect and complete, lacking in nothing. But if any of you lacks wisdom, let him ask of God, who gives to all generously and without reproach, and it will be given to him. (NASB)
Galatians 6:1

8. Work at keeping an open relationship and communication with your children. Then when God gives the opportunity, they may listen.

1 Corinthians 13:4–7 Love suffers long and is kind; love does not envy; love does not parade itself, is not puffed up; does not behave rudely, does not seek its own, is not provoked, thinks no evil; does not rejoice in iniquity, but rejoices in the truth; bears all things, believes all things, hopes all things, endures all things. (NKJV)
Proverbs 29:11 Fools vent their anger, but the wise quietly hold it back. (NLT)
1 Peter 4:8 And above all things have fervent love for one another, for "love will cover a multitude of sins." (NKJV)
Psalm 37:8 Cease from anger, and forsake wrath; do not fret —it only causes harm. (NKJV)
Proverbs 20:3; Galatians 5:22–23; James 5:19–20

9. Pray constantly for your child, not necessarily for what you want as a parent, but for what God wants to do in your child's life.

1 Samuel 1:27–28 For this boy I prayed, and the LORD has given me my petition which I asked of Him. So I have also dedicated him to the LORD; as long as he lives he is dedicated to the LORD. (NASB)
Romans 8:26 In the same way the Spirit also helps our weakness; for we do not know how to pray as we should, but the Spirit

Himself intercedes for us with groanings too deep for words. (NASB)

> Matthew 7:7–11; 2 Corinthians 12:8–10

10. Have hope—God desires for your child to be restored. Anticipate what he can do.

> **Jeremiah 32:27** Behold, I am the LORD, the God of all flesh; is anything too difficult for Me? (NASB)
>
> **Lamentations 3:25–26** The LORD is good to those who wait for Him, to the person who seeks Him. It is good that he waits silently for the salvation of the LORD. (NASB)
>
> **Romans 15:13** Now may the God of hope fill you with all joy and peace in believing, so that you will abound in hope by the power of the Holy Spirit. (NASB)
>
> 2 Peter 3:9

11. When a child does come home and experiences God's renewed blessings, parents must be prepared for the reactions of people who do not understand (or like) grace and have adopted the "elder brother" attitude.

> Luke 15:25–30

Biblical Narratives

- Lost sheep, Matthew 18:10–14
- Prodigal son, Luke 15:11–32

Practical Steps

- Don't push for a quick resolution; be willing to wait as God does his work. Unwise pushing can stiffen your child's resistance.
- Seek wise counsel. Consider—are you majoring on externals or the heart of your child?
- Show consistent love—spend time with your child; show affection by touching; send notes; use words that build up.

- Guard your walk and time with God so you are not brought down to discouragement, depression, defeat, or self-blame.

Resources

- *Engaging Today's Prodigal: Clear Thinking, New Approaches, and Reasons for Hope.* Carol Barnier. Moody.
- *Parents with Broken Hearts.* William L. Coleman. BMH.
- *Prayers for Prodigals: 90 Days of Prayer for Your Child.* James Banks. Discovery House.
- *Prodigals and Those Who Love Them.* Ruth Graham. Focus on the Family.
- *When Your Kid's in Trouble* (booklet). William Smith. New Growth.

Profanity

See also Anger, Speech

The basic meaning of the word *holy* in the Old Testament is "apart, separate, other." In reference to God's holy name, it places him as far above and beyond, distinct, separated, totally other, uncommon in comparison to common, ordinary, sinful mankind. God in his essence, his very being, is separated from all that is sinful, and is pure, just, and right, and perfect!

1. Since the name of God represents who he is in his holy character and perfection, we must be careful not to speak that name in a profane (or common) manner. We must not denigrate his holy name.

   Deuteronomy 5:11 You shall not take the name of the LORD your God in vain, for the LORD will not hold him guiltless who takes his name in vain. (ESV)
   Leviticus 19:12 You shall not swear by my name falsely, and so profane the name of your God: I am the LORD. (ESV)
   Leviticus 22:1–2; Psalm 74:18; 138:2; 1 Peter 1:15–16

2. All through Scripture, the people of God spontaneously praise and glorify his name. Our response should be the same, to revere and respect, never to profane. In the Psalms, the "name" of God is used in this way 106 times.

   Psalm 5:11 Let all who take refuge in You be glad, let them ever sing for joy; and may You shelter them, that those who love Your name may exult in You. (NASB)
   Psalm 29:2 Ascribe to the LORD the glory due to His name; worship the LORD in holy array. (NASB)
   Psalm 9:2; 45:17

3. Proper respect is due the name of God, never the flippant words "Oh my God" or "By God."

Luke 11:2 He said to them, "When you pray, say: 'Father, hallowed be your name, your kingdom come.'" (NIV)

Jeremiah 10:6–7 No one is like you, Lᴏʀᴅ; you are great, and your name is mighty in power. Who should not fear you, King of the nations? This is your due. Among all the wise leaders of the nations and in all their kingdoms, there is no one like you. (NIV)

4. The name of Jesus must also be given proper respect, never used in vain or in contempt.

Philippians 2:9–11 Therefore God has highly exalted him and bestowed on him the name that is above every name, so that at the name of Jesus every knee should bow, in heaven and on earth and under the earth, and every tongue confess that Jesus Christ is Lord, to the glory of God the Father. (ESV)

Hebrews 10:28–29

5. God is not pleased with coarse and perverted speech, that which is foul or vulgar.

Psalm 1:1–2 Blessed is the man who walks not in the counsel of the wicked, nor stands in the way of sinners, nor sits in the seat of scoffers; but his delight is in the law of the Lᴏʀᴅ, and on his law he meditates day and night. (ESV)

Proverbs 10:31–32 The mouth of the righteous brings forth wisdom, but the perverse tongue will be cut off. The lips of the righteous know what is acceptable, but the mouth of the wicked, what is perverse. (ESV)

Ephesians 4:29–30 Let no unwholesome word proceed from your mouth, but only such a word as is good for edification according to the need of the moment, so that it will give grace to those who hear. Do not grieve the Holy Spirit of God, by whom you were sealed for the day of redemption. (NASB)

Psalm 17:3; 39:1; Proverbs 8:13; 12:13; James 3:8–11

6. God knows our thoughts. Profanity must be removed from our minds. Thinking the words is as bad as saying them.

> Psalm 139:1–4 O LORD, you have searched me and known me! You know when I sit down and when I rise up; you discern my thoughts from afar. You search out my path and my lying down and are acquainted with all my ways. Even before a word is on my tongue, behold, O LORD, you know it altogether. (ESV)
> Romans 12:2; 2 Corinthians 10:5; Hebrews 4:13

7. There is much more involved in taking God's name in vain than profanity. Study the third commandment further using appropriate resources.

Practical Steps

- A good way to curtail the habit of profanity is keeping accountable to another Christian. Having to admit one has been using profanity or vulgar speech is embarrassing.

- Do further study on the biblical concept of holiness. Look up the word in the *Evangelical Dictionary of Theology* (Walter Elwell, Baker).

- Write on a card and memorize Exodus 20:7 and Ephesians 4:29. Keep the card close as a reminder.

Resources

- "Avoiding Foul Language" in *Measure of a Young Man*. Gene and Kenton Getz. Regal.

- "The Third Commandment" in *The Ten Commandments*. G. Campbell Morgan. Baker.

- "What's in a Name?" in *Pathway to Freedom: How God's Laws Guide Our Lives*. Alistair Begg. Moody.

Prostitution

See also Confession, Forgiveness from God, Integrity, Lust, Sexual Purity, Temptation

1. **Going to a prostitute is dangerously sinful. Nothing is more clearly stated in God's Word.**

   Proverbs 5:3–5 For the lips of an immoral woman are as sweet as honey, and her mouth is smoother than oil. But in the end she is as bitter as poison, as dangerous as a double-edged sword. Her feet go down to death; her steps lead straight to the grave. (NLT)

   1 Corinthians 6:15 Do you not know that your bodies are members of Christ? Shall I then take away the members of Christ and make them members of a prostitute? May it never be! (NASB)

   Leviticus 19:29; Proverbs 23:27–28; Jeremiah 13:27

2. **As in Bible times, many in our world today flaunt and rationalize sin.**

   Isaiah 3:9 The look on their faces testifies against them; they parade their sin like Sodom; they do not hide it. Woe to them! They have brought disaster upon themselves. (NIV)

   Isaiah 5:20 Woe to those who call evil good and good evil, who put darkness for light and light for darkness, who put bitter for sweet and sweet for bitter! (ESV)

   Proverbs 17:15; Jeremiah 6:15

3. **Presumptuous or willful sins are extremely dangerous. Going to a prostitute is a premeditated, planned, heinous sin.**

   Psalm 19:13 Keep back your servant also from presumptuous sins; let them not have dominion over me! Then I shall be blameless, and innocent of great transgression. (ESV)

   Numbers 15:30–31 But those who brazenly violate the LORD's will, whether native-born Israelites or foreigners, have blasphemed the LORD, and they must be cut off from the community. Since they have treated the LORD's word with contempt and deliberately disobeyed his command, they must be completely cut off and suffer the punishment for their guilt. (The context is Sabbath breaking, but the principle applies to other areas of life.) (NLT)

4. **We need to be on the alert for unexpected attacks of temptation.**

   1 Peter 5:8 Be of sober spirit, be on the alert. Your adversary, the devil, prowls around like a roaring lion, seeking someone to devour. (NASB)
   2 Corinthians 11:3; Ephesians 6:10–18; James 4:7–8

5. **Repentance and confession must take place as first steps to freedom.**

   Proverbs 28:13 He who conceals his transgressions will not prosper, but he who confesses and forsakes them will find compassion. (NASB)
   Matthew 11:28–30 Come to Me, all who are weary and heavy-laden, and I will give you rest. Take My yoke upon you and learn from Me, for I am gentle and humble in heart, and you will find rest for your souls. For My yoke is easy and My burden is light. (NASB)
   Romans 6:23 For the wages of sin is death, but the free gift of God is eternal life in Christ Jesus our Lord. (NASB)
   Romans 6:6–8, 19

6. **The amazing thing is that God so completely forgives any sin.**

   1 John 1:9 If we confess our sins, He is faithful and righteous to forgive us our sins and to cleanse us from all unrighteousness. (NASB)
   Micah 7:18–19 Who is a God like you, pardoning iniquity and passing over transgression for the remnant of his inheritance? He does not retain his anger forever, because he delights in steadfast love. He will again have compassion on us; he will tread our iniquities under foot. You will cast all our sins into the depths of the sea. (ESV)
   Isaiah 38:17; 43:25

Biblical Narratives

- Judah and Tamar, Genesis 38
- Rahab, Joshua 2; Hebrews 11:31
- Men of Israel sinning, Jeremiah 5:7–8
- Parable of two sisters, Ezekiel 23
- Gomer, Hosea 1–3
- Grave warnings, Proverbs 5–7
- Prodigal son, Luke 15:13, 30

Practical Steps

- When traveling without your family, avoid being out in the city alone, especially at night. Stay away from sleazy neighborhoods. Make frequent calls home to wife and kids.
- Our movies and other entertainment media have trivialized the sin of prostitution. Make sure you are firm on what God's Word teaches about it. Always keep in mind the debilitating and heinous nature of this sin.
- Guard your mind; monitor your thinking according to Philippians 4:8.
- If you have committed this sin, evaluate what brought you to this point in your life. Take steps not to repeat it.
- Take responsibility if you have become infected with STDs. Medical care is necessary. Openness and honesty with your physician and spouse are essential so that proper testing can be done.

Resources

- *Free at Last*. Tony Evans. Moody.
- *Sexual Addiction* (booklet). David Powlison. New Growth.
- *Think before You Look: Avoiding the Consequences of Secret Temptation*. Daniel Henderson. Living Ink.

Purpose for Living

Goals and Dreams

See also Decision Making, Disappointment, Materialism, Self-Worth, Spiritual Gifts

Why has God placed us here? What should we want to accomplish in life? What are our goals, dreams, and ambitions? We must understand the biblical answer to *why* we are here on earth!

1. **We must first know God as the "root drive" and everything else as simply "file folders" beneath him. He is the great and sovereign Father-God creator.**

   Isaiah 44:6 Thus says the LORD, the King of Israel and his Redeemer, the LORD of hosts: "I am the first and I am the last, and there is no God besides Me." (NASB)

   Isaiah 42:8 I am the LORD, that is My name; I will not give My glory to another, nor My praise to graven images. (NASB)

   Isaiah 43:10–13 "You are my witnesses," declares the LORD, "and my servant whom I have chosen, so that you may know and believe me and understand that I am he. Before me no god was formed, nor will there be one after me. I, even I, am the LORD, and apart from me there is no savior. I have revealed and saved and proclaimed—I, and not some foreign god among you. You are my witnesses," declares the LORD, "that I am God. Yes, and from ancient days I am he. No one can deliver out of my hand. When I act, who can reverse it?" (NIV)

2. Our lives are therefore lived before an audience of One. Our purpose for living must be to bring glory to God as we serve him. All dreams and goals must reflect this.

Psalm 115:1 Not to us, O LORD, not to us, but to your name give glory, for the sake of your steadfast love and your faithfulness! (ESV)

1 Chronicles 16:24–25, 28–29 Declare his glory among the nations, his marvelous works among all the peoples! For great is the LORD, and greatly to be praised, and he is to be feared above all gods. . . . Ascribe to the LORD, O families of the peoples, ascribe to the LORD glory and strength! Ascribe to the LORD the glory due his name. (ESV)

Colossians 3:23 Whatever you do, work heartily, as for the Lord and not for men. (ESV)

Isaiah 43:7; Haggai 1:8; Ephesians 5:7–8; 6:5–7; 1 Corinthians 10:31; 2 Corinthians 5:9; Hebrews 13:15–16, 20–21; 1 Peter 4:10–11

3. God is honored when we purpose to walk closely with him.

Micah 6:8 He has told you, O man, what is good; and what does the LORD require of you but to do justice, to love kindness, and to walk humbly with your God? (NASB)

Colossians 1:9–10 For this reason also, since the day we heard of it, we have not ceased to pray for you and to ask that you may be filled with the knowledge of His will in all spiritual wisdom and understanding, so that you will walk in a manner worthy of the Lord, to please Him in all respects, bearing fruit in every good work and increasing in the knowledge of God. (NASB)

John 15:4–5; Ephesians 5:10

4. We bring glory to God when we are conformed to the image of his Son.

Romans 8:29 For those whom he foreknew he also predestined to be conformed to the image of his Son, in order that he might be the firstborn among many brothers. (ESV)

Hebrews 13:20–21 Now may the God of peace who brought again from the dead our Lord Jesus, the great shepherd of the sheep, by the blood of the eternal covenant, equip you with everything good that you may do his will, working in us that which is pleasing in his sight, through Jesus Christ, to whom be glory forever and ever. Amen. (ESV)

5. **God is honored when we serve others.**

Philippians 2:3–4 Don't be selfish; don't try to impress others. Be humble, thinking of others as better than yourselves. Don't look out only for your own interests, but take an interest in others, too. (NLT)

Romans 12:10, 13 Be devoted to one another in brotherly love; give preference to one another in honor; . . . contributing to the needs of the saints, practicing hospitality. (NASB)

Galatians 5:13–14

6. **God is honored when we take him into account as we dream and plan for the future.**

James 4:13–15 Look here, you who say, "Today or tomorrow we are going to a certain town and will stay there a year. We will do business there and make a profit." How do you know what your life will be like tomorrow? Your life is like the morning fog—it's here a little while, then it's gone. What you ought to say is, "If the Lord wants us to, we will live and do this or that." (NLT)

Proverbs 27:1

7. **Whatever circumstances in life we endure, if disappointments come, it is good to know that God will be glorified through them.**

2 Corinthians 12:9–10 But he said to me, "My grace is sufficient for you, for my power is made perfect in weakness." Therefore I will boast all the more gladly of my weaknesses, so that the power of Christ may rest upon me. For the sake of Christ, then, I am content with weaknesses, insults, hardships, persecutions, and calamities. For when I am weak, then I am strong. (ESV)

Ephesians 3:20–21 Now to him who is able to do far more abundantly than all that we ask or think, according to the power at work within us, to him be glory in the church and in Christ Jesus throughout all generations, forever and ever. Amen. (ESV)

Romans 11:36; 16:27; Philippians 4:19–20; 1 Timothy 1:17; 2 Timothy 4:18; Jude 1:24–25

Biblical Narratives

- David's celebration for God's glory, 1 Chronicles 16
- Paul, who always sought God's glory, Philippians 1:21, Galatians 2:20
- Jude's praise, Jude 1:24–25

Practical Steps

- Pray each morning, "Lord, I give this day back to you!" Get started with your focus on him.
- Look back as you end your day. Evaluate, looking for areas that need improvement. What steps should you take to be more honoring to God—in word, attitude, thinking, actions?
- Always include God in the equation for your dreams and goals. What does he want? What will bring him glory?

Resources

- *The Cross Centered Life*. C. J. Mahaney. Multnomah.
- "Cry for a Kingdom Man" in *Kingdom Man: Every Man's Destiny, Every Woman's Dream*. Tony Evans. Focus on the Family.
- *Gospel Treason: Betraying the Gospel with Hidden Idols*. Brad Bigney. P & R.
- *Holy Ambition: Turning God-Shaped Dreams into Reality*. Chip Ingram. Moody.
- *A Quest for More: Living for Something Bigger than You*. Paul Tripp. New Growth.
- *Who Do You Think You Are? Finding Your True Identity in Christ*. Mark Driscoll. Thomas Nelson.

Reputation

See also Decision Making, Entertainment, Flirting, Integrity, Leadership

1. Note the desirability and value of a good name.

> Proverbs 22:1 A good name is to be chosen rather than great riches, and favor is better than silver or gold. (ESV)
> Ecclesiastes 7:1 A good reputation is more valuable than costly perfume. (NLT)
> Proverbs 20:11

2. People who obey God and accomplish good things for others establish a valuable legacy.

> Psalm 112:6 Such people will not be overcome by evil. Those who are righteous will be long remembered. (NLT) (For "such people," see context.)
> Proverbs 10:7

3. A good reputation is the essential and overriding qualification for men who can be trusted for key church leadership. "Above reproach" means no one can lay a charge of wrongdoing against this person. Note that this is the first quality mentioned in the lists in 1 Timothy and Titus.

> 1 Timothy 3:1–2 The saying is trustworthy: If anyone aspires to the office of overseer, he desires a noble task. Therefore an overseer must be above reproach, the husband of one wife, sober-minded, self-controlled, respectable, hospitable, able to teach. (ESV)
> Titus 1:5–9

4. A good reputation is critical to engage our culture as valid witnesses for Christ.

> **Philippians 2:14–15** Do all things without grumbling or disputing, that you may be blameless and innocent, children of God without blemish in the midst of a crooked and twisted generation, among whom you shine as lights in the world. (ESV)

> **Titus 2:6–8** Similarly, encourage the young men to be self-controlled. In everything set them an example by doing what is good. In your teaching show integrity, seriousness and soundness of speech that cannot be condemned, so that those who oppose you may be ashamed because they have nothing bad to say about us. (NIV)

> **1 Thessalonians 4:11–12; 1 Peter 2:12, 15**

Biblical Narratives

- Enoch, known for walking with God, Genesis 5:21–24
- Mordecai, known as an able administrator, Esther 9:4 (NIV)
- Solomon wanted his name to endure, Psalm 72:17 (It did, with both a good and bad reputation.)
- Men, chosen to serve, were above reproach, Acts 6:2–3
- John Mark, a bad reputation, but improved, Acts 15:36–40; 2 Timothy 4:11
- Timothy, well spoken of, Acts 16:2
- Paul, careful for his reputation in money matters, 2 Corinthians 8:16–22

Practical Steps

- If you've had a bad reputation from the past, you will need to work very hard to reestablish yourself as above reproach. Make sure you are making careful, godly decisions every day.
- Associations with people, places you frequent, and entertainment activities must all be chosen with care. If necessary, separate

yourself from those that are questionable. If you are married and have children, go the family-oriented route in your choices.

- If you are in a city and away from family, take decisive steps to avoid questionable activities that could damage a reputation.
- Bad judgment in business and financial dealings must be avoided. Keep debt to a minimum; have a balanced budget, not spending more than you make. Always pay your taxes and pay on time.
- Ask yourself often throughout the day, *Am I bringing glory to God?*

Resources

- "Building a Good Reputation" in *The Measure of a Man*. Gene Getz. Regal.
- *Disciplines of a Godly Man*. Kent Hughes. Crossway.
- *Good to Great in God's Eyes: 10 Practices Great Christians Have in Common*. Chip Ingram. Baker.

Self-Control/Discipline

See also Anger, Materialism, Money, Peer Pressure, Purpose for Living, Sexual Purity, Temptation

Self-control and discipline are two sides of the same coin. The former includes the qualities of restraint, nonimpulsive behavior, thinking through one's options before acting, and deferred gratification. Discipline includes careful planning, staying the course, a determination to succeed, doing what it takes to get the job done.

1. **Lack of self-control leads to sinful attitudes and behaviors. Broken lives result.**

   Proverbs 25:28 A man without self-control is like a city broken into and left without walls. (ESV)

   2 Timothy 3:1–3 But understand this, that in the last days there will come times of difficulty. For people will be lovers of self, . . . unappeasable, slanderous, without self-control, brutal, not loving good. (ESV)

   Galatians 5:19–21

2. **Self-control in the use of the tongue is essential.**

   Proverbs 17:27 Whoever restrains his words has knowledge, and he who has a cool spirit is a man of understanding. (ESV)

   Proverbs 10:19

3. **Knowing and obeying God's Word are critical to maintaining self-control.**

   Psalm 119:101–2 I have restrained my feet from every evil way, that I may keep Your word. I have not turned aside from Your ordinances, for You Yourself have taught me. (NASB)

Psalm 119:9, 11 How can a young man keep his way pure? By keeping it according to Your word. . . . Your word I have treasured in my heart, that I may not sin against You. (NASB)
Proverbs 6:23; 2 Timothy 3:16–17

4. We must depend on God's Spirit and accept his control in our lives.

Galatians 5:16 But I say, walk by [by means of, depend on] the Spirit, and you will not gratify the desires of the flesh. (ESV)
Ephesians 5:18 (The issue is: what controls us, the things of this world or God?)

5. Possessing self-control is included in lists of positive Christian qualities.

Galatians 5:22–24 But the fruit of the Spirit is love, joy, peace, patience, kindness, goodness, faithfulness, gentleness, self-control; against such things there is no law. And those who belong to Christ Jesus have crucified the flesh with its passions and desires. (ESV)
1 Timothy 4:7–8; 2 Peter 1:5–8

6. The lifestyle of mature, godly men includes self-control.

Titus 2:2, 6, 11–12 Older men are to be sober-minded, dignified, self-controlled, sound in faith, in love, and in steadfastness. . . . Likewise, urge the younger men to be self-controlled. . . . For the grace of God has appeared, bringing salvation for all people, training us to renounce ungodliness and worldly passions, and to live self-controlled, upright, and godly lives in the present age. (ESV)
1 Timothy 3:2; 1 Peter 1:13–16

7. The apostle Paul was a man who appreciated the discipline necessary for athletic contests and for the Christian life!

1 Corinthians 9:24–25 Surely you know that many runners take part in a race, but only one of them wins the prize. Run, then, in such a way as to win the prize. Every athlete in training submits

to strict discipline, in order to be crowned with a wreath that will not last; but we do it for one that will last forever. (GNT)

Biblical Narratives

- King Ahaz, a poor example to Israel, 2 Chronicles 28:19
- Paul, giving his testimony to Felix, Acts 24:24–25

Practical Steps

- Set realistic goals for what you want to accomplish, with reasonable, attainable steps for completion.
- Make lists for each day and check off items completed. This will give a sense of progress toward the goal.
- If lack of self-control in areas of ethics or morality is the problem, seek accountability with your wife or with mature men in your church. Meet with them often to confess, pray, and discuss progress.

Resources

- "Becoming a Disciplined Man" in *The Measure of a Man*. Gene Getz. Regal.
- "Essential Qualities of Leadership" in *Spiritual Leadership*. J. Oswald Sanders. Moody.
- "Lack of Self-Control" in *Respectable Sins*. Jerry Bridges. NavPress.
- *Motives: Why Do I Do the Things I Do?* (booklet). Ed Welch. P & R.

Selfishness/Subjectivity

See also Compassion, Jealousy, Pride, Purpose for Living

The concept of selfishness is not difficult to grasp—one's own self-centered interests come first. Subjectivity is seeing everything from your point of view—other points of view being not that important. The two easily fit together, and, simply stated, God is not pleased with either.

1. A self-seeking attitude is wrong.

James 3:14–16 But if you harbor bitter envy and selfish ambition in your hearts, do not boast about it or deny the truth. Such "wisdom" does not come down from heaven but is earthly, unspiritual, demonic. For where you have envy and selfish ambition, there you find disorder and every evil practice. (NIV)
Romans 2:8

2. God expects us to put him first.

Luke 9:23–24 And he said to them all, "If you want to come with me, you must forget yourself, take up your cross every day, and follow me. For if you want to save your own life, you will lose it, but if you lose your life for my sake, you will save it." (GNT)
Matthew 6:33; 22:37–38

3. God expects us to put others ahead of ourselves.

Philippians 2:3–4 Don't be selfish; don't try to impress others. Be humble, thinking of others as better than yourselves. Don't look out only for your own interests, but take an interest in others, too. (NLT)
Romans 12:9–13; 15:1–3; 1 Corinthians 10:24; 13:4–6

257

Biblical Narratives

Negative

- Lot chose the best land for himself, Genesis 13
- Jacob stole the birthright, Genesis 27
- Shepherds of Israel fed themselves, not the flock, Ezekiel 34:1–10
- James and John wanted to rule in the coming kingdom, Mark 10:35–45

Positive

- Jonathan, selfless for David, 1 Samuel 19–20
- Paul, willing to be lost if kinsmen would come to Christ, Romans 9:1–3
- Jesus gave up much to come to earth, Philippians 2:5–8
- Dorcas served others, Acts 9:36

Practical Steps

- Are there warning signs in your life of too much focus on self? Ask yourself: *Am I easily angered in conversation, jealous, suspicious of the motives of others, unaccepting of criticism? Do I carry grudges?* Affirmative answers would point to a need to concentrate more on others.
- Be on the alert for cultural influences that are constantly pushing you toward self-centeredness and subjectivity. Commit to resisting these influences.
- Consider carefully these contrasting aspects of subjectivity and objectivity. Use them to evaluate your progress toward being more objective.

Subjectivity	Objectivity
based on feelings	based on fact
my point of view	looking at the other's point of view
illogical	logical
emotional	rational
self-absorbed	concerned for others

Resources

- *The Freedom of Self-Forgetfulness*. Timothy Keller. 10Publishing.
- *Selfishness* (booklet). Lou Priolo. P & R.
- "Selfishness" in *Respectable Sins*. Jerry Bridges. NavPress.
- *Feelings and Faith*. Brian Borgman. Crossway.
- *When People Are Big and God Is Small*. Ed Welch. P & R.

Self-Worth

See also Anxiety, Pride, Purpose for Living, Selfishness

1. The foundation for all self-worth is the awareness that we are God's own creation, made in his own image.

> **Genesis 1:27** God created man in His own image, in the image of God He created him; male and female He created them. (NASB)
>
> **Genesis 2:7** Then the LORD God formed man of dust from the ground, and breathed into his nostrils the breath of life; and man became a living being. (NASB)
>
> **Genesis 2:21–22; Luke 12:7; Psalm 139:13–14**

2. Knowing that God valued us enough to send his own Son to die for us makes life truly meaningful.

> **John 3:16** For God so loved the world, that he gave his only Son, that whoever believes in him should not perish but have eternal life. (ESV)
>
> **Jeremiah 31:3** The LORD appeared to him from afar, saying, "I have loved you with an everlasting love; therefore I have drawn you with lovingkindness." (NASB)
>
> **Ephesians 1:6; 2:4–7; 1 Peter 1:18–20; 1 John 4:10**

3. We must find significance in our relationship to God, not in ourselves or in others.

> **Micah 6:8** He has told you, O man, what is good; and what does the LORD require of you but to do justice, and to love kindness, and to walk humbly with your God? (ESV)
>
> **1 Peter 2:9** But you are a chosen people, a royal priesthood, a holy nation, God's special possession, that you may declare the

praises of him who called you out of darkness into his wonderful light. (NIV)

John 15:15–16; 2 Corinthians 5:17–18; Ephesians 2:10

4. **Knowing God personally makes life truly meaningful, not physical qualities, intellect, or achievements.**

    Jeremiah 9:23–24 Thus says the LORD: "Let not the wise man boast in his wisdom, let not the mighty man boast in his might, let not the rich man boast in his riches, but let him who boasts boast in this, that he understands and knows me, that I am the LORD who practices steadfast love, justice, and righteousness in the earth. For in these things I delight, declares the LORD." (ESV)

    Ephesians 1:18 I pray that the eyes of your heart may be enlightened in order that you may know the hope to which he has called you, the riches of his glorious inheritance in his holy people. (NIV)

    Ephesians 3:17–20; Philippians 3:8–10

5. **Reliance on self can be a dangerous trap.**

    Romans 12:3 For through the grace given to me I say to everyone among you not to think more highly of himself than he ought to think; but to think so as to have sound judgment, as God has allotted to each a measure of faith. (NASB)

    2 Corinthians 1:8–9

Biblical Narratives

- Elijah, deeply discouraged, 1 Kings 19:4, 10
- Job, feeling worthless, Job 3:11–13; 9:21
- David's struggles, Psalm 22:6; 31:11

Practical Steps

- Work on being a man of sacrificial living, thinking of the needs of others and doing something about those needs. When you are giving out, it becomes less about you and more about others.

- Keep a daily journal of meaningful expressions of service and kindness you have accomplished for others.
- Memorize and meditate on Jeremiah 9:23–24. Consider carefully why intellect, power, and riches don't cut it for true meaning in life.

Resources

- *Changed into His Image*. Jim Berg. BJU.
- *Christ Esteem: Where the Search for Self-Esteem Ends*. Don Matzat. Harvest House.
- "Finding the Real You" in *Lost in the Middle*. Paul Tripp. Shepherd.
- *Free at Last*. Tony Evans. Moody.
- "When You Feel Like a Nobody Going Nowhere" in *Finding God When You Need Him the Most*. Chip Ingram. Baker.
- *Who Do You Think You Are? Finding Your True Identity in Christ*. Mark Driscoll. Thomas Nelson.

Sex Life

See also Boundaries, Marriage, Sexual Purity, Temptation

In a sex-obsessed society it is easy to forget that male and female, marriage and sex, are a part of God's plan, his creation. Our moral slide as a nation is moving more quickly than ever away from the absolutes of biblical morality. Satan's counterfeits are everywhere. Christian men, more than ever, need a solid commitment to a biblical sexuality as designed by God.

1. **Sexual relations must be between a married couple only, a man and a woman.**

   Proverbs 5:15–18 Drink water from your own cistern, running water from your own well. Should your springs overflow in the streets, your streams of water in the public squares? Let them be yours alone, never to be shared with strangers. May your fountain be blessed, and may you rejoice in the wife of your youth. (NIV)

   1 Corinthians 7:2 But since sexual immorality is occurring, each man should have sexual relations with his own wife, and each woman with her own husband. (NIV)

   Hebrews 13:4

2. **Sexual intimacy in marriage is God's design. Creation as male and female was his plan.**

   Genesis 1:27 So God created man in his own image, in the image of God he created him; male and female he created them. (ESV)

   Genesis 2:24–25

263

3. There are three biblical reasons for sexual intimacy.

PROCREATION (BABIES)

Genesis 9:1, 7 And God blessed Noah and his sons and said to them, "Be fruitful and multiply and fill the earth. . . . And you, be fruitful and multiply, increase greatly on the earth and multiply in it." (ESV)

Psalm 127:3 Behold, children are a heritage from the LORD, the fruit of the womb a reward. (ESV)

RECREATION (ENJOYMENT)

Proverbs 5:18–19 Let your fountain be blessed, and rejoice in the wife of your youth, a lovely deer, a graceful doe. Let her breasts fill you at all times with delight; be intoxicated always in her love. (ESV)

PURITY (TO AVOID IMMORALITY)

1 Corinthians 7:2 But because of the temptation to sexual immorality, each man should have his own wife and each woman her own husband. (ESV)

4. **The husband is responsible to satisfy his wife sexually, and the wife to satisfy her husband.**

1 Corinthians 7:3–4 The husband should give to his wife her conjugal rights, and likewise the wife to her husband. For the wife does not have authority over her own body, but the husband does. Likewise the husband does not have authority over his own body, but the wife does. (ESV)

5. **Frequent sex is crucial. Otherwise temptation will be a problem.**

1 Corinthians 7:5 Do not deprive one another, except perhaps by agreement for a limited time, that you may devote yourselves to prayer; but then come together again, so that Satan may not tempt you because of your lack of self-control. (ESV)

Proverbs 5:19 (Note "all times" and "always.")

6. Sexual activity is seen as beautiful and to be delighted in by the couple.

Song of Solomon 7:1–8

7. While intimacy should be a constant in the marriage, there will be times where illness or personal crisis makes having sex difficult. Sex is never to be demanded.

1 Corinthians 13:4–5 Love is patient and kind; love does not envy or boast; it is not arrogant or rude. It does not insist on its own way. (ESV)
Philippians 2:3–4

Biblical Narratives

- Isaac and Rebekah, Genesis 26:8
- Song of Solomon

Practical Steps

- Be thankful for God's unique creation of humans: 1. Most mammals mate only when the female is in heat (ovulating); humans mate quite often. 2. Humans are the only mammals that mate face-to-face! God's plan was intimacy.
- Read Song of Solomon out loud in a modern translation—each spouse reading a part. What is God's plan for intimacy?
- Each spouse needs to communicate freely what is pleasing to them. Enjoy what is mutually pleasurable.
- Since men are extremely sensitive to the visual image of the female body, communicate clearly to your wife your needs in this area. See Song of Solomon 7:6–8.
- Plan times away from home as a couple, even if it is a weekend retreat.
- If you experience physical problems or your wife experiences pain when having sex, see your physician.

- Sexual intimacy is a barometer of the health of the marriage. Be sure to practice good communication, forgiveness, resolving of conflicts, and agreeing on issues of handling children.

- Understand that intimacy is God's design and he gives no timetable for it ending. Sexual activity should continue all of one's married life.

Resources

- *A Biblical Guide to Love, Sex, and Marriage.* Derek and Rosemary Thomas. Evangelical Press.

- *His Needs, Her Needs: Building an Affair-Proof Marriage.* Willard Harley. Revell.

- *Love, Sex, and Lasting Relationships.* Chip Ingram. Baker.

- "Sexuality" in *Secrets Men Keep.* Steve Arterburn. Thomas Nelson.

- *Song of Solomon: God's Best for Love, Marriage, Sex, and Romance.* (4-DVD series). Tommy Nelson.

Sexual Purity

See also Adultery, Forgiveness from God, Integrity, Peer Pressure, Temptation

The title for one of the resources listed below, *Every Man's Battle*, says it all. No matter how young or how old the man, the battle for sexual purity never goes away!

1. **The problem is real; the temptation is strong—a certainty in this present life.**

   1 Corinthians 10:13 No temptation has overtaken you except such as is common to man. (NKJV)
   Romans 7:18–20; Galatians 5:19–21; Ephesians 4:17–19; James 1:14–15

2. **God requires purity of heart, mind, actions.**

   1 Thessalonians 4:3 God wants you to be holy and completely free from sexual immorality. (GNT) (See verses 2–10.)
   Romans 13:14 Take up the weapons of the Lord Jesus Christ, and stop paying attention to your sinful nature and satisfying its desires. (GNT)

3. **Our bodies belong to God and must be used for his honor.**

   1 Corinthians 6:19–20 Don't you realize that your body is the temple of the Holy Spirit, who lives in you and was given to you by God? You do not belong to yourself, for God bought you with a high price. So you must honor God with your body. (NLT)
   1 Peter 1:14–16 So you must live as God's obedient children. Don't slip back into your old ways of living to satisfy your own desires. You didn't know any better then. But now you must be

holy in everything you do, just as God who chose you is holy. For the Scriptures say, "You must be holy because I am holy." (NLT)

4. Do not even get close to sexual impurity.

Ephesians 5:3 But among you there must not be even a hint of sexual immorality, or of any kind of impurity. (NIV)

Proverbs 6:27 Can a man scoop fire into his lap without his clothes being burned? (NIV)

5. Don't let others pressure you into doing something impure.

Isaiah 51:7 Listen to me, you who know right from wrong, you who cherish my law in your hearts. Do not be afraid of people's scorn, nor fear their insults. (NLT)

Proverbs 1:10 My child, if sinners entice you, turn your back on them! (NLT)

James 4:17

6. Guard purity of the eyes as well as the body.

Job 31:1 I made a covenant with my eyes not to look lustfully at a young woman. (NIV)

Matthew 5:28 I tell you that anyone who looks at a woman lustfully has already committed adultery with her in his heart. (NIV)

Psalm 101:3–4

7. Make good choices to flee from impurity and pursue what is right.

1 Corinthians 6:18 Flee from sexual immorality. Every other sin a person commits is outside the body, but the sexually immoral person sins against his own body. (ESV)

Romans 6:13 Do not offer any part of yourself to sin as an instrument of wickedness, but rather offer yourselves to God as those who have been brought from death to life; and offer every part of yourself to him as an instrument of righteousness. (NIV)

Colossians 3:5–6; 2 Timothy 2:22; 1 Peter 2:11

8. Knowing and applying God's Word makes all the difference.

Psalm 119:9 How can a young person stay on the path of purity? By living according to your word. (NIV)

Deuteronomy 32:46–47 He said to them, "Take to heart all the words I have solemnly declared to you this day, so that you may command your children to obey carefully all the words of this law. They are not just idle words for you—they are your life." (NIV)

Joshua 1:8; James 1:21; 1 Peter 2:1–2

9. Determine to be obedient with God's help.

Isaiah 50:7 Because the Sovereign LORD helps me, I will not be disgraced. Therefore, I have set my face like a stone, determined to do his will. And I know that I will not be put to shame. (NLT)

1 Corinthians 10:13 The temptations in your life are no different from what others experience. And God is faithful. He will not allow the temptation to be more than you can stand. When you are tempted, he will show you a way out so that you can endure. (NLT)

Ephesians 6:10–13; Hebrews 4:15–16

10. As with other sins, God forgives completely.

Isaiah 38:17 Yes, this anguish was good for me, for you have rescued me from death and forgiven all my sins. (NLT)

Isaiah 44:22 I have swept away your sins like a cloud. I have scattered your offenses like the morning mist. Oh, return to me, for I have paid the price to set you free. (NLT)

Psalm 86:5; 130:3–4; Isaiah 43:25; Lamentations 3:22; Micah 7:18–19; Romans 8:1–2; Colossians 1:13–14

Biblical Narrative

• Joseph, standing firm, Genesis 39

Practical Steps

- Seek out a strong brother in Christ for strict accountability. If the Internet is a problem, ask him to hold you accountable in this area as well.

- If you are single and in a relationship, think through and write out your guidelines for staying pure. Discuss them with the person you are dating.

- Avoid being alone with your date for any length of time. Seek out activities where others are present.

- If you are married, your wife is your best accountability. If you fail in this area, think how hurt she would be.

- Monitor carefully your known triggers for sexual temptation.

- Be alert for catalogs that are selling their product by using the female body. Either stop them from coming or throw them away without looking.

- Make a strong commitment to obey the scriptural commands regarding the Holy Spirit—not to grieve, to be controlled by, to depend on, and not to quench his conviction in your life. (Eph. 4:30; 5:18; Gal. 5:16; 1 Thess. 5:19)

- If you travel alone, ask that the cable TV in your hotel room be turned off.

Resources

- "A Powerful Response to Temptation" in *The Hand of God: Finding His Care in All Circumstances*. Alistair Begg. Moody.

- *Hope and Help for Sexual Temptation*. Mark Shaw. Focus.

- *Every Man's Battle: Winning the War on Sexual Temptation One Victory at a Time* (workbook available). Stephen Arterburn. WaterBrook.

- *Living Together: A Guide to Counseling Unmarried Couples*. Jeff VanGoethem. Kregel.

- "Maintaining Moral Purity" in *Measure of a Man*. Gene Getz. Regal.

- *Think before You Look*. Daniel Henderson. Living Ink.

Single Father

See also Anxiety, Decision Making, Loneliness, Fathering

1. Single parenting can be a lonely responsibility, but God's loving presence is guaranteed.

   Deuteronomy 31:8 It is the LORD who goes before you. He will be with you; he will not leave you or forsake you. Do not fear or be dismayed. (ESV)

   Isaiah 43:1–2 But now thus says the LORD, he who created you, O Jacob, he who formed you, O Israel: "Fear not, for I have redeemed you; I have called you by name, you are mine. When you pass through the waters, I will be with you; and through the rivers, they shall not overwhelm you; when you walk through fire you shall not be burned, and the flame shall not consume you." (ESV)

   Joshua 1:6–9; Hebrews 13:5–6

2. God is in control of every situation and cares for you because you are his child.

   Jeremiah 29:11–12 "For I know the plans I have for you," says the LORD. "They are plans for good and not for disaster, to give you a future and a hope. In those days when you pray, I will listen." (NLT)

   Romans 8:28 And we know that God causes everything to work together for the good of those who love God and are called according to his purpose for them. (NLT)

3. If your present situation is the result of your sin, make sure you have repented and confessed, seeking God's restoration. (See the topic Forgiveness from God.)

1 John 1:9 If we confess our sins, he is faithful and just to forgive us our sins and to cleanse us from all unrighteousness. (ESV)
Psalm 51:1–2

4. If your present situation is the result of someone else's sin, make sure you have forgiven that person. (See the topic Forgiving Others.)

Ephesians 4:31–32 Let all bitterness and wrath and anger and clamor and slander be put away from you, along with all malice. Be kind to one another, tenderhearted, forgiving one another, as God in Christ forgave you. (ESV)
Colossians 3:12–14

5. Whatever the reason for being a single parent, you and your child are special in the eyes of God.

Jeremiah 31:3 The LORD has appeared of old to me, saying: "Yes, I have loved you with an everlasting love; therefore with lovingkindness I have drawn you." (NKJV)
Psalm 127:3 Behold, children are a heritage from the LORD, the fruit of the womb is a reward. (NKJV)
Luke 18:15–16

6. Since it is God's plan for believers to assist other believers in vital needs, be willing to seek out others for assistance.

1 Corinthians 12:25–26 This makes for harmony among the members, so that all the members care for each other. If one part suffers, all the parts suffer with it, and if one part is honored, all the parts are glad. (NLT)
1 Thessalonians 5:11 Therefore encourage one another and build one another up, just as you are doing. (ESV)
Romans 12:9–13; Galatians 6:2

7. **God's peace is possible in every situation.**

> 2 Thessalonians 3:16 Now may the Lord of peace Himself continually grant you peace in every circumstance. The Lord be with you all! (NASB)
> John 14:27; Galatians 5:22–23; Philippians 4:6–7

Biblical Narratives

- Single parent Hagar blessed by God, Genesis 21:15–20
- Woman and son with Elijah, 1 Kings 17

Practical Steps

- Seek out others to provide your children with a female, motherly influence. This will reduce the pressure to fill both roles.
- If they are available, keep in close contact with godly grandparents from both sides. They can be a great source of support and assistance.
- To avoid quick decision making in future relationships, make sure you understand any feelings of rejection, replacement, loneliness, insecurity, or abandonment and have handled them biblically.
- Invest faithfully and consistently in your children. Spend time listening and learning from them. They need a father strongly committed to them.

Resources

- *Children and Divorce: Helping When Life Interrupts* (booklet). Amy Baker. New Growth.
- *How Do I Stop Losing It with My Kids: Getting to the Heart of Your Discipline Problems* (booklet). William Smith. New Growth.
- "Rest in God's Sovereignty" in *Broken-Down House*. Paul Tripp. Shepherd.
- *Single Parenting That Works*. Kevin Leman. Tyndale.
- *Single Parents: Daily Grace for the Hardest Job* (booklet). Robert D. Jones. New Growth.

Singleness

See also Anxiety, Contentment, Loneliness, Sexual Purity, Trust

For most men, remaining single and celibate throughout their lives would be a difficult calling. If such were to be God's will for you, he who called you is faithful—always, guaranteed.

1. **Paul presents both the single life or being married as viable options.**

    1 Corinthians 7:1, 8–9 Now for the matters you wrote about: "It is good for a man not to have sexual relations with a woman." . . . Now to the unmarried and the widows I say: It is good for them to stay unmarried, as I do. But if they cannot control themselves, they should marry, for it is better to marry than to burn with passion. (NIV)

2. **Singleness should be viewed as the gift of living undivided for the Lord.**

    1 Corinthians 7:25–35

3. **God always has our best interests at heart.**

    Jeremiah 29:11 "For I know the plans that I have for you," declares the LORD, "plans for welfare and not for calamity to give you a future and a hope." (NASB)

    Isaiah 41:9–10 I have called you back from the ends of the earth, saying, "You are my servant." For I have chosen you and will not throw you away. Don't be afraid, for I am with you. Don't be discouraged, for I am your God. I will strengthen you and help you. I will hold you up with my victorious right hand. (NLT)

4. God's love, kindness, and commitment to his children never change.

Deuteronomy 31:8 The LORD is the one who goes ahead of you; He will be with you. He will not fail you or forsake you. Do not fear or be dismayed. (NASB)

Romans 8:38–39 For I am convinced that neither death, nor life, nor angels, nor principalities, nor things present, nor things to come, nor powers, nor height, nor depth, nor any other created thing, will be able to separate us from the love of God, which is in Christ Jesus our Lord. (NASB)

Isaiah 40:28–31; Jeremiah 31:3; Haggai 2:4

5. We can enjoy contentment with ourselves and with our present state.

Philippians 4:12–13 I know how to be brought low, and I know how to abound. In any and every circumstance, I have learned the secret of facing plenty and hunger, abundance and need. I can do all things through him who strengthens me. (ESV)

Psalm 139:14–15

6. Contentment is found in a close walk with God. We must be convinced that he will meet all our needs, including our needs for intimacy.

Psalm 17:15 As for me, I shall behold Your face in righteousness; I will be satisfied with Your likeness when I awake. (NASB)

Psalm 62:5–8 My soul, wait in silence for God only, for my hope is from Him. He only is my rock and my salvation, my stronghold; I shall not be shaken. On God my salvation and my glory rest; the rock of my strength, my refuge is in God. Trust in Him at all times, O people; pour out your heart before Him; God is a refuge for us. (NASB)

Psalm 4:8; 46:10–11; 84:10–11; 103:2–5; 2 Corinthians 12:9; Hebrews 10:24–25

Biblical Narratives

- Paul, 1 Corinthians 7
- Philip's daughters, Acts 21:8–9

Practical Steps

- If you are single, list opportunities you have for serving. Thank God for them and commit to them without distraction.
- Evaluate your leadership potential and involvement in your local church and community—Bible studies, mission trips, caregiving. Are you using your singleness to its fullest potential?
- Keep a list of current blessings; add to it often.

Resources

- *Being Single and Satisfied* (booklet). Tony Evans. Moody.
- *Believing God for His Best: How to Marry Contentment and Singleness.* William Thrasher. Moody.
- *They Were Single Too: 8 Biblical Role Models.* David Hoffeditz. Kregel.
- "Undivided Devotion to the Lord: The Divine Gift of Singleness" in *God, Marriage and Family* (a scholarly volume). Andreas Kostenberger. Crossway.
- *We're Just Friends and Other Dating Lies.* Chuck Milian. New Growth Press.

Sleep Struggles

See also Anxiety, Fear, Health, Trust

Medical studies are constantly showing that enough sleep and quality sleep are essential to every aspect of our lives—physical, spiritual, mental, emotional, social.

1. **How we conduct ourselves during the day will help us sleep better at night. Wise and godly choices are critical.**

   Proverbs 3:23–24 Then you will walk in your way securely and your foot will not stumble. When you lie down, you will not be afraid; when you lie down, your sleep will be sweet. (NASB) (The context is wisdom.)

   Proverbs 19:23 The fear of the LORD leads to life, so that one may sleep satisfied, untouched by evil. (NASB)

   Proverbs 1:33; 6:20–22

2. **Knowing that God who made the night guards the night helps us sleep peacefully.**

   Psalm 74:16 The day is Yours, the night also is Yours; You have prepared the light and the sun. (NKJV)

   Psalm 4:8 I will both lie down in peace, and sleep; for You alone, O LORD, make me dwell in safety. (NKJV)

   Psalm 91:4–5; 121:3–8; Isaiah 41:10, 13

3. **Prayer, coupled with carefully monitored thinking, will assist getting to sleep.**

   Philippians 4:6–8 Don't worry about anything; instead, pray about everything. . . . Then you will experience God's peace, which exceeds anything we can understand. His peace will guard your hearts and minds as you live in Christ Jesus. . . . Fix your thoughts on what is true, and honorable, and right, and pure, and lovely, and admirable. Think about things that are excellent and worthy of praise. (NLT)

Psalm 88:1–3 O LORD, God of my salvation, I cry out to you by day. I come to you at night. Now hear my prayer; listen to my cry. For my life is full of troubles. (NLT)

4. **Trusting in God's sovereignty for all the details of our lives is a huge factor for better sleeping.**

Psalm 3:3–5 But you, O LORD, are a shield for me, my glory and the One who lifts up my head. I cried to the LORD with my voice, and He heard me from His holy hill. I lay down and slept; I awoke, for the LORD sustained me. (NKJV)

Psalm 74:16; 90:1–2; 127:1–2; Matthew 6:33–34

5. **God can use our times of sleeplessness for guidance and instruction.**

Psalm 16:7 I will bless the LORD who has given me counsel; my heart also instructs me in the night seasons. (NKJV)

Isaiah 26:9 With my soul I have desired You in the night, yes, by my spirit within me I will seek You early; for when Your judgments are in the earth, the inhabitants of the world will learn righteousness. (NKJV)

Psalm 17:1–3; 1 Samuel 3:1–10

6. **When sleep will not come, it helps to spend time praying, giving thanks, reflecting on Scripture, and singing.**

Psalm 42:8 The LORD will command His lovingkindness in the daytime; and His song will be with me in the night, a prayer to the God of my life. (NASB)

Psalm 63:6–8 When I remember You on my bed, I meditate on You in the night watches, for You have been my help, and in the shadow of Your wings I sing for joy. My soul clings to You; Your right hand upholds me. (NASB)

Psalm 1:2; 77:6; 91:1–2; 119:148; 149:5

7. When sleep does not come because of indecision, worry, or stress, we must trust in the Holy Spirit's intercession to the Father for us.

Romans 8:26 Likewise the Spirit helps us in our weakness. For we do not know what to pray for as we ought, but the Spirit himself intercedes for us with groanings too deep for words. (ESV)

Biblical Narratives

- Samuel couldn't sleep because God wanted to talk to him, 1 Samuel 3:1–10
- God uses an insomniac king to help save the Jews from destruction, Esther 6:1–3. (This is the turning point in the book; read the book of Esther for the complete story.)
- David, weeping at night, Psalm 6:6–7

Practical Steps

- Exercise consistently. Physical labor is a great stress reducer.
- Evaluate use of caffeine, alcohol, sugar in hours before sleep.
- After 9:00 p.m. decrease mental activity—no electronics, action movies, work, etc.
- Seek a physician's evaluation to make sure that medications or supplements are not keeping you awake.
- Be sure that anger and conflicts have been resolved.

Resources

- *The Knowledge of the Holy*. A. W. Tozer. Harper Collins.
- *Can God Be Trusted in Our Trials?* Tony Evans. Moody.
- "Exercise, Eating and Sleeping" in *Character Counts*. Rod Handley. Cross Training.
- *Trusting God: Even When Life Hurts*. Jerry Bridges. NavPress.

Spiritual Disciplines

See also Church Involvement, Money, Purpose for Living, Spiritual Gifts

Staying close to God is the key for success for every man in his actions, relationships, and responsibilities. This closeness requires certain consistent disciplines.

Discipline for Time Alone with God

1. **Meeting with God alone frequently is important (every day, if possible).**

   Psalm 42:1–2 As the deer pants for streams of water, so my soul pants for you, my God. My soul thirsts for God, for the living God. When can I go and meet with God? (NIV)
   Jeremiah 29:13 You will seek me and find me when you seek me with all your heart. (NIV)
   Psalm 63:1; Habakkuk 2:20

2. **Waiting on God is a similar concept.**

   Psalm 27:14 Wait for the LORD; be strong, and let your heart take courage; wait for the LORD! (ESV)
   Isaiah 40:31 They who wait for the LORD shall renew their strength; they shall mount up with wings like eagles; they shall run and not be weary; they shall walk and not faint. (ESV)
   Psalm 40:1

Discipline for Time in God's Word

1. **Spending time in Scripture—reading, meditation, study—gives guidance for each day.**

   Joshua 1:8 This Book of the Law shall not depart from your mouth, but you shall meditate on it day and night, so that you may be careful to do according to all that is written in it. For then you will make your way prosperous, and then you will have good success. (ESV)
   Psalm 119:105 Your word is a lamp to my feet and a light to my path. (ESV)
   Psalm 1:2–3; 19:9–11; 119:9–11, 129–30; Isaiah 55:1–2; 2 Timothy 3:16–17; Hebrews 4:12

2. **Committing God's Word to memory is a further step.**

   Psalm 119:11 I have stored up your word in my heart, that I might not sin against you. (ESV)
   Deuteronomy 6:6–9; Psalm 37:31

Discipline for Time to Talk to God

1. **Spending time daily in prayer is essential.**

   Psalm 5:2–3 Heed the sound of my cry for help, my King and my God, for to You I pray. In the morning, O LORD, You will hear my voice; in the morning I will order my prayer to You and eagerly watch. (NASB)
   Psalm 88:13; 119:47; Jeremiah 33:3; Ephesians 6:18; Hebrews 4:16

2. **Prayer is the Christian's lifeline. We must pray—consistently and constantly.**

   Psalm 55:17 Evening and morning and at noon I will pray, and cry aloud, and He shall hear my voice. (NKJV)
   1 Thessalonians 5:17 Pray without ceasing. (NKJV)
   Psalm 86:3–6; Matthew 7:7; Luke 18:1

3. We must pray in Jesus's name, that is, according to his holy character and will, not selfishly.

John 14:13 Whatever you ask in my name, this I will do, that the Father may be glorified in the Son. (ESV)

1 John 5:14–15 And this is the confidence that we have toward him, that if we ask anything according to his will he hears us. And if we know that he hears us in whatever we ask, we know that we have the requests that we have asked of him. (ESV)

4. Sin can hinder our prayers.

Psalm 66:18; Isaiah 59:1–2

5. We can pray about anything that concerns us.

Philippians 4:6–7 Don't worry about anything; instead, pray about everything. Tell God what you need, and thank him for all he has done. Then you will experience God's peace, which exceeds anything we can understand. His peace will guard your hearts and minds as you live in Christ Jesus. (NLT)

Matthew 7:7–11

Discipline for Time to Be with God's People

1. Being a part of a local church and attending with consistency is commanded.

Hebrews 10:24–25 Let us think of ways to motivate one another to acts of love and good works. And let us not neglect our meeting together, as some people do, but encourage one another, especially now that the day of his return is drawing near. (NLT)

Psalm 42:4; 122:1; 1 Thessalonians 5:11

2. In Acts and throughout the Epistles, the existence of the local church and every believer's involvement in it is assumed.

Acts 6:5; 13:1; 14:23; 1 Corinthians 11:18; 1 Thessalonians 1:1; James 5:14

Discipline for Giving Back to God

1. Giving financially to the Lord's work is a principle strongly supported in Scripture.

   2 Corinthians 9:7 You should each give, then, as you have decided, not with regret or out of a sense of duty; for God loves the one who gives gladly. (GNT)

   Proverbs 3:9 Honor the LORD by making him an offering from the best of all that your land produces. (GNT)

2. While Old Testament tithing is not the law for God's people under the New Covenant, the laws of tithing do help us understand God's mind and heart on the question of giving. They represent his thinking on the matter.

   Leviticus 27:30–33; Malachi 3:8; Romans 6:14–15

Discipline to Be the Witness God Wants Us to Be

1. Sharing our faith in Jesus is a commanded spiritual discipline.

   Acts 1:8 But when the Holy Spirit comes upon you, you will be filled with power, and you will be witnesses for me in Jerusalem, in all of Judea and Samaria, and to the ends of the earth. (GNT)

   1 Peter 3:15 But have reverence for Christ in your hearts, and honor him as Lord. Be ready at all times to answer anyone who asks you to explain the hope you have in you. (GNT)

   Matthew 5:16

Biblical Narratives

- Israelites, giving for the tabernacle, Exodus 35:29; 36:4–7
- Ezra, his decision to study, obey, and teach the Word, Ezra 7:10
- Hezekiah, asking for deliverance from the Assyrians, Isaiah 37:14–20
- Daniel, consistent in prayer, Daniel 6:10

- Habakkuk, his time alone waiting on God, Habakkuk 2:1
- Jesus, praying and seeking time alone with the Father, Matthew 14:23; Mark 1:35

Practical Steps

- Set reminders in your cell phone and other devices for taking time in prayer, meditation, solitude, and time in God's Word.
- If your times with God become mediocre or ineffective, think creatively to enhance those disciplines.
- Get a plan going to study books of the Bible or to read through the Bible in a year.
- For state-of-the-art help in memorizing Scripture, get acquainted with the Navigators.
- Make giving back to God a part of your budget and financial planning. There's no time like the present to get started.
- Work at keeping Sundays free for local church involvement. Ask your employer to allow you the time to worship with others on that day.
- Ask God for passion to reach out to the lost. Make a list of people to pray to faith.

Resources

- *A Man's Guide to the Spiritual Disciplines*. Patrick Morely. Moody.
- *The Bare Bones Bible Handbook*. Jim George. Harvest House.
- *Basics for Believers*. William Thrasher. Moody.
- *Disciplines of a Godly Man*. Kent Hughes. Crossway.
- *Good to Great in God's Eyes: 10 Practices Great Christians Have in Common*. Chip Ingram. Baker.
- *Spiritual Disciplines for the Christian Life*. Don Whitney. NavPress.

Spiritual Gifts

See also **Church Involvement**

"You did not choose Me but I chose you, and appointed you that you would go and bear fruit, and that your fruit would remain, so that whatever you ask of the Father in My name He may give to you" (John 15:16 NASB).

1. **Every believer has at least one spiritual gift.**

    1 Corinthians 12:4–7, 11 There are different kinds of gifts, but the same Spirit distributes them. There are different kinds of service, but the same Lord. There are different kinds of working, but in all of them and in everyone it is the same God at work. Now to each one the manifestation of the Spirit is given for the common good. . . . All these are the work of one and the same Spirit, and he distributes them to each one, just as he determines. (NIV)
    Ephesians 4:7–8

2. **We need to know what spiritual gifts are available and how to use them to be able to effectively serve in the body of Christ.**

    Romans 12:6–8 We have different gifts, according to the grace given to each of us. If your gift is prophesying, then prophesy in accordance with your faith; if it is serving, then serve; if it is teaching, then teach; if it is to encourage, then give encouragement; if it is giving, then give generously; if it is to lead, do it diligently; if it is to show mercy, do it cheerfully. (NIV)
    1 Peter 4:10–11

3. Loving others takes priority over gifts.

> 1 Corinthians 13:1–3 If I speak in the tongues of men or of angels, but do not have love, I am only a resounding gong or a clanging cymbal. If I have the gift of prophecy and can fathom all mysteries and all knowledge, and if I have a faith that can move mountains, but do not have love, I am nothing. If I give all I possess to the poor and give over my body to hardship that I may boast, but do not have love, I gain nothing. (NIV)

4. The absence of a specific spiritual gift in our life does not mean that we can ignore biblical commands for ministry. For example, we should all be involved in evangelism, sharing our faith.

> Matthew 28:19–20 Go, then, to all peoples everywhere and make them my disciples: baptize them in the name of the Father, the Son, and the Holy Spirit, and teach them to obey everything I have commanded you. And I will be with you always, to the end of the age. (GNT)
> Isaiah 44:8; Acts 1:8

Biblical Narratives

- Lists of gifts, Romans 12:6–8; 1 Corinthians 12:8–10, 28–30; Ephesians 4:11
- Love has priority over gifts, 1 Corinthians 13

Practical Steps

- Begin serving in different areas of ministry in which you have interest.
- Take a spiritual gifts inventory that will identify your strengths.
- Study the lists of gifts in Romans 12 and 1 Corinthians 12.
- Ask other godly men where they see strengths and possible spiritual gifts in your life.

Resources

- *Keeping in Step with the Spirit*. J. I. Packer. Baker.
- *The Promise: Experiencing God's Greatest Gift*. Tony Evans. Moody.
- "The Holy Spirit's Gifts" in *Theology You Can Count On*. Tony Evans. Moody.
- "The Spirit Gives Gifts" in *The Holy Spirit*. Charles Ryrie. Moody.

Spiritual Warfare

See also Temptation

That the Christian life is a battle is well attested in Scripture. Satan seeks to defeat us. He destroys, deceives, corrupts, and counterfeits what God has made. Illustrations and metaphors abound from "fighting the good fight" to "putting on the full armor"; we must seek God's protection from the forces that would tear us down.

Satan Seeks to Destroy

1. **Satan's first line of attack has always been to deny and distort God's Word.**

   Genesis 3:1 Now the serpent was more crafty than any of the wild animals the LORD God had made. He said to the woman, "Did God really say, 'You must not eat from any tree in the garden'?" (NIV)
   2 Corinthians 11:3; Revelation 12:9

2. **Satan is a liar and murderer, our enemy who seeks our destruction.**

   John 8:44 You are of your father the devil, and your will is to do your father's desires. He was a murderer from the beginning, and does not stand in the truth, because there is no truth in him. When he lies, he speaks out of his own character, for he is a liar and the father of lies. (ESV)
   1 Peter 5:8

3. Satan attempts to deceive us with his counterfeits.

> **Isaiah 14:13–14** For you said to yourself, "I will ascend to heaven and set my throne above God's stars. I will preside on the mountain of the gods far away in the north. I will climb to the highest heavens and be like the Most High." (NLT)
>
> **2 Corinthians 11:14** But I am not surprised! Even Satan disguises himself as an angel of light. (NLT)
>
> **Deuteronomy 13:1–3; 1 Timothy 4:1; 1 John 4:1**

4. Satan controls this present world system and seeks to control us.

> **1 John 5:19** We know that we are children of God and that the world around us is under the control of the evil one. (NLT)
>
> **John 12:31; 17:15; 1 John 2:15–16**

5. Satan uses demons in his schemes to defeat Christians and to keep people from coming to Christ.

> **Revelation 12:9** And the great dragon was thrown down, that ancient serpent, who is called the devil and Satan, the deceiver of the whole world—he was thrown down to the earth, and his angels were thrown down with him. (ESV)
>
> **Ephesians 2:1–2; 6:10–12**

The Battle Can Be Won

1. Our strength and freedom come from the Lord.

> **Luke 4:18–19** The Spirit of the Lord is upon me, because he has anointed me to proclaim good news to the poor. He has sent me to proclaim liberty to the captives and recovering of sight to the blind, to set at liberty those who are oppressed, to proclaim the year of the Lord's favor. (ESV)
>
> **2 Thessalonians 3:3** But the Lord is faithful. He will establish you and guard you against the evil one. (ESV)
>
> **Psalm 62:6–8; Ephesians 6:10–18**

2. We must be on guard and dependent on his Spirit.

1 Peter 5:7–9 Give all your worries and cares to God, for he cares about you. Stay alert! Watch out for your great enemy, the devil. He prowls around like a roaring lion, looking for someone to devour. Stand firm against him, and be strong in your faith. (NLT)
Galatians 5:16; Ephesians 4:27; James 4:7–8

Areas to Avoid and Action to Take

1. We must be sure there is no unconfessed sin in our life. Keeping short accounts with God is crucial to prevent Satan from gaining inroads of influence.

   1 John 1:8–10 If we say we have no sin, we deceive ourselves, and the truth is not in us. If we confess our sins, he is faithful and just to forgive us our sins and to cleanse us from all unrighteousness. If we say we have not sinned, we make him a liar, and his word is not in us. (ESV)
   Psalm 32; 66:18; Ephesians 4:27; James 4:7

2. God forbids any involvement with satanic practices, occult mediums, or beliefs, including games, movies, and reading materials that have pro-satanic content.

   Deuteronomy 18:10–12 There shall not be found among you anyone who burns his son or his daughter as an offering, anyone who practices divination or tells fortunes or interprets omens, or a sorcerer or a charmer or a medium or a necromancer or one who inquires of the dead, for whoever does these things is an abomination to the LORD. (ESV)
   Isaiah 8:19; Galatians 5:19–21

3. God, not astrology, is in control of the events of our lives.

   Isaiah 47:13–14 You are wearied in the multitude of your counsels; let now the astrologers, the stargazers, and the monthly prognosticators stand up and save you from what shall come upon you. Behold, they shall be as stubble, the fire shall burn them;

they shall not deliver themselves from the power of the flame; it shall not be a coal to be warmed by, nor a fire to sit before! (NKJV)
Deuteronomy 4:19; Job 42:1–2; Jeremiah 10:2; Daniel 4:35

4. **The heavenly bodies (stars, planets, sun, and moon) were created by God to light the world and express God's glory, not to reveal or guide us to our destiny.**

    Genesis 1:16–18 God made the two great lights, the greater light to govern the day, and the lesser light to govern the night; He made the stars also. God placed them in the expanse of the heavens to give light on the earth, and to govern the day and the night, and to separate the light from the darkness; and God saw that it was good. (NASB)
    Psalm 19:1; 108:4–5; Isaiah 40:26

5. **Reincarnation is not taught in Scripture.**

    Genesis 3:19 By the sweat of your face you will eat bread, till you return to the ground, because from it you were taken; for you are dust, and to dust you shall return. (NASB)
    Hebrews 9:27 And inasmuch as it is appointed for men to die once and after this comes judgment. (NASB)

6. **Destroy all items related to the occult and its practices.**

    James 1:21 So get rid of every filthy habit and all wicked conduct. Submit to God and accept the word that he plants in your hearts, which is able to save you. (GNT)
    Acts 19:18–20; 2 Corinthians 6:14–17

Biblical Narratives

- David, who knew that the battle was the Lord's, 1 Samuel 17:44–45
- Jesus and demonic activity, Mark 5:1–20 (among many other Scriptures)
- Peter's need to resist, Luke 22:31–34

- Simon, the magician, Acts 8:9–24
- Slave girl, Acts 16:16–18
- Events at Ephesus, Acts 19:13–20

Practical Steps

- Study each piece of the armor of God from Ephesians 6:13–18. Thank God every day for his protection, and ask him to make that armor effective in your life.
- Study each of the four commands in the New Testament regarding the Holy Spirit, asking God to help you obey them. See Ephesians 4:30; 5:18; Galatians 5:16; 1 Thessalonians 5:19.
- Protect your family by removing occult items from your house. Stay away from such Internet sites. Destroy ungodly DVDs and CDs. Prohibit occult games.
- Reflect daily on the price Jesus paid to redeem you with his blood. Know that the gospel is sufficient for the battle.

Resources

- *Free Indeed: Escaping Bondage and Brokenness for Freedom in Christ*. Richard Ganz. Shepherd.
- "Occultism: Superstition or Deception" in *Seven Snares of the Enemy*. Erwin Lutzer. Moody.
- *Overcoming the Adversary*. Mark Bubeck. Moody.
- *Stealth Attack: Protecting Yourself against Satan's Plan to Destroy Your Life*. Ray Pritchard. Moody.
- *Victory in Spiritual Warfare*. Tony Evans. Harvest House.

Substance Abuse

See also Temptation

1. A Christian's body, as a temple of the Holy Spirit, must not be subjected to the harmful effects of drug and alcohol abuse.

   Romans 13:13–14 Because we belong to the day, we must live decent lives for all to see. Don't participate in the darkness of wild parties and drunkenness, or in sexual promiscuity and immoral living, or in quarreling and jealousy. Instead, clothe yourself with the presence of the Lord Jesus Christ. And don't let yourself think about ways to indulge your evil desires. (NLT)

   1 Corinthians 6:19–20 Do you not know that your bodies are temples of the Holy Spirit, who is in you, whom you have received from God? You are not your own; you were bought at a price. Therefore honor God with your bodies. (NIV)

   Ephesians 5:18

2. Negative effects from drunkenness are abundant.

   Isaiah 28:7–8 And these also reel with wine and stagger from strong drink: the priest and the prophet reel with strong drink, they are confused by wine, they stagger from strong drink; they reel while having visions, they totter when rendering judgment. For all the tables are full of filthy vomit, without a single clean place. (NASB)

   Proverbs 23:29–35

3. Note these associations with drunkenness that are disgusting and lead to further sin. (The same would apply to drug use.)

   Genesis 9:21—exposure, nakedness
   Job 12:25—staggering

Psalm 107:27—reeling, staggering, at wits' end
Proverbs 23:21—poverty, drowsiness
Proverbs 23:33–35—addiction
Isaiah 19:14—staggering in vomit
Isaiah 24:20—reeling, swaying, and falling
Jeremiah 25:27—vomiting
Lamentations 4:21—stripped naked
Ezekiel 23:33—ruin, desolation
Romans 13:13—indecent behavior
Ephesians 5:18—debauchery

4. Drunkenness is sinful and evidence of a deep spiritual problem.

Galatians 5:19, 21 What human nature does is quite plain. It shows itself in immoral, filthy, and indecent actions. . . . They are envious, get drunk, have orgies, and do other things like these. I warn you now as I have before: those who do these things will not possess the Kingdom of God. (GNT)

Isaiah 5:11–12, 22 Woe to those who rise early in the morning to run after their drinks, who stay up late at night till they are inflamed with wine. They have harps and lyres at their banquets, pipes and timbrels and wine. . . . Woe to those who are heroes at drinking wine and champions at mixing drinks. (NIV)

Proverbs 20:1; 1 Corinthians 6:9–11; 1 Peter 4:1–3

5. We must not let others pressure us.

Isaiah 51:7 Listen to me, you who know right from wrong, you who cherish my law in your hearts. Do not be afraid of people's scorn, nor fear their insults. (NLT)

Proverbs 1:10; Habakkuk 2:15–16; James 4:17

6. It is God's will for people to be released from these habits.

1 Corinthians 10:13 The temptations in your life are no different from what others experience. And God is faithful. He will not allow the temptation to be more than you can stand. When you are tempted, he will show you a way out so that you can endure. (NLT)

Romans 12:1–2

7. **Our part is to know that Christ's death included provision for victory over sin.**

   John 8:36 So if the Son sets you free, you will be free indeed. (NIV)
   Romans 6:6–13

8. **Repentance is necessary.**

   Ezekiel 14:6 Therefore say to the people of Israel, "This is what the Sovereign LORD says: Repent! Turn from your idols and renounce all your detestable practices!" (NIV)
   Isaiah 1:16–18; Acts 3:19

9. **God's strength is available to those in great need.**

   Isaiah 40:31 Yet those who wait for the LORD will gain new strength; they will mount up with wings like eagles, they will run and not get tired, they will walk and not become weary. (NASB)
   Philippians 4:13 I can do all things through Him who strengthens me. (NASB)
   Isaiah 41:10

Biblical Narratives

- Noah, Genesis 9:18–27
- Lot, Genesis 19:30–38
- Drunkards of Israel, Isaiah 5:11–12, 22

Practical Steps

- Advise the counselee to see a physician.
- Counselors should provide opportunities for those involved to see the long-term effects in people who are dying from alcohol, tobacco, or drugs.
- Spend much time in reading and study of Scripture. Memorize key portions. Search out relevant Psalms.

- Seek help in finding solutions for your problems other than in drugs or drinking. Other mature believers and church leaders would be able to help for accountability.
- Avoid relationships and places for sinning. Commit to cutting these off.
- Review your life goals and how these will not be achieved if you continue in this sin.

Resources

- *Addictions: A Banquet in the Grave*. Ed Welch. P & R.
- "Alcoholism: Quitting Tomorrow" in *Seven Snares of the Enemy*. Erwin Lutzer. Moody.
- *Breaking the Addictive Cycle* (booklet). David Powlison. New Growth.
- *Cross Talking: A Devotional for Transforming Addicts*. Mark Shaw. Focus.
- *Divine Intervention: Hope and Help for Families of Addicts*. Mark Shaw. Focus.
- *Freedom from Addiction* (booklet). Ed Welch. New Growth.
- *The Heart of Addiction*. Mark Shaw. Focus.

Suffering/Trials/Adversity

See also Anxiety, Disappointment, Fear, Health, Natural Disasters, Purpose for Living, Trust

Difficult Times a Part of Life

1. **Living in a fallen world means that tough times are inevitable.**

   Genesis 3:17 Then to Adam He said, "Because you have heeded the voice of your wife, and have eaten from the tree of which I commanded you, saying, 'You shall not eat of it': Cursed is the ground for your sake; in toil you shall eat of it all the days of your life." (NKJV)

   Job 5:7 For man is born for trouble, as sparks fly upward. (NASB)
   Job 14:1–2; John 15:18–21; 16:33; Romans 8:18–23

2. **Trials are to be expected and remind us of the sufferings of Christ.**

   1 Peter 4:12–13 My dear friends, do not be surprised at the painful test you are suffering, as though something unusual were happening to you. Rather be glad that you are sharing Christ's sufferings, so that you may be full of joy when his glory is revealed. (GNT)

   2 Timothy 2:3 Take your part in suffering, as a loyal soldier of Christ Jesus. (GNT)

Why God Allows Trials

1. **Our faith will be strengthened.**

   1 Peter 1:6–7 In all this you greatly rejoice, though now for a little while you may have had to suffer grief in all kinds of trials.

These have come so that the proven genuineness of your faith—of greater worth than gold, which perishes even though refined by fire—may result in praise, glory and honor when Jesus Christ is revealed. (NIV)

James 1:2–5

2. **Trials enable us to develop into the person God wants us to be.**

Job 23:8–10 Look, I go forward, but He is not there, and backward, but I cannot perceive Him; when He works on the left hand, I cannot behold Him; when He turns to the right hand, I cannot see Him. But He knows the way that I take; when He has tested me, I shall come forth as gold. (NKJV)

3. **Through trials we are driven to focus more on heaven and eternity.**

2 Corinthians 4:17–18 And this small and temporary trouble we suffer will bring us a tremendous and eternal glory, much greater than the trouble. For we fix our attention, not on things that are seen, but on things that are unseen. What can be seen lasts only for a time, but what cannot be seen lasts forever. (GNT)

4. **A possible reason for trials is God's discipline that moves us to repentance and confession of sin.**

Hebrews 12:10–11

5. **The comfort that God provides for us can be passed on to help others.**

2 Corinthians 1:4 He helps us in all our troubles, so that we are able to help others who have all kinds of troubles, using the same help that we ourselves have received from God. (GNT)

How We Must Respond

1. **Resting in God's presence and strength is crucial.**

Psalm 3:4–5 I cried aloud to the LORD, and he answered me from his holy hill. I lay down and slept; I woke again, for the LORD sustained me. (ESV)

Psalm 9:9–10 The LORD is a stronghold for the oppressed, a stronghold in times of trouble. And those who know your name put their trust in you, for you, O LORD, have not forsaken those who seek you. (ESV)
Psalm 31:9–10; 61:2; 86:3

2. We can trust God's sovereign wisdom and support.

Jeremiah 10:23 LORD, I know that none of us are the master of our own destiny; none of us have control over our own life. (GNT)
2 Thessalonians 3:16 Now may the Lord of peace Himself continually grant you peace in every circumstance. The Lord be with you all! (NASB)
2 Timothy 4:17–18 But the Lord stayed with me and gave me strength. . . . And the Lord will rescue me from all evil and take me safely into his heavenly Kingdom. (GNT)
Psalm 23; 56:8; 71:20–21; Isaiah 43:1–2; John 14:27

3. His grace is our sufficiency. Count on it!

Psalm 55:22 Cast your burden on the LORD, and he will sustain you; he will never permit the righteous to be moved. (ESV)
2 Corinthians 12:9

4. As we are strong through adversity, God's reward will be evident.

James 1:12 Blessed is the man who remains steadfast under trial, for when he has stood the test he will receive the crown of life, which God has promised to those who love him. (ESV)

Biblical Narratives

Consider the response of each of the following people to their suffering.

- Job, Job 1:21; 2:10; James 5:11
- Joseph, Genesis 37–50
- David, 1 Samuel 19–30
- Apostles, Acts 5:27–42

- Paul and Silas, Acts 16
- Paul, 2 Corinthians 11:25–33; 12:7–10

Practical Steps

- Keep a daily prayer journal, noting your pain and struggles. Record answers as God responds. Every day, list items of thanksgiving.
- Memorize Philippians 4:6–7. Write it on a card and keep it close at hand.
- Be open with other believers. Enlist them to empathize and pray for you.
- Seek out others going through trials; encourage them by listening to their journeys and praying faithfully for them.
- Meditate on Romans 8:28 and write down a past difficult event in your life that God has used for good.
- Center your Bible reading in the Psalms where the authors experienced adversity, see especially 13; 34; 46; 55; 73; 91; 121; 143; 145.

Resources

- *A Shelter in the Time of Storm*. Paul Tripp. Crossway.
- *Can God Be Trusted in Our Trials?* Tony Evans. Moody.
- *Finding God When You Need Him the Most*. Chip Ingram. Baker.
- *Making Sense of Suffering* (pamphlet). Joni Eareckson Tada. Rose.
- *Trusting God: Even When Life Hurts*. Jerry Bridges. NavPress.
- *When Will My Life Not Suck?* Ramon Presson. New Growth.

Suicide

See also Depression, Fear, Hope, Loneliness, Purpose for Living, Self-Worth

Current secular thinking (without God or moral absolutes in the picture) sees little wrong with ending one's own life, especially if that life is rife with pain and suffering. You have a "right to die," if you so determine. Yet we have a loving heavenly Father who has revealed himself to us through his Word. Factoring God into the equation makes all the difference in this world and the next.

1. **Human beings are God's highest creation, made in his image. We are his possession. We have no right to end this life that belongs to him.**

   Genesis 1:27 So God created human beings in his own image. In the image of God he created them; male and female he created them. (NLT)
   Ezekiel 18:4 The life of every person belongs to me. (GNT)
   Genesis 2:7; Job 41:11; Psalm 139:13–16

2. **God showed how much he loves us by sending his Son to die for us.**

   Romans 5:8 But God shows his love for us in that while we were still sinners, Christ died for us. (ESV)
   Ephesians 2:4–5 But God, being rich in mercy, because of the great love with which he loved us, even when we were dead in our trespasses, made us alive together with Christ— by grace you have been saved. (ESV)
   John 3:16; 1 Peter 2:9

3. Christians have a special relationship with God that gives us great hope.

1 Corinthians 6:19–20 Do you not know that your body is a temple of the Holy Spirit within you, whom you have from God? You are not your own, for you were bought with a price. So glorify God in your body. (ESV)

1 Corinthians 10:13 No temptation has overtaken you that is not common to man. God is faithful, and he will not let you be tempted beyond your ability, but with the temptation he will also provide the way of escape, that you may be able to endure it. (ESV)

Ephesians 3:20–21

4. Though we may feel guilty for some great sin, we must not take our life. There is no sin too great for God to forgive. Jesus took the punishment for all sin.

Micah 7:18–19 Who is a God like You, who pardons iniquity and passes over the rebellious act of the remnant of His possession? He does not retain His anger forever, because He delights in unchanging love. He will again have compassion on us; He will tread our iniquities under foot. Yes, You will cast all their sins into the depths of the sea. (NASB)

Isaiah 43:25 I, even I, am the one who wipes out your transgressions for My own sake, and I will not remember your sins. (NASB)

Psalm 145:8; 1 Corinthians 6:9–11; 1 John 1:9; Isaiah 53

5. God's presence is guaranteed, even when darkness overwhelms us. He will never leave us.

Psalm 139:7–12 Where could I go to escape from you? Where could I get away from your presence? If I went up to heaven, you would be there; if I lay down in the world of the dead, you would be there. If I flew away beyond the east or lived in the farthest place in the west, you would be there to lead me, you would be there to help me. I could ask the darkness to hide me or the light around me to turn into night, but even darkness is not dark for

you, and the night is as bright as the day. Darkness and light are the same to you. (GNT)
Deuteronomy 31:8; Joshua 1:9; Haggai 2:4

6. **There is no problem too great for God to handle. Our strength comes from him.**

    Jeremiah 32:17 Ah, Lord God! It is you who has made the heavens and the earth by your great power and by your outstretched arm! Nothing is too hard for you. (ESV)
    Isaiah 43:18–19; Ephesians 6:10; 2 Timothy 2:1

7. **Our future is secure with God on our side.**

    Jeremiah 29:11–13 For I know the plans I have for you, declares the LORD, plans for welfare and not for evil, to give you a future and a hope. Then you will call upon me and come and pray to me, and I will hear you. You will seek me and find me when you seek me with all your heart. (ESV)
    Romans 8:31–39

8. **God's Word provides the answers for relief from life's difficulties.**

    Joshua 1:8 This book of the law shall not depart from your mouth, but you shall meditate on it day and night, so that you may be careful to do according to all that is written in it; for then you will make your way prosperous, and then you will have success. (NASB)
    Deuteronomy 32:46–47; Psalm 119:105; Hebrews 4:12

9. **If suicide does occur, God's grace extends even to that sin. A Christian who takes his or her own life will still be secure in the love of God.**

    Romans 8:38–39 For I am certain that nothing can separate us from his love: neither death nor life, neither angels nor other heavenly rulers or powers, neither the present nor the future, neither the world above nor the world below—there is nothing in all creation that will ever be able to separate us from the love of God which is ours through Christ Jesus our Lord. (GNT)
    John 10:27–29

Practical Steps

For the Counselee

- Research Scripture on God's sovereignty. Suicidal thoughts ultimately come because of a lack of hope. Something in life is too huge or too awful to imagine surviving. Hope in God will provide relief.
- Know that a very practical help for feelings of depression is intense, consistent physical exercise to help relieve the symptoms. Get a plan going and stick to it.
- Write down how you are feeling and how the Bible describes Jesus and his love for you. Take to heart that you are totally valuable and precious in his sight!

For the Counselor

- Pay attention to the counselee's life-changing situations. Take every threat or call for help seriously.
- This person must have a physical examination, with extensive blood work involved.
- Emphasize community, with others involved—civil authorities, family members, and church leaders, as necessary.
- Encourage the person to journal God's promises. Direct them to specific texts of comfort, such as John 10:10.

Resources

- *Finding God When You Need Him the Most*. Chip Ingram. Baker.
- *Grieving a Suicide*. Albert Hsu. IVP.
- *Grieving a Suicide: Help for the Aftershock* (booklet). David Powlison. CCEF.
- *Suicide: Understanding and Intervening* (booklet). Jeffrey S. Black. P & R.
- *I Just Want to Die: Replacing Suicidal Thoughts with Hope* (booklet). David Powlison. CCEF.

Temptation

See also Integrity, Lust, Sexual Purity, Spiritual Warfare

Being tempted to sin is not a sin in itself. How we handle it when it comes is key.

1. **We need to recognize the weaknesses of our sinful nature, taking care to monitor our thoughts and desires.**

    Romans 7:18–19 And I know that nothing good lives in me, that is, in my sinful nature. I want to do what is right, but I can't. I want to do what is good, but I don't. (NLT)

    James 1:14–15 Temptation comes from our own desires, which entice us and drag us away. These desires give birth to sinful actions. And when sin is allowed to grow, it gives birth to death. (NLT)

    Proverbs 23:7 For as he thinks within himself, so he is. (NASB)
    Philippians 4:8

2. **Achan's failure to resist is a classic example of the progression of sin in one's life.**

    Joshua 7:20–21 So Achan answered Joshua and said, "Truly, I have sinned against the LORD, the God of Israel, and this is what I did: when I saw among the spoil a beautiful mantle from Shinar and two hundred shekels of silver and a bar of gold fifty shekels in weight, then I coveted them and took them; and behold, they are concealed in the earth inside my tent with the silver underneath it." (NASB) (Note the verbs—*saw, coveted, took, concealed.*)

3. God has made provision for us to resist. We need courage and commitment to follow through.

1 Corinthians 10:13 The temptations in your life are no different from what others experience. And God is faithful. He will not allow the temptation to be more than you can stand. When you are tempted, he will show you a way out so that you can endure. (NLT)

2 Peter 1:3 His divine power has given us everything we need for a godly life through our knowledge of him who called us by his own glory and goodness. (NIV)

Ephesians 6:10–11; Hebrews 12:1–2; 1 John 4:4

4. Knowing and obeying God's Word are essential to our resisting.

Psalm 37:31 The law of his God is in his heart; his steps do not slip. (ESV)

Psalm 40:8 I delight to do your will, O my God; your law is within my heart. (ESV)

Psalm 119:9–11; Hebrews 4:12

5. Though Christ never sinned, he understands temptation and is able to help us through it.

Hebrews 2:18 For since He Himself was tempted in that which He has suffered, He is able to come to the aid of those who are tempted. (NASB)

Hebrews 4:15 For we do not have a high priest who cannot sympathize with our weaknesses, but One who has been tempted in all things as we are, yet without sin. (NASB)

6. His death included provision for victory over sin.

Romans 6:6, 11–13 For we know that our old self was crucified with him so that the body ruled by sin might be done away with, that we should no longer be slaves to sin. . . . In the same way, count yourselves dead to sin but alive to God in Christ Jesus. Therefore do not let sin reign in your mortal body so that you obey its evil desires. Do not offer any part of yourself to sin as an instrument of wickedness, but rather offer yourselves to God as those who have been brought from death to life; and offer every part of yourself to him as an instrument of righteousness. (NIV) (Note the "know," "count," "offer" sequence for action steps.)

7. **Concerted prayer is critical for help in resisting.**

   Mark 14:38 Keep watching and praying that you may not come into temptation; the spirit is willing, but the flesh is weak. (NASB)
   Ephesians 6:18; James 5:16–17

8. **Choosing to obey God rather than sin is vital for resisting temptation.**

   Psalm 37:27 Depart from evil and do good, so you will abide forever. (NASB)
   Joshua 24:14–15

9. **We must not let others pressure us.**

   Isaiah 51:7 Listen to me, you who know right from wrong, you who cherish my law in your hearts. Do not be afraid of people's scorn, nor fear their insults. (NLT)
   Proverbs 1:10; James 4:17

10. **Lack of sexual intimacy in a marriage can be a cause of sexual temptation.**

    1 Corinthians 7:5 Do not deprive each other of sexual relations. (NLT)

11. **Use caution in helping others flee temptation; do not be caught yourself.**

    Psalm 141:9–10 Keep me safe from the traps set by evildoers, from the snares they have laid for me. Let the wicked fall into their own nets, while I pass by in safety. (NIV)
    Galatians 6:1–2

Biblical Narratives

- Joseph resisted, Genesis 39:7–10
- Achan failed to resist, Joshua 7 (See number 2 above.)

- Jesus, Matthew 4
- Disciples in Gethsemane, Mark 14:37–38

Practical Steps

- Do a scriptural study of the three enemies of the believer—the world, the flesh, and the devil. Note how the three relate to each other and how we must be vigilant in the battle.
- Know your own weaknesses. From 1 John 2:15–17, study the three areas of temptation (in verse 16). List your own personal battles with each.
- Accountability is a must! Find someone who will be ruthless with you.
- Remove temptations from your home, office, auto, cell phone. Evaluate places you go to frequently; commit to staying away from those that lead to temptation.
- Memorize Psalm 55:22. Write it on a card to keep close at hand.
- Spend time reading Romans 6–8 out loud.

Resources

- "A Powerful Response to Temptation" in *The Hand of God: Finding His Care in All Circumstances*. Alistair Begg. Moody.
- *Temptation: Fighting the Urge* (booklet). Timothy Lane. CCEF.
- *Christ and Your Problems* (booklet). Jay Adams. P & R.
- *Winning the Inner War: How to Say No to a Stubborn Habit*. Erwin Lutzer. Cook.

Thought Life/Fantasizing

See also Anxiety, Lust, Materialism, Pornography, Sexual Purity

That no one knows our thoughts is a comforting reality but it also moves us into dangerous ground spiritually. It is tempting to think about a sin we would never actually commit. God is concerned with what we think, and his Word supplies extended warnings and instruction.

1. There are no thoughts or secrets hidden from God.

> **Psalm 139:1–4** LORD, you have examined me and you know me. You know everything I do; from far away you understand all my thoughts. You see me, whether I am working or resting; you know all my actions. Even before I speak, you already know what I will say. (GNT)
>
> **Jeremiah 23:23–24** I am a God who is everywhere and not in one place only. No one can hide where I cannot see them. Do you not know that I am everywhere in heaven and on earth. (GNT)
>
> **2 Chronicles 16:9; Hebrews 4:13**

2. Our thought life reflects who we are.

> **Proverbs 23:7** For as he thinks within himself, so he is. (NASB) (The context is eating, but the principle applies.)
>
> **Mark 7:20–23**

3. We must discipline ourselves to think biblically.

> **2 Corinthians 10:5** We demolish arguments and every pretension that sets itself up against the knowledge of God, and we take captive every thought to make it obedient to Christ. (NIV)
>
> **Philippians 4:8; 1 Peter 1:13**

4. Thinking as God thinks should be our standard. Put evil fantasies aside.

Isaiah 55:7–8 Let the wicked forsake their ways and the unrighteous their thoughts. Let them turn to the LORD, and he will have mercy on them, and to our God, for he will freely pardon. "For my thoughts are not your thoughts, neither are your ways my ways," declares the LORD. (NIV)
Ephesians 4:22–24

5. Covetous, lustful, worldly thoughts are sinful and must be removed.

Matthew 5:28 But I tell you that anyone who looks at a woman lustfully has already committed adultery with her in his heart. (NIV)
Job 31:1 I made a covenant with my eyes not to look lustfully at a young woman. (NIV)
Deuteronomy 5:21; Romans 12:1–2; 1 Corinthians 3:18–19; 1 Thessalonians 4:3–5

6. We should not think more highly of ourselves than we ought to think.

Romans 12:3 Don't think you are better than you really are. Be honest in your evaluation of yourselves, measuring yourselves by the faith God has given us. (NLT)
Galatians 6:3 For if anyone thinks he is something, when he is nothing, he deceives himself. (ESV)
1 Corinthians 10:12

7. Our lives must reflect sacrificial thinking.

Philippians 2:5–7 (Jesus at his incarnation).

8. Mature thinking is an intellectual and spiritual goal.

1 Corinthians 13:11 When I was a child, I spoke and thought and reasoned as a child. But when I grew up, I put away childish things. (NLT)

1 Corinthians 14:20 Brothers, do not be children in your think-ing. Be infants in evil, but in your thinking be mature. (ESV)
Proverbs 22:17

Practical Steps

- A key area for spiritual and emotional health is exercise. Set aside time and follow through.

- Complete a concordance study of the hundreds of uses of *mind*, *thinking*, and *thoughts* to understand better how God wants us to think.

- When tempting thoughts come, ask God to control your mind. Pray, "Lord, please remove that thought from me" or "Lord, through your Spirit, I reject that thought."

- Study *sanctification* in Scripture. Center on renewing your mind by memorizing Philippians 4:8 and Romans 12:2.

- Evaluate your thought patterns, life situation, or physical locations that are triggers for faulty thinking. Sort out and discard those that are troubling to your thought life.

Resources

- "Changing Your Thought Patterns" (booklet). George Sanchez. NavPress.
- *How People Change*. Timothy Lane. New Growth.
- *Right Thinking in a World Gone Wrong*. John MacArthur. Harvest House.
- *You Can Change: God's Transforming Power for Our Sinful Behavior and Negative Emotions*. Tim Chester. Crossway.

Time Management

See also Burnout, Priorities, Wisdom, Workplace

1. **The time we have on earth, the days of our lives, are a gift from God and determined by him.**

   Job 14:1–2, 5 How frail is humanity! How short is life, how full of trouble! We blossom like a flower and then wither. Like a passing shadow, we quickly disappear. . . . You have decided the length of our lives. You know how many months we will live, and we are not given a minute longer. (NLT)
   Psalm 31:14–15 But as for me, I trust in you, O LORD, I say, "You are my God." My times are in Your hand. (NASB)
   Psalm 39:4 LORD, remind me how brief my time on earth will be. Remind me that my days are numbered—how fleeting my life is. (NLT)
   Psalm 90:3–12; 144:4

2. **It is God's plan that we use our time wisely.**

   Psalm 90:12 So teach us to number our days, that we may gain a heart of wisdom. (NKJV)
   Ephesians 5:15–18

3. **As we make plans, depending on God and asking for his wisdom are critical to success.**

   Psalm 90:17 Let the favor of the LORD our God be upon us; and confirm for us the work of our hands; yes, confirm the work of our hands. (NASB)
   James 1:5 But if any of you lack wisdom, you should pray to God, who will give it to you; because God gives generously and graciously to all. (GNT)
   Proverbs 16:9; James 4:13–15

4. Staying balanced is crucial for time management.

Ecclesiastes 7:18 It is good to grasp the one and not let go of the other. Whoever fears God will avoid all extremes. (NIV)
Nehemiah 4:8–9 (Note the balance of praying and working.)

Biblical Narrative

- Moses, taking Jethro's advice for delegation, Exodus 18:13–24; Deuteronomy 1:9–18

Practical Steps

- Admit your need for a planner. Use it consistently to manage your time wisely and efficiently.
- Use a monthly/weekly calendar to help your family keep organized.
- Evaluate often how much time is spent on various activities, searching out and eliminating time wasters.

Resources

- *Balancing Life's Demands: Biblical Priorities for a Busy Life*. DVD series. Chip Ingram. Living on the Edge Ministries.
- *The Overload Syndrome: Learning to Live within Your Limits*. Richard Swenson. NavPress.
- *Priorities: Mastering Time Management* (booklet). James Petty. P & R.

Trust/Confidence

See also Anxiety, Fear, Hope, Suffering

Trust is a confident reliance on that which is perceived to be firm, safe, and secure. Self-reliance, trusting in one's own abilities and assets, is seen by many men as a mark of masculinity, but for a follower of Christ, trusting God first and foremost is the priority.

1. **Trust in self alone, or in others, can be unreliable. Ultimate trust must center on God.**

    Psalm 118:8–9 It is better to take refuge in the LORD than to trust in man. It is better to take refuge in the LORD than to trust in princes. (NASB)

    Jeremiah 17:5, 7 Thus says the LORD: "Cursed is the man who trusts in man and makes flesh his strength, whose heart departs from the LORD. . . . Blessed is the man who trusts in the LORD, and whose hope is the LORD." (NKJV)

    Psalm 20:7

2. **God is worthy of our trust. His presence in our lives is guaranteed.**

    Psalm 9:10 And those who know your name put their trust in you, for you, O LORD, have not forsaken those who seek you. (ESV)

    Joshua 1:7–9; Deuteronomy 31:8; Hebrews 13:5

3. **Faith brings certainty and reality to that which is otherwise unknown, and faith is necessary to please God.**

    Hebrews 11:1, 6 Now faith is confidence in what we hope for and assurance about what we do not see. . . . And without faith it is impossible to please God, because anyone who comes to him must believe that he exists and that he rewards those who earnestly seek him. (NIV)

Philippians 1:6

4. **Trusting God for the unknown is a characteristic of faith.**

Hebrews 11:8 By faith Abraham, when called to go to a place he would later receive as his inheritance, obeyed and went, even though he did not know where he was going. (NIV)

Matthew 17:20 "You don't have enough faith," Jesus told them. "I tell you the truth, if you had faith even as small as a mustard seed, you could say to this mountain, 'Move from here to there,' and it would move. Nothing would be impossible." (NLT)

2 Corinthians 5:7

5. **Trust in God must be constant, unwavering. This faith gets us through tough times.**

Psalm 26:1 Vindicate me, O LORD, for I have walked in my integrity, and I have trusted in the LORD without wavering. (ESV)

Habakkuk 3:17–18 Though the fig tree should not blossom and there be no fruit on the vines, though the yield of the olive should fail and the fields produce no food, though the flock should be cut off from the fold and there be no cattle in the stalls, yet I will exult in the LORD, I will rejoice in the God of my salvation. (NASB)

Job 23:8–10; Psalm 33:4–5; 119:41–42; Isaiah 26:4

6. **Trusting God expresses confidence that his timing is perfect.**

Habakkuk 2:3 For the vision is yet for the appointed time; it hastens toward the goal and it will not fail. Though it tarries, wait for it; for it will certainly come, it will not delay. (NASB)

Psalm 31:15; 130:5–6

7. **Results of a life of trust:**

SHELTER

Psalm 5:11 But let all who take refuge in You be glad, let them ever sing for joy; and may You shelter them, that those who love Your name may exult in You. (NASB)

Psalm 91:1–2

Guidance

Psalm 143:8 Let me hear Your lovingkindness in the morning; for I trust in You; teach me the way in which I should walk; for to You I lift up my soul. (NASB)

Stability

Psalm 125:1–2 Those who trust in the Lord are as Mount Zion, which cannot be moved but abides forever. As the mountains surround Jerusalem, so the Lord surrounds His people from this time forth and forever. (NASB)

Overcoming fear

Psalm 56:2–4 My foes have trampled upon me all day long, for they are many who fight proudly against me. When I am afraid, I will put my trust in You. In God, whose word I praise, in God I have put my trust; I shall not be afraid. What can mere man do to me? (NASB)

Gladness

Psalm 64:10 The righteous man will be glad in the Lord and will take refuge in Him; and all the upright in heart will glory. (NASB)

Peace

Isaiah 26:3 You will keep him in perfect peace, whose mind is stayed on You, because he trusts in You. (NKJV)

Blessing

Jeremiah 17:7 Blessed is the man who trusts in the Lord, and whose hope is the Lord. (NKJV)
Psalm 84:12

Confidence in the future

Psalm 112:7 He will not be afraid of evil tidings; his heart is steadfast, trusting in the Lord. (NKJV)

CONFIDENCE IN PRAYER

Hebrews 4:16 Let us therefore come boldly to the throne of grace, that we may obtain mercy and find grace to help in time of need. (NKJV)

OVERCOMING PHYSICAL LIMITATIONS

Hebrews 11:11 By faith Sarah herself also received strength to conceive seed, and she bore a child when she was past the age, because she judged Him faithful who had promised. (NKJV)

Biblical Narratives

- Abraham trusted God's promises, Genesis 17:15–19; Romans 4:3
- David, Psalm 18
- Three young men, Daniel 3:13–18
- Centurion trusted Christ to heal, Matthew 8:5–10
- Peter walked on water, Matthew 14:24–32

Practical Steps

- Study the names of God in the Old Testament, reflecting on his trustworthiness.
- Study *trust* in the Psalms using a concordance. List and categorize the verses that relate to your crisis situation.
- Meet with believing men who have similar work responsibilities as you. Pray and share with them.
- Paraphrase Psalm 145 as it relates to your trust issue. Select key verses to memorize. Keep them close at hand to remind you of God's faithfulness.

Resources

- *The Attributes of God: A Journey into the Father's Heart*. A. W. Tozer. Christian Publications.
- "The Faithfulness of God" in *God as He Longs for You to See Him*. Chip Ingram. Baker.
- *Finding God When You Need Him the Most*. Chip Ingram. Baker.
- *God Cannot Be Trusted (and Five Other Lies of Satan)*. Tony Evans. Moody.
- "Replacing a Doubtful Heart . . . with an Attitude of Trust" in *Lord, Change My Attitude*. James MacDonald. Moody.
- *Trusting God: Even When Life Hurts*. Jerry Bridges. NavPress.

Unbelieving Spouse

See also Anxiety, Marriage

1. **Divorce or leaving an unbelieving wife is not an option.**

   1 Corinthians 7:12–13 But to the rest I say, not the Lord, that if any brother has a wife who is an unbeliever, and she consents to live with him, he must not divorce her. And a woman who has an unbelieving husband, and he consents to live with her, she must not send her husband away. (NASB)

2. **Consistent living because of God's grace is required in every believer's life.**

   1 Peter 1:14–16 As obedient children, do not be conformed to the former lusts which were yours in your ignorance, but like the Holy One who called you, be holy yourselves also in all your behavior; because it is written, "YOU SHALL BE HOLY, FOR I AM HOLY." (NASB)
   Titus 2:11–14

3. **Consistent living because of God's grace is a testimony to an unbelieving wife.**

   1 Peter 3:1–2 Wives, in the same way submit yourselves to your own husbands so that, if any of them do not believe the word, they may be won over without words by the behavior of their wives, when they see the purity and reverence of your lives. (NIV) (Though this is addressed to wives, it would be true for a husband with an unbelieving wife.)
   1 Corinthians 7:12–18; Matthew 5:16; John 13:35

4. It is comforting to know that what seems impossible to us is certainly not impossible with God.

> Jeremiah 32:17 Ah, Lord GOD! It is you who have made the heavens and the earth by your great power and by your outstretched arm! Nothing is too hard for you. (ESV)
> **Genesis 18:14; Job 42:2; Matthew 19:26**

Practical Steps

- Don't nag your wife. Be quiet (1 Peter 3:1–2) and let God do his work in his time.
- Being consistent in your patience and love to her can be the successful bridge in her coming to faith.
- Develop accountability with other believing men who can provide wisdom and prayer support.
- Do not permit church or ministry to come between you and your wife.

Resources

- *Living with an Angry Spouse* (booklet). Ed Welch. New Growth.
- *Surviving a Spiritual Mismatch in Marriage*. Lee and Leslie Strobel. Zondervan.

Widower

See also Anxiety, Bitterness, Grief, Loneliness, Purpose for Living, Suffering

Marriage is one of the closest of human relationships. A happily married man would agree that there is no one on earth he would rather spend time with than his wife. Best friend, lover, companion, and confidante she is to him, and to lose all of that at her death is one of the most devastating of experiences.

1. **Being alone is difficult, yet as believers we are never really alone.**

    Psalm 68:5–6 A father of the fatherless and a judge for the widows, is God in His holy habitation. God makes a home for the lonely; He leads out the prisoners into prosperity, only the rebellious dwell in a parched land. (NASB)
    Deuteronomy 31:6; Psalm 73:25–26; Hebrews 13:5

2. **Grief is difficult, yet God's comfort is available.**

    Isaiah 40:1 "Comfort, O comfort My people," says your God. (NASB)
    Psalm 55:22 Cast your burden on the LORD, and He shall sustain you; He shall never permit the righteous to be moved. (NKJV)
    Nehemiah 8:10; Psalm 31; 2 Corinthians 1:3–4; Philippians 4:13, 19

3. **When our hearts are submissive, God will provide the direction we need.**

    Psalm 48:14 For this God is our God forever and ever; he will be our guide even to the end. (NIV)
    Proverbs 4:11–13; Psalm 25:12–15; Jeremiah 10:23

4. Even though the loss is great, we must keep focused on Christ and our present life with him.

Hebrews 12:1–2. Let us run with endurance the race that is set before us, looking unto Jesus, the author and finisher of our faith. (NKJV)
Philippians 3:12–14

5. As difficult as it is, a widower must accept death, grief, and his loss as being a part of life.

Ecclesiastes 3:1–2, 4 There is an appointed time for everything. And there is a time for every event under heaven—a time to give birth and a time to die. . . . A time to weep and a time to laugh; a time to mourn and a time to dance. (NASB)
Hebrews 9:27 Everyone must die once, and after that be judged by God. (GNT)
Psalm 116:15 Precious in the sight of the LORD is the death of his saints. (ESV)
1 Peter 5:10

6. Recovery is assisted by focusing on the certainty of resurrection when Christ returns. There is life beyond death because of Christ's resurrection.

Job 19:25–26 For I know that my Redeemer lives, and He shall stand at last on the earth; and after my skin is destroyed, this I know, that in my flesh I shall see God. (NKJV)
1 Thessalonians 4:16, 18 For the Lord himself will come down from heaven, with a loud command, with the voice of the archangel and with the trumpet call of God, and the dead in Christ will rise first. . . . Therefore encourage one another with these words. (NIV)
1 Corinthians 13:12 Now we see things imperfectly, like puzzling reflections in a mirror, but then we will see everything with perfect clarity. All that I know now is partial and incomplete, but then I will know everything completely, just as God now knows me completely. (NLT)
John 11:25–26; 14:1–3; 2 Corinthians 13:4; 1 Peter 1:3

7. Remarriage in the Lord is an acceptable possibility.

> 1 Corinthians 7:39 A woman is bound to her husband as long as he lives. But if her husband dies, she is free to marry anyone she wishes, but he must belong to the Lord. (NIV)
> **Romans 7:2–3**

Biblical Narrative

- Abraham remarried, Genesis 25:1

Practical Steps

- Deepen your hope of heaven with study of Scripture and books on heaven.
- If you are discouraged and depressed, get out often for fellowship with friends and fellow believers. Being alone too much is one of the worst things you can do. Make yourself get out.
- Find volunteer service projects you can do. Go on a mission trip. Ask church leaders for tasks you can do at church.
- Do not quickly pursue remarriage. Avoid online relationships. Seek counsel from trusted, mature Christians.

Resources

- "The Sovereignty of God" and "The Wisdom of God" in *God as He Longs for You to See Him.* Chip Ingram. Baker.
- *The Strength of a Man: 50 Devotionals to Help Men Find Their Strength in God.* David Roper. Discovery House.
- *The Widow's Toolbox: Repairing Your Life after Losing Your Spouse.* (This is nuts and bolts, good practical advice, but not strong Christian content.) Gerald Schaefer. New Horizon.

Wisdom

See also Integrity

Descriptive terms for wisdom include understanding, discernment, common sense, sound judgment, insight, and discretion. While knowledge is the possession of facts and information, wisdom is the application of knowledge to life situations. Godly wisdom is viewing life from God's perspective.

1. **God himself is the source of the wisdom we need to live a productive life.**

   Proverbs 2:6–8 For the LORD gives wisdom; from his mouth come knowledge and understanding; he stores up sound wisdom for the upright; he is a shield to those who walk in integrity, guarding the paths of justice and watching over the way of his saints. (ESV)
   James 1:5–6 If any of you lacks wisdom, let him ask God, who gives generously to all without reproach, and it will be given him. But let him ask in faith, with no doubting, for the one who doubts is like a wave of the sea that is driven and tossed by the wind. (ESV)
   Ecclesiastes 2:26

2. **It is God's desire that we seek and search after wisdom.**

   Proverbs 2:2 Make your ear attentive to wisdom, incline your heart to understanding. (NASB)
   Proverbs 8:12–21

3. **Wisdom begins with submissive obedience, a proper relationship to God.**

   Psalm 111:10 The fear of the LORD is the beginning of wisdom; all those who practice it have a good understanding. His praise endures forever! (ESV)
   Micah 6:9

4. The wisdom of God resides in the Word of God.

   Psalm 19:7–8 The law of the LORD is perfect, reviving the soul; the testimony of the LORD is sure, making wise the simple; the precepts of the LORD are right, rejoicing the heart; the commandment of the LORD is pure, enlightening the eyes. (ESV)
   Deuteronomy 4:5–6; Psalm 37:30–31; 119:98–100; 2 Timothy 3:16–17

5. Those who are wise readily accept counsel and instruction.

   Proverbs 9:9 Give instruction to a wise man, and he will be still wiser; teach a righteous man, and he will increase in learning. (ESV)
   Proverbs 11:14

6. Wisdom will prevent reckless, foolish decisions.

   Ecclesiastes 7:5 It is better for a man to hear the rebuke of the wise than to hear the song of fools. (ESV)
   Proverbs 7:4–5; 29:8–10; Ecclesiastes 7:19

7. Applied to life's needs and concerns, wisdom brings great blessing.

   Proverbs 3:13 Blessed is the one who finds wisdom, and the one who gets understanding. (ESV) (See verses 13–18.)
   James 3:17–18 But the wisdom from above is first pure, then peaceable, gentle, open to reason, full of mercy and good fruits, impartial and sincere. And a harvest of righteousness is sown in peace by those who make peace. (ESV)
   Proverbs 8:32–36

8. Wise use of time assists in having a more productive life.

   Ephesians 5:15–17 Look carefully then how you walk, not as unwise but as wise, making the best use of the time, because the days are evil. Therefore do not be foolish, but understand what the will of the Lord is. (ESV)
   Psalm 90:12; Ecclesiastes 10:10

9. Paul compares the foolish wisdom of this world with true wisdom from above, that is, the message of the cross.

> **1 Corinthians 1:18–19** For the message of the cross is foolishness to those who are perishing, but to us who are being saved it is the power of God. For it is written: "I will destroy the wisdom of the wise, and bring to nothing the understanding of the prudent." (NKJV)
> **Colossians 2:2–3**

Biblical Narratives

- Job's friends, who lacked wisdom, Job 17:10
- Solomon, who prayed for wisdom above material gain, 1 Kings 3:2–15
- Men of Issachar, who understood the times, 1 Chronicles 12:32
- Daniel, who depended on God for wisdom, Daniel 1:17–21.

Practical Steps

- Wisdom is a recurring theme in Proverbs. Study that word, underlining every time it is used, asking God to help you apply these truths to your current needs. Notice especially sections 1:20–23; 2:1–22; 3:13–24; 8:1–36; 9:1–6. Find a good commentary on Proverbs to assist you.
- For each decision you make, pray for wisdom, asking God for his will and direction.

Resources

- "Demonstrating Wisdom" in *The Measure of a Man*. Gene Getz. Regal.

Words That Hurt

Gossip and Rumors

See also Anger, Lying, Profanity, Speech

Remember that it is not only what we say (the content), but how we say it (tone, inflection, body language) that is crucial in avoiding damaging words.

Consequences of Using Hurtful Words

1. **Words used inappropriately can bring hurt, even destruction, into the lives of all involved.**

   Leviticus 19:16 Do not go about spreading slander among your people. Do not do anything that endangers your neighbor's life. I am the LORD. (NIV)

   Obadiah 1:12 You should not gloat over your brother in the day of his misfortune, nor rejoice over the people of Judah in the day of their destruction, nor boast so much in the day of their trouble. (NIV)

   James 3:6 And the tongue is a fire, the very world of iniquity. (NASB) (See verses 5–12.)

   Exodus 23:1; Proverbs 13:3; 26:20–22; Galatians 5:14–15

2. **Using words appropriately will safeguard our daily walk with God.**

   Psalm 15:1–3 LORD, who may dwell in your sacred tent? Who may live on your holy mountain? The one . . . who speaks the

truth from their heart; whose tongue utters no slander, who does no wrong to a neighbor, and casts no slur on others. (NIV)
Psalm 24:3–4; Isaiah 33:15–16

3. **Gossip and unwholesome speech produce ungodly results.**

   Proverbs 18:21 The tongue can bring death or life; those who love to talk will reap the consequences. (NLT)
   Galatians 5:15 But if you are always biting and devouring one another, watch out! Beware of destroying one another. (NLT)
   Proverbs 21:23; Matthew 12:35–36; 2 Timothy 2:16–17; James 3:11

4. **Gossip is included in lists of disturbing sins.**

   2 Timothy 3:2–3 For men will be lovers of self, lovers of money, boastful, arrogant, revilers, disobedient to parents, ungrateful, unholy, unloving, irreconcilable, malicious gossips, without self-control, brutal. (NASB)
   Psalm 50:16–20; Romans 1:28–29

Avoiding Use of Hurtful Words

1. **We must choose carefully the words we use—a reasoned, Spirit-led response.**

   James 1:26 Those who consider themselves religious and yet do not keep a tight rein on their tongues deceive themselves, and their religion is worthless. (NIV)
   1 Peter 3:10 Whoever would love life and see good days must keep their tongue from evil and their lips from deceitful speech. (NIV)
   Psalm 17:3; 1 Peter 2:1

2. **Choosing not to associate with gossips is wise.**

   Proverbs 20:19 A gossip goes around telling secrets, so don't hang around with chatterers. (NLT)
   Psalm 141:3–4 Take control of what I say, O LORD, and guard my lips. Don't let me drift toward evil or take part in acts of

wickedness. Don't let me share in the delicacies of those who do wrong. (NLT)

3. **Damaging words must be replaced with positive, productive words.**

Ephesians 4:29 Do not let any unwholesome talk come out of your mouths, but only what is helpful for building others up according to their needs, that it may benefit those who listen. (NIV)

Proverbs 12:18; 16:24; 17:9

Responding to Words That Hurt

1. **God is our best refuge when others use words that hurt.**

Psalm 31:19–20 Oh, how great is Your goodness, which You have laid up for those who fear You, which You have prepared for those who trust in You in the presence of the sons of men! You shall hide them in the secret place of Your presence from the plots of man; You shall keep them secretly in a pavilion from the strife of tongues. (NKJV)

Luke 6:22 Blessed are you when men hate you, and ostracize you, and insult you, and scorn your name as evil, for the sake of the Son of Man. (NASB)

Psalm 62:5–7; 140:12

2. **A plan for relief.**

Proverbs 12:16 A fool is quick-tempered, but a wise person stays calm when insulted. (NLT)

Psalm 120:1–2 I took my troubles to the LORD; I cried out to him, and he answered my prayer. Rescue me, O LORD, from liars and from all deceitful people. (NLT)

Luke 6:27–28 But to you who are willing to listen, I say, love your enemies! Do good to those who hate you. Bless those who curse you. Pray for those who hurt you. (NLT)

Psalm 119:69; Romans 12:17–21

Biblical Narratives

- Hannah, hurt deeply by words, 1 Samuel 1:1–18
- Jesus, his controlled response, 1 Peter 2:21–23

Practical Steps

- If you have the problem of using harsh words, be willing to admit that it is sin, no more excuses. Confess and ask forgiveness from God. Ask your wife, children, and others to forgive you.
- Commit to obeying commands of nonretaliation and responding peacefully. See Matthew 5:38–44 and Romans 12:14, 17.
- To help break the sinful pattern of gossip, write on a card, "What is my motivation for sharing this?" Keep this close at hand to monitor your conversations throughout the day.
- Avoid places where gossip often occurs, such as break rooms at work.
- If someone begins to gossip, have the courage to explain tactfully that you prefer not to listen and then walk away, or just walk away.

Resources

- *Communication and Conflict Resolution* (booklet). Stewart Scott. Focus.
- "Discipline of Tongue" in *Disciplines of a Godly Man*. Kent Hughes. Crossway.
- "Sins of the Tongue" in *Respectable Sins*. Jerry Bridges. NavPress.
- *War of Words*. Paul Tripp. P & R.
- *Words That Cut* (booklet). Alfred Poirier. Peace Maker Ministries.

Work Ethic/Workplace

See also Career, Flirting, Laziness, Lying, Integrity, Purpose for Living, Sexual Purity, Temptation, Thought Life

Working responsibly should be characteristic of those who follow Jesus. Issues to handle with diligence include integrity, faithfulness, dependability, relationships with co-workers and work authorities, time used wisely, and a good testimony for Christ.

1. **God's plan for work was established from the very beginning as a part of his creation of mankind and therefore work is good.**

   Genesis 2:15 The LORD God took the man and put him in the garden of Eden to work it and keep it. (ESV)
   Genesis 1:26–31

2. **Hard work continued to be God's plan even after sin entered the world.**

   Genesis 3:17–19 Cursed is the ground because of you; in pain you shall eat of it all the days of your life; thorns and thistles it shall bring forth for you; and you shall eat the plants of the field. By the sweat of your face you shall eat bread. (ESV)
   Psalm 104:23

3. **Work will be enjoyed and bring satisfaction when we understand it as God's gift to us.**

   Psalm 62:12 Lovingkindness is Yours, O Lord, for You recompense a man according to his work. (NASB)
   Ecclesiastes 5:18–19 Here is what I have seen to be good and fitting: to eat, to drink and enjoy oneself in all one's labor in which he toils under the sun during the few years of his life which

God has given him; for this is his reward. Furthermore, as for every man to whom God has given riches and wealth, He has also empowered him to eat from them and to receive his reward and rejoice in his labor; this is the gift of God. (NASB)
Psalm 90:17; Ecclesiastes 3:12–13

4. Respectful obedience is due our employer. An employer owes justice and fairness to employees. (For today's culture application, substitute "workers" for "slaves" and "employers" for "masters" in Scripture verses.)

Colossians 3:22–23 Slaves, obey your earthly masters in every-thing. . . . Whatever you do, work at it with all your heart, as working for the Lord, not for human masters. (NIV)
Colossians 4:1 Masters, provide your slaves with what is right and fair, because you know that you also have a Master in heaven. (NIV)
Ephesians 6:5–9; Titus 2:9–10; 1 Timothy 6:1–2; 1 Peter 2:18–19

5. Our testimony in the workplace must be exemplary. Integrity, honesty, and responsibility must be in place.

Proverbs 3:3–4 Never let loyalty and kindness leave you! Tie them around your neck as a reminder. Write them deep within your heart. Then you will find favor with both God and people, and you will earn a good reputation. (NLT)
2 Corinthians 8:21; 1 Timothy 3:7

6. All work must be done for God's glory and with his reputation in mind.

1 Corinthians 10:31 So, whether you eat or drink, or whatever you do, do all to the glory of God. (ESV)
Ecclesiastes 12:13–14 The end of the matter; all has been heard. Fear God and keep his commandments, for this is the whole duty of man. For God will bring every deed into judgment, with every secret thing, whether good or evil. (ESV)
Colossians 3:17

7. **Paul's example and instructions are timeless.**

> **Acts 18:3** Paul lived and worked with them, for they were tent makers just as he was. (NLT)
> **1 Thessalonians 2:9** Don't you remember, dear brothers and sisters, how hard we worked among you? Night and day we toiled to earn a living so that we would not be a burden to any of you as we preached God's Good News to you. (NLT)
> **1 Thessalonians 4:11–12; 2 Thessalonians 3:7–13**

Biblical Narratives

- Lot and Abram couldn't get along in their "workplace" and had to separate, Genesis 13
- Jacob worked hard for father-in-law Laban, Genesis 29–31
- Jesus, in subjection to Joseph and Mary, would have learned a trade, most likely the same as his legal father, Luke 2:51–52; Matthew 13:55
- Peter worked hard at fishing, Luke 5:5
- Paul did double duty as a tent maker and evangelist, Acts 18:3; 1 Corinthians 4:12

Practical Steps

- Paying for food, shelter, and clothing and taking care of your family are basic motivations for being a good employee. Keep a positive attitude, even for a job you don't like very much, thanking God for his provision.
- When you go home at night, do your best to leave work behind, in both a physical and mental sense. When you walk in the door to your family, focus on them alone. Taking work cell phones home will be a killer to relationships.
- To help resist temptation with women at work, have pictures of your wife and family all over the place. If you go on business trips, have pictures in your pocket to look at and show others.

333

- Write Genesis 39:9 and Ephesians 5:28 on cards. Keep them posted at work as constant reminders.
- Keep involvement in workplace activities at a reasonable, minimum level. Always be mindful of your reputation as one who puts in a full day's work for a full day's wages. Listen to your boss.

Resources

- "Building a Good Reputation" and "Becoming a Disciplined Man" in *The Measure of a Man*. Gene Getz. Regal.
- "Discipline of Work" in *Disciplines of a Godly Man*. Kent Hughes. Crossway.
- "It's a Worker's World" in *The Secrets Men Keep*. Steve Arterburn. Thomas Nelson.
- *Work Matters*. Tom Nelson. Crossway.

The *Quick* SCRIPTURE REFERENCE COLLECTION

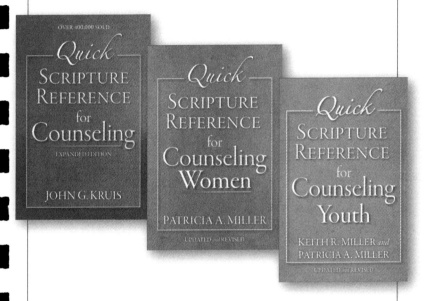

Absolutely essential reference books for parents, pastors, or counselors.